Lambert M. Surhone, Mariam T. Tennoe,
Susan F. Henssonow (Ed.)

Software Testing Automation Framework

Lambert M. Surhone, Mariam T. Tennoe,
Susan F. Henssonow (Ed.)

Software Testing Automation Framework

Open Source, Cross-Platform, Software Test, Distributed Computing

Betascript Publishing

Imprint

All parts of this book are extracted from Wikipedia, the free encyclopedia (www.wikipedia.org).

You can get detailed informations about the authors of this collection of articles at the end of this book. The editors (Ed.) of this book are no authors. They have not modified or extended the original texts.

Pictures published in this book can be under different licences than the GNU Free Documentation License. You can get detailed informations about the authors and licences of pictures at the end of this book.

The content of this book was generated collaboratively by volunteers. Please be advised that nothing found here has necessarily been reviewed by people with the expertise required to provide you with complete, accurate or reliable information. Some information in this book maybe misleading or wrong. The Publisher does not guarantee the validity of the information found here. If you need specific advice (f.e. in fields of medical, legal, financial, or risk management questions) please contact a professional who is licensed or knowledgeable in that area.

Cover image: www.ingimage.com
Concerning the licence of the cover image please contact ingimage.

Contact:
VDM Publishing House Ltd.,17 Rue Meldrum, Beau Bassin,1713-01 Mauritius
Email: info@vdm-publishing-house.com
Website: www.vdm-publishing-house.com

Published in 2010
Printed in: U.S.A., U.K., Germany. This book was not produced in Mauritius.

ISBN: 978-613-3-09417-8

Contents

Articles

References

Article Licenses

Software Testing Automation Framework

Developer(s)	IBM
Initial release	Initial Release in 1998. Version 3.0 initial release in 2005.
Written in	Core application: C++. Public APIs available in Java, C, C++, Python, Perl, Tcl, Rexx.
Operating system	Cross-platform
Available in	English
Type	Test Automation Framework
License	As of v3.2.5, STAF uses the Eclipse Public License V1.0. Additional details here [1].
Website	Software Testing Automation Framework (STAF) [2]

Introduction

The **Software Testing Automation Framework (STAF)** is an open source project that enables users to create cross-platform, distributed software test environments.

Services

STAF includes a number of services that provide specific functionality. The most prominent of these is called the STAf eXecution engine (STAX), which executes test scripts. Other services provide cron, file system, inter-process communication, e-mail, and HTML support, among others. The documentation includes instructions and guidelines for developers to generate their own custom services, as well.

Support

IBM supports users of STAF through extensive online documentation and user forums, accessible via the STAF website [2].

External links

- Software Testing Automation Framework (STAF) [2]

References

[1] http://staf.sourceforge.net/license.php
[2] http://staf.sourceforge.net/index.php

Open source

Open source describes practices in production and development that promote access to the end product's source materials. Some consider open source a philosophy, others consider it a pragmatic methodology. Before the term *open source* became widely adopted, developers and producers used a variety of phrases to describe the concept; *open source* gained hold with the rise of the Internet, and the attendant need for massive retooling of the computing source code. Opening the source code enabled a self-enhancing diversity of production models, communication paths, and interactive communities.[1] Subsequently, a new, three-word phrase "open source software" was born to describe the environment that the new copyright, licensing, domain, and consumer issues created.

The open source model includes the concept of concurrent yet different agendas and differing approaches in production, in contrast with more centralized models of development such as those typically used in commercial software companies.[2] A main principle and practice of open source software development is peer production by bartering and collaboration, with the end-product, source-material, "blueprints" and documentation available at no cost to the public. This is increasingly being applied in other fields of endeavor, such as biotechnology.[3]

History

The concept of open source and free sharing of technological information existed long before computers. For example, cooking recipes have been shared since the beginning of human culture. Open source can pertain to businesses and to computers, software and technology.

In the early years of automobile development, a group of capital monopolists owned the rights to a 2 cycle gasoline engine patent originally filed by George B. Selden.[4] By controlling this patent, they were able to monopolize the industry and force car manufacturers to adhere to their demands, or risk a lawsuit. In 1911, independent automaker Henry Ford won a challenge to the Selden patent. The result was that the Selden patent became virtually worthless and a new association (which would eventually become the Motor Vehicle Manufacturers Association) was formed.[4] The new association instituted a cross-licensing agreement among all US auto manufacturers: although each company would develop technology and file patents, these patents were shared openly and without the exchange of money between all the manufacturers.[4] Until the US entered World War 2, 92 Ford patents were being used freely by other manufacturers and were in turn making use of 515 patents from other companies, all without lawsuits or the exchange of money.[4]

Very similar to open standards, researchers with access to the Advanced Research Projects Agency Network (ARPANET) used a process called Request for Comments to develop telecommunication network protocols. This collaborative process of the 1960s led to the birth of the Internet in 1969.

Early instances of open source and free software include IBM's source releases of its operating systems and other programs in the 1950s and 1960s, and the SHARE user group that formed to facilitate the exchange of software.[5] [6] Open source on the Internet began when the Internet was just a message board, and progressed to more advanced presentation and sharing forms like a Web site. There are now many Web sites, organizations and businesses that promote open source sharing of everything from computer code to mechanics of improving a product, technique, or medical advancement.

The label “open source” was adopted by some people in the free software movement at a strategy session[7] held at Palo Alto, California, in reaction to Netscape's January 1998 announcement of a source code release for Navigator. The group of individuals at the session included Christine Peterson who suggested “open source”, Todd Anderson, Larry Augustin, Jon Hall, Sam Ockman, Michael Tiemann and Eric S. Raymond. Over the next week, Raymond and others worked on spreading the word. Linus Torvalds gave an all-important sanction the following day. Phil Hughes offered a pulpit in *Linux Journal*. Richard Stallman, pioneer of the free software movement, flirted with adopting the term, but changed his mind.[8] Those people who adopted the term used the opportunity before the release of

Navigator's source code to free themselves of the ideological and confrontational connotations of the term "free software". Netscape released its source code under the Netscape Public License and later under the Mozilla Public License.[9]

The term was given a big boost at an event organized in April 1998 by technology publisher Tim O'Reilly. Originally titled the "Freeware Summit" and later known as the "Open Source Summit",[10] The event brought together the leaders of many of the most important free and open source projects, including Linus Torvalds, Larry Wall, Brian Behlendorf, Eric Allman, Guido van Rossum, Michael Tiemann, Paul Vixie, Jamie Zawinski of Netscape, and Eric Raymond. At that meeting, the confusion caused by the name free software was brought up. Tiemann argued for "sourceware" as a new term, while Raymond argued for "open source." The assembled developers took a vote, and the winner was announced at a press conference that evening. Five days later, Raymond made the first public call to the free software community to adopt the new term.[11] The Open Source Initiative was formed shortly thereafter.[7]

Starting in the early 2000s, a number of companies began to publish a portion of their source code to claim they were open source, while keeping key parts closed. This led to the development of the now widely used terms *free open source software* and *commercial open source software* to distinguish between truly open and hybrid forms of open source.

Economic analysis

Most economists agree that open source candidates have an information good[12] (also termed 'knowledge good') aspect. In general, this suggests that the original work involves a great deal of time, money, and effort. However, the cost of reproducing the work is very low, so that additional users may be added at zero or near zero cost — this is referred to as the marginal cost of a product. At this point, it is necessary to consider a copyright. The idea of copyright for works of authorship is to protect the incentive of making these original works. Copyright restriction then creates access costs on consumers who value the original more than making an additional copy but value the original less than its price. Thus, they will pay an access cost of this difference. Access costs also pose problems for authors who wish to create something based on another work but are not willing to pay the copyright holder for the rights to the copyrighted work. The second type of cost incurred with a copyright system is the cost of administration and enforcement of the copyright.

Being organised effectively as a consumers' cooperative, the idea of open source is then to eliminate the access costs of the consumer and the creator by reducing the restrictions of copyright. This will lead to creation of additional works, which build upon previous work and add to greater social benefit. Additionally some proponents argue that open source also relieves society of the administration and enforcement costs of copyright. Organizations such as Creative Commons have websites where individuals can file for alternative "licenses", or levels of restriction, for their works.[13] These self-made protections free the general society of the costs of policing copyright infringement. Thus, on several fronts, there is an efficiency argument to be made on behalf of open sourced goods.

Others argue that society loses through open sourced goods. Because there is a loss in monetary incentive to the creation of new goods, some argue that new products will not be created. This argument seems to apply particularly well to the business model where extensive research and development is done, e.g. pharmaceuticals. However, this argument ignores the fact that cost reduction for all concerned is perhaps an even better monetary incentive than is a price increase. In addition, others argue that visual art and other works of authorship should be free. These proponents of extensive open source ideals argue that monetary incentive for artists would perhaps better be derived from performances or exhibitions, in a similar fashion to the funding of provision of other types of services.

Case study

An investigation of open source industrial symbiosis is performed by Doyle and Pearce [14] using Google Earth (GE). This paper found that virtual globes coupled with open source waste information can be used to:

1. reduce embodied transport energy by reducing distances to recycling facilities,
2. choose end of life at recycling facilities rather than landfills, and
3. establish industrial symbiosis and eco-industrial parks on known by-product synergies.

Ultimately, open source sharing of information in virtual globes provide a means to identify economically and environmentally beneficial opportunities for waste management if the data have been made available.

Applications

Many fields of study and social and political views have been affected by the growth of the concept of open source. Advocates in one field often support the expansion of open source in other fields. For example, Linus Torvalds is quoted as saying, "the future is open source everything."[15] But Eric Raymond and other founders of the open source movement have sometimes publicly argued against speculation about applications outside software, saying that strong arguments for software openness should not be weakened by overreaching into areas where the story is less compelling. The broader impacts of the open source movement, and the extent of its role in the development of new information sharing procedures, remains to be seen.

The open source movement has inspired increased transparency and liberty in other fields, including the release of biotechnology research by CAMBIA,[16] Wikipedia,[17] and other projects. The open-source concept has also been applied to media other than computer programs, e.g., by Creative Commons.[18] It also constitutes an example of user innovation (see for example the book *Democratizing Innovation*).[19] Often, open source is an expression where it simply means that a system is available to all who wish to work on it. The difference between crowdsourcing and open source is that open source production is a cooperative activity initiated and voluntarily undertaken by members of the public

Computer software

Open source software is software whose source code is published and made available to the public, enabling anyone to copy, modify and redistribute the source code without paying royalties or fees. Open source code evolves through community cooperation. These communities are composed of individual programmers as well as very large companies. Examples of open-source software products are:[20]

- GNU Project — "a sufficient body of free software"
- FreeBSD — operating system derived from Unix
- Apache — HTTP web server
- Tomcat web server — web container
- Drupal — content management system
- Eclipse — software development environment comprising an integrated development environment (IDE)
- Joomla — content management system
- Linux — operating system based on Unix
- Mediawiki — wiki server software, the software that runs Wikipedia
- MongoDB — document-oriented, non-relational database
- Moodle — course management system or virtual learning environment
- Mozilla Firefox — web browser
- Mozilla Thunderbird — e-mail client
- OpenBSD — operating system derived from Unix
- OpenOffice.org — office suite

- OpenSolaris — Unix Operating System from Sun Microsystems
- osCommerce — ecommerce
- PeaZip — File archiver
- Stockfish — chess engine series, considered to be one of the strongest chess programs of the world
- Symbian — real time mobile operating system
- TYPO3 — content management system
- WordPress — content management system — blog software
- 7-Zip — File archiver
- Many, many more

Computer hardware

Open source hardware is hardware whose initial specification, usually in a software format, are published and made available to the public, enabling anyone to copy, modify and redistribute the hardware and source code without paying royalties or fees. Open source hardware evolves through community cooperation. These communities are composed of individual hardware/software developers, hobbyists, as well as very large companies. Examples of open source hardware initiatives are:

- Openmoko: a family of open source mobile phones, including the hardware specification and the operating system.
- Sun Microsystems's OpenSPARC T1 Multicore processor. Sun has released it under GPL.[21]
- Arduino, a microcontroller platform for hobbyists, artists and designers.[22]
- Simputer, an open hardware handheld computer, designed in India for use in environments where computing devices such as personal computers are deemed inappropriate.[23]

Beverages

- OpenCola — a cola soft drink, similar to Coca-Cola and Pepsi, whose recipe[24] is open source and developed by volunteers. The taste is said to be comparable to that of the standard beverages. Most corporations producing beverages, hold their formulas as closely guarded secrets.[25]
- Vores Øl beer — a beer created by students at the IT-University in Copenhagen together with Superflex, a Copenhagen-based artist collective, to illustrate how open source concepts might be applied outside the digital world.[26] [27] [28]
- In 2002, the beer company Brewtopia in Australia started an open source brewery and invited the general population to be involved in the development and ownership of the brewery, and to vote on the development of every aspect of its beer, Blowfly, and its road to market. In return for their feedback and input, individuals received shares in the company, which is now publicly traded on a stock exchange in Australia. The company has always adhered to its Open Source roots and is the only beer company in the world that allows the public to design, customise and develop its own beers online.[29]
- Coffee — capsule-based beverage systems such as Nestle's *Nespresso* or Krups' *Tassimo* turn home-brewed coffee from an inherently "open-source" beverage into a product limited by the specific range of capsules made available by the system manufacturers.[30]

Digital content

- Open-content projects organized by the Wikimedia Foundation [31] — Sites such as Wikipedia and Wiktionary have embraced the open-content GFDL and Creative Commons content licenses. These licenses were designed to adhere to principles similar to various open-source software development licenses. Many of these licenses ensure that content remains free for re-use, that source documents are made readily available to interested parties, and that changes to content are accepted easily back into the system. An important site embracing open source-like ideals is Project Gutenberg[32] , which posts many books on which the copyright has expired and are thus in the Public Domain, ensuring that anyone can use that content for any purpose whatsoever.

Health and science

Medicine

- Pharmaceuticals — There have been several proposals for open-source pharmaceutical development,[33] [34] which led to the establishment of the Tropical Disease Initiative [35]. There are also a number of not-for-profit "virtual pharmas" such as the Institute for One World Health [36] and the Drugs for Neglected Diseases Initiative [37].

Science

- Research — The Science Commons was created as an alternative to the expensive legal costs of sharing and reusing scientific works in journals etc.[38]
- Research — The Open Source Science Project was created to increase the ability for students to participate in the research process by providing them access to microfunding — which, in turn, offers non-researchers the opportunity to directly invest, and follow, cutting-edge scientific research. All data and methodology is subsequently published in an openly accessible manner under a Creative Commons fair use license.

Other

- Open source principles can be applied to technical areas such as digital communication protocols and data storage formats.
- Open design — which involves applying open source methodologies to the design of artifacts and systems in the physical world. Very nascent but has huge potential.[39]
- Open source appropriate technology (OSAT) refers to technologies that are designed in the same fashion as free and open-source software. These technologies must be "appropriate technology" (AT) — meaning technology that is designed with special consideration to the environmental, ethical, cultural, social, political, and economical aspects of the community it is intended for.

MediaWiki logo

- Teaching — which involves applying the concepts of open source to instruction using a shared web space as a platform to improve upon learning, organizational, and management challenges. An example of an Open Source Courseware is the Java Education & Development Initiative (JEDI).[40]
- There are few examples of business information (methodologies, advice, guidance, practices) using the open source model, although this is another case where the potential is enormous. ITIL is close to open source. It uses the Cathedral model (no mechanism exists for user contribution) and the content must be bought for a fee that is small by business consulting standards (hundreds of British pounds). Various checklists are published by government, banks or accounting firms. Possibly the only example of free, bazaar-model open source business information is Core Practice [41].

Society and culture

Open source culture is the creative practice of appropriation and free sharing of found and created content. Examples include collage, found footage film, music, and appropriation art. Open source culture is one in which fixations, works entitled to copyright protection, are made generally available. Participants in the culture can modify those products and redistribute them back into the community or other organizations.

The rise of open-source culture in the 20th century resulted from a growing tension between creative practices that involve appropriation, and therefore require access to content that is often copyrighted, and increasingly restrictive intellectual property laws and policies governing access to copyrighted content. The two main ways in which intellectual property laws became more restrictive in the 20th century were extensions to the term of copyright (particularly in the United States) and penalties, such as those articulated in the Digital Millennium Copyright Act (DMCA), placed on attempts to circumvent anti-piracy technologies.[42]

Although artistic appropriation is often permitted under fair use doctrines, the complexity and ambiguity of these doctrines creates an atmosphere of uncertainty among cultural practitioners. Also, the protective actions of copyright owners create what some call a "chilling effect" among cultural practitioners.[43]

In the late 20th century, cultural practitioners began to adopt the intellectual property licensing techniques of free software and open-source software to make their work more freely available to others, including the Creative Commons.

The idea of an "open source" culture runs parallel to "Free Culture," but is substantively different. *Free culture* is a term derived from the free software movement, and in contrast to that vision of culture, proponents of Open Source Culture (OSC) maintain that some intellectual property law needs to exist to protect cultural producers. Yet they propose a more nuanced position than corporations have traditionally sought. Instead of seeing intellectual property law as an expression of instrumental rules intended to uphold either natural rights or desirable outcomes, an argument for OSC takes into account diverse goods (as in "the Good life") and ends.

One way of achieving the goal of making the fixations of cultural work generally available is to maximally utilize technology and digital media. In keeping with Moore's law's prediction about processors, the cost of digital media and storage plummeted in the late 20th Century. Consequently, the marginal cost of digitally duplicating anything capable of being transmitted via digital media dropped to near zero. Combined with an explosive growth in personal computer and technology ownership, the result is an increase in general population's access to digital media. This phenomenon facilitated growth in open source culture because it allowed for rapid and inexpensive duplication and distribution of culture. Where the access to the majority of culture produced prior to the advent of digital media was limited by other constraints of proprietary and potentially "open" mediums, digital media is the latest technology with the potential to increase access to cultural products. Artists and users who choose to distribute their work digitally face none of the physical limitations that traditional cultural producers have been typically faced with. Accordingly, the audience of an open source culture faces little physical cost in acquiring digital media.

Open source culture precedes Richard Stallman's codification of the concept with the creation of the Free Software Foundation. As the public began to communicate through Bulletin Board Systems (BBS) like FidoNet, places like Sourcery Systems BBS were dedicated to providing source code to Public Domain, Shareware and Freeware programs.

Essentially born out of a desire for increased general access to digital media, the Internet is open source culture's most valuable asset. It is questionable whether the goals of an open source culture could be achieved without the Internet. The global network not only fosters an environment where culture can be generally accessible, but also allows for easy and inexpensive redistribution of culture back into various communities. Some reasons for this are as follows.

First, the Internet allows even greater access to inexpensive digital media and storage. Instead of users being limited to their own facilities and resources, they are granted access to a vast network of facilities and resources, some free.

Sites such as Archive.org offer up free web space for anyone willing to license their work under a Creative Commons license. The resulting cultural product is then available to download free (generally accessible) to anyone with an Internet connection.

Second, users are granted unprecedented access to each other. Older analog technologies such as the telephone or television have limitations on the kind of interaction users can have. In the case of television there is little, if any interaction between users participating on the network. And in the case of the telephone, users rarely interact with any more than a couple of their known peers. On the Internet, however, users have the potential to access and meet millions of their peers. This aspect of the Internet facilitates the modification of culture as users are able to collaborate and communicate with each other across international and cultural boundaries. The speed in which digital media travels on the Internet in turn facilitates the redistribution of culture.

Through various technologies such as peer-to-peer networks and blogs, cultural producers can take advantage of vast social networks in order to distribute their products. As opposed to traditional media distribution, redistributing digital media on the Internet can be virtually costless. Technologies such as BitTorrent and Gnutella take advantage of various characteristics of the Internet protocol (TCP/IP) in an attempt to totally decentralize file distribution.

Government

- Open politics (sometimes known as *Open source politics*) — is a term used to describe a political process that uses Internet technologies such as blogs, email and polling to provide for a rapid feedback mechanism between political organizations and their supporters. There is also an alternative conception of the term *Open source politics* which relates to the development of public policy under a set of rules and processes similar to the Open Source Software movement.
- Open source governance — is similar to open source politics, but it applies more to the democratic process and promotes the freedom of information.

Ethics

Open Source ethics is split into two strands:

- Open Source Ethics as an Ethical School — Charles Ess and David Berry are researching whether ethics can learn anything from an open source approach. Ess famously even defined the AoIR Research Guidelines as an example of open source ethics.[44]
- Open Source Ethics as a Professional Body of Rules — This is based principally on the computer ethics school, studying the questions of ethics and professionalism in the computer industry in general and software development in particular.[45]

Media

Open source journalism — referred to the standard journalistic techniques of news gathering and fact checking, and reflected a similar term that was in use from 1992 in military intelligence circles, open source intelligence. It is now commonly used to describe forms of innovative publishing of online journalism, rather than the sourcing of news stories by a professional journalist. In the December 25, 2006 issue of TIME magazine this is referred to as user created content and listed alongside more traditional open source projects such as OpenSolaris and Linux.

Weblogs, or blogs, are another significant platform for open source culture. Blogs consist of periodic, reverse chronologically ordered posts, using a technology that makes webpages easily updatable with no understanding of design, code, or file transfer required. While corporations, political campaigns and other formal institutions have begun using these tools to distribute information, many blogs are used by individuals for personal expression, political organizing, and socializing. Some, such as LiveJournal or WordPress, utilize open source software that is open to the public and can be modified by users to fit their own tastes. Whether the code is open or not, this format represents a nimble tool for people to borrow and re-present culture; whereas traditional websites made the illegal reproduction of culture difficult to regulate, the mutability of blogs makes "open sourcing" even more uncontrollable since it allows a larger portion of the population to replicate material more quickly in the public sphere.

Messageboards are another platform for open source culture. Messageboards (also known as discussion boards or forums), are places online where people with similar interests can congregate and post messages for the community to read and respond to. Messageboards sometimes have moderators who enforce community standards of etiquette such as banning users who are spammers. Other common board features are private messages (where users can send messages to one another) as well as chat (a way to have a real time conversation online) and image uploading. Some messageboards use phpBB, which is a free open source package. Where blogs are more about individual expression and tend to revolve around their authors, messageboards are about creating a conversation amongst its users where information can be shared freely and quickly. Messageboards are a way to remove intermediaries from everyday life — for instance, instead of relying on commercials and other forms of advertising, one can ask other users for frank reviews of a product, movie or CD. By removing the cultural middlemen, messageboards help speed the flow of information and exchange of ideas.

OpenDocument is an open document file format for saving and exchanging editable office documents such as text documents (including memos, reports, and books), spreadsheets, charts, and presentations. Organizations and individuals that store their data in an open format such as OpenDocument avoid being locked in to a single software vendor, leaving them free to switch software if their current vendor goes out of business, raises their prices, changes their software, or changes their licensing terms to something less favorable.

Open source movie production is either an open call system in which a changing crew and cast collaborate in movie production, a system in which the end result is made available for re-use by others or in which exclusively open source products are used in the production. The 2006 movie Elephants Dream is said to be the "world's first open movie",[46] created entirely using open source technology.

An open source documentary film has a production process allowing the open contributions of archival material, footage, and other filmic elements, both in unedited and edited form. By doing so, on-line contributors become part of the process of creating the film, helping to influence the editorial and visual material to be used in the documentary, as well as its thematic development. The first open source documentary film to go into production "The American Revolution" [47][48] ," which will examine the role that WBCN-FM in Boston played in the cultural, social and political changes locally and nationally from 1968 to 1974, is being produced by Lichtenstein Creative Media and the non-profit The Fund for Independent Media. Open Source Cinema [49] is a website to create Basement Tapes, a feature documentary about copyright in the digital age, co-produced by the National Film Board of Canada [50]. Open Source Filmmaking refers to a form of filmmaking that takes a method of idea formation from open source software, but in this case the 'source' for a film maker is raw unedited footage rather than programming code. It can also refer to a method of filmmaking where the process of creation is 'open' i.e. a disparate group of contributors, at different times contribute to the final piece.

Open-IPTV is IPTV that is not limited to one recording studio, production studio, or cast. Open-IPTV uses the Internet or other means to pool efforts and resources together to create an online community that all contributes to a show.

Education

Within the academic community, there is discussion about expanding what could be called the "intellectual commons" (analogous to the Creative Commons). Proponents of this view have hailed the Connexions Project at Rice University, OpenCourseWare project at MIT, Eugene Thacker's article on "Open Source DNA", the "Open Source Cultural Database" and Wikipedia as examples of applying open source outside the realm of computer software.

Open source curricula are instructional resources whose digital source can be freely used, distributed and modified.

Another strand to the academic community is in the area of research. Many funded research projects produce software as part of their work. There is an increasing interest in making the outputs of such projects available under an open source license. In the UK the Joint Information Systems Committee (JISC) has developed a policy on open source software. JISC also funds a development service called OSS Watch which acts as an advisory service for higher and further education institutions wishing to use, contribute to and develop open source software.

Innovation communities

The principle of sharing predates the open source movement; for example, the free sharing of information has been institutionalized in the scientific enterprise since at least the 19th century. Open source principles have always been part of the scientific community. The sociologist Robert K. Merton described the four basic elements of the community — universalism (an international perspective), communism (sharing information), disinterestedness (removing one's personal views from the scientific inquiry) and organized skepticism (requirements of proof and review) that accurately describe the scientific community today. These principles are, in part, complemented by US law's focus on protecting expression and method but not the ideas themselves. There is also a tradition of publishing research results to the scientific community instead of keeping all such knowledge proprietary. One of the recent initiatives in scientific publishing has been open access — the idea that research should be published in such a way that it is free and available to the public. There are currently many open access journals where the information is available free online, however most journals do charge a fee (either to users or libraries for access). The Budapest Open Access Initiative is an international effort with the goal of making all research articles available free on the Internet. The National Institutes of Health has recently proposed a policy on "Enhanced Public Access to NIH Research Information." This policy would provide a free, searchable resource of NIH-funded results to the public and with other international repositories six months after its initial publication. The NIH's move is an important one because there is significant amount of public funding in scientific research. Many of the questions have yet to be answered — the balancing of profit vs. public access, and ensuring that desirable standards and incentives do not diminish with a shift to open access.

Farmavita.Net — Community of Pharmaceuticals Executives have recently proposed new business model of Open Source Pharmaceuticals[51] . The project is targeted to development and sharing of know-how for manufacture of essential and life saving medicines. It is mainly dedicated to the countries with less developed economies where local pharmaceutical research and development resources are insufficient for national needs. It will be limited to generic (off-patent) medicines with established use. By the definition, medicinal product have a “well-established use” if is used for at least 15 years, with recognized efficacy and an acceptable level of safety. In that event, the expensive clinical test and trial results could be replaced by appropriate scientific literature.

Benjamin Franklin was an early contributor eventually donating all his inventions including the Franklin stove, bifocals and the lightning rod to the public domain.

New NGO communities are starting to use the open source technology as a tool. One example is the Open Source Youth Network started in 2007 in Lisboa by ISCA members[52] .

Open innovation is also a new emerging concept which advocate putting R&D in a common pool. The Eclipse platform is openly presenting itself as an Open innovation network[53] .

Arts and recreation

Copyright protection is used in the performing arts and even in athletic activities. Some groups have attempted to remove copyright from such practices.[54]

See also

Lists

- List of commercial open source applications
- List of Open Source eCommerce Software
- List of open source healthcare software
- List of open source software packages
- List of open source video games
- List of trademarked open source software

Terms based on open source

- Open source appropriate technology
- Open source governance
- Open source hardware
- Open Source Initiative
- Open source license
- Open source political campaign
- Open source record label
- Open source religion
- Open source software
- Open-sourcing

Other

- Business models for open source software
- *Code: Collaborative Ownership and the Digital Commons* (book)
- Collaborative intelligence
- Commons-based peer production
- Commercial open source applications
- Community source
- Digital freedom
- Embrace, extend and extinguish
- Free Beer
- Free software
- Gift economy
- Glossary of legal terms in technology
- Halloween Documents
- Linux
- Network effect
- Open access (publishing)
- Open content
- Open data
- Open design

- Open format
- Open implementation
- Open innovation
- Open JDK
- Open research
- Open Solaris
- Open Source as a Service
- Open source vs. closed source
- Open system (computing)
- Open standard
- OpenDWG
- Openness
- Shared software
- Shared source
- Vendor lock-in

Further reading

- David M. Berry (2008). *Copy, Rip, Burn: The Politics of Copyleft and Open Source* [55]. London:Pluto Press.
- Karl Fogel. Producing Open Source Software [56] (How to Run a Successful Free Software Project). Free PDF version available.
- Ron Goldman and Richard P. Gabriel (2005). *Innovation Happens Elsewhere* [57]. Richard P. Gabriel. ISBN 1558608893.
- Isaac Hunter Dunlap (2006). *Open Source Database Driven Web Development* [58]. Oxford: Chandos. ISBN 1843341611.
- Steven Weber (2005). *The Success of Open Source* [59]. Harvard: Harvard University Press.
- Nettingsmeier, Jörn. "So What? I Don't Hack!." *eContact! 11.3 — Logiciels audio « open source » / Open Source for Audio Application* [60] (September 2009). Montréal: CEC.
- Richard M. Stallman. *Free Software Free Society* [61].
- Various authors. *eContact! 11.3 — Logiciels audio « open source » / Open Source for Audio Application* [62] (September 2009). Montréal: CEC.
- Various authors. "Open Source Travel Guide [wiki] [63]." *eContact! 11.3 — Logiciels audio « open source » / Open Source for Audio Application* [62] (September 2009). Montréal: CEC.

Literature on legal and economic aspects

- François Letellier (2008), Open Source Software: the Role of Nonprofits in Federating Business and Innovation Ecosystems [64], AFME 2008 (in Adobe pdf format).
- Benkler, Y. (2002): "Coase's Penguin, or, Linux and The Nature of the Firm." Yale Law Journal 112.3 (Dec 2002): p367(78) [65] (in Adobe pdf format)
- Berry, D. M & Moss, G. (2008). Libre Culture: Meditations on Free Culture. Canada: Pygmalion Books. [66] (in Adobe pdf format)
- Bitzer, J. & Schröder, P. J.H. (2005): "The Impact of Entry and Competition by Open Source Software on Innovation Activity", Industrial Organization 0512001, EconWPA. [67] (in Adobe Systems pdf format)
- v. Engelhardt, S. (2008): "The Economic Properties of Software", Jena Economic Research Papers, Volume 2 (2008), Number 2008-045. [68] (in Adobe pdf format)
- v. Engelhardt, S. (2008): "Intellectual Property Rights and Ex-Post Transaction Costs: the Case of Open and Closed Source Software", Jena Economic Research Papers 2008-047 [69]. (in Adobe pdf format)

- v. Engelhardt, S. & Swaminathan, S. (2008): "Open Source Software, Closed Source Software or Both: Impacts on Industry Growth and the Role of Intellectual Property Rights", Discussion Papers of DIW Berlin 799. [70] (in Adobe Systems pdf format)
- Feller, J., Fitzgerald, B. & Hissam, S. A. (eds), (2005): Perspectives on Free and Open Source Software, MIT Press.
- Ghosh, R. A. (2006): Study on the: Economic impact of open source software on innovation and the competitiveness of the Information and Communication Technologies (ICT) sector in the EU [71]
- v. Hippel, E. & v. Krogh, G. (2003): 'Open source software and the "private-collective" innovation model: Issues for organization science', Organization Science 14(2), 209–223.
- Lerner J. & Pathak P. A. & Tirole, J. (2006): "The Dynamics of Open Source Contributors", American Economic Review, vol. 96 (2), p. 114-118.
- Lerner, J. & Tirole, J. (2002): 'Some simple economics on open source', Journal of Industrial Economics 50(2), p 197–234. Download of an earlier version. [72]
- Lerner, J. & Tirole, J. (2005): "The Scope of Open Source Licensing", The Journal of Law, Economics, and Organization, vol. 21, p. 20-56.
- Lerner, J. & Tirole, J. (2005): "The Economics of Technology Sharing: Open Source and Beyond", Journal of Economic Perspectives, vol. 19(2), p. 99-120.
- Maurer, S. M. (2008): 'Open source biology: Finding a niche (or maybe several)', UMKC Law Review 76(2). (download an online version) [73] (in Adobe pdf format)
- Osterloh, M. & Rota, S. (2007): "Open source software development--Just another case of collective invention?", Research Policy, vol. 36(2), pages 157-171. Download of an earlier version [74]
- Riehle, D. (2007): "The Economic Motivation of Open Source: Stakeholder Perspectives [75]", IEEE Computer, vol. 40, no. 4 (April 2007), p. 25-32.
- Rossi, M. A. (2006): Decoding the free/open source software puzzle: A survey of theoretical and empirical contributions, in J. Bitzer P. Schröder, eds, 'The Economics of Open Source Software Development', p 15–55. (download an online version) [76] (in Adobe pdf format)
- Schiff, A. (2002): "The Economics of Open Source Software: A Survey of the Early Literature," [77] Review of Network Economics, vol. 1(1), p 66-74.

External links

- An open-source shot in the arm? [78] The Economist, Jun 10th 2004,
- SDForum Distinguished Speaker talks on Open Source Software by Guido van Rossum, Howard Rheingold, and Bruce Perens, 2005. [79]
- SDForum Global Open Source, March 24, 2008 [80]
- Machine Learning Open Source Software [81]
- Google-O'Reilly Open Source Awards [82]
- QualiPSo European Initiative [83]
- International Institute for Software Technology / United Nations University [84]
- UNU/IIST Open Source Software Certification [85]
- Calls for open source government [86]
- Open Source Open World — Open Standards Throughout the Globe [87]
- How to Contribute to Open Source Without Coding [88]

References

[1] The complexity of such communication relates to Brooks' law, and it is also described by Eric S. Raymond, "Brooks predicts that as your number of programmers N rises, work performed scales as N but complexity and vulnerability to bugs rises as N-squared. N-squared tracks the number of communications paths (and potential code interfaces) between developers' code bases." — "The Revenge of the Hackers" (http://catb.org/~esr/faqs/hacker-revenge.html). 2000.

[2] Raymond, Eric S. *The Cathedral and the Bazaar*. ed 3.0. 2000.

[3] "Science 2.0 is here as CSIR resorts to open source drug research for TB" Business Standard, 1 March 2009 (http://www.business-standard.com/india/news/sreelatha-menon-researchers-sans-borders/00/19/350429/)

[4] James J. Flink *The Car Culture* (MIT Press, 1977) ISBN 0-262-56015-1

[5] Fisher, Franklin M.; James W. McKie, Richard B. Mancke (1983). *IBM and the U.S. Data Processing Industry: An Economic History*. Praeger. ISBN 0-03-063059-2. pages 172-179 IBM unbundled (began charging for) software June 23, 1969

[6] Dave Pitts' IBM 7090 support (http://www.cozx.com/~dpitts/ibm7090.html) – An example of distributed source: Page contains a link to IBM 7090/94 IBSYS source, including COBOL and FORTRAN compilers.

[7] Tiemann, Michael (September 19, 2006). "History of the OSI" (http://www.opensource.org/history). Open Source Initiative. . Retrieved August 23, 2008.

[8] http://opensource.org/history

[9] Muffatto, Moreno (2006). *Open Source: A Multidisciplinary Approach*. Imperial College Press. ISBN 1860946658.

[10] Open Source Summit (http://linuxgazette.net/issue28/rossum.html) Linux Gazette. 1998.

[11] Goodbye, "free software"; hello, "open source" (http://www.catb.org/~esr/open-source.html)

[12] Grandstrand, 1999

[13] About the Creative Commons Licenses (http://creativecommons.org/about/licenses/)

[14] http://me.queensu.ca/people/pearce/publications/documents/as21.pdf

[15] http://www.sciencelive.org/component/option,com_mediadb/task,view/idstr,S-517352/Itemid,26

[16] http://www.cambia.org/daisy/cambia/470.html

[17] http://www.linux.com/archive/feed/40486

[18] http://creativecommons.org/software

[19] http://mitpress.mit.edu/catalog/item/default.asp?ttype=2&tid=10446

[20] Open-Source Watch — Examples of Open-Source Software (http://www.oss-watch.ac.uk/resources/softwareexamples.xml)

[21] An Open Source Processor used in Sun SPARC Servers (http://www.opensparc.net/)

[22] http://www.arduino.cc/

[23] http://www.dmoz.org/Computers/Systems/Handhelds/Open_Source/Simputer/

[24] http://alfredo.octavio.net/soft_drink_formula.pdf

[25] OpenCola Softdrink (http://www.colawp.com/colas/400/cola467_recipe.html)

[26] The concept expands upon a statement found in the Free Software Definition: "Free software is a matter of liberty, not price. To understand the concept, you should think of 'free' as in 'free speech' not as in 'free beer.'"

[27] Stallman, Richard M. The Free Software Definition (http://www.gnu.org/philosophy/free-sw.html). Free Software Foundation. 2005.

[28] Cohn, David. " Free Beer for Geeks (http://www.wired.com/news/business/0,1367,68144,00.html?tw=wn_17culthead)", Wired News, 18 July 2005.

[29] About Brewtopia (http://brewtopia.com.au/about-brewtopia.php)

[30] Formats-ouverts.org (http://formats-ouverts.org/blog/2004/09/26/131-prisonnier-dune-capsule) **(French)**

[31] http://wikimediafoundation.org/wiki/Our_projects

[32] Free eBooks by Project Gutenberg (http://www.gutenberg.org/)

[33] Can open-source R&D reinvigorate drug research? (http://www.ncbi.nlm.nih.gov/entrez/query.fcgi?cmd=Retrieve&db=pubmed&dopt=Abstract&list_uids=16915233)

[34] Finding Cures for Tropical Diseases: Is Open Source an Answer? (http://medicine.plosjournals.org/perlserv/?request=get-document&doi=10.1371/journal.pmed.0010056)

[35] http://www.tropicaldisease.org/

[36] http://www.iowh.org/

[37] http://www.dndi.org/

[38] Science Commons (http://sciencecommons.org/)

[39] http://www.adciv.org/Open_collaborative_design

[40] http://kenai.com/projects/jedi

[41] http://www.corepractice.org

[42] http://www.copyright.gov/legislation/dmca.pdf

[43] http://www.chillingeffects.org/

[44] Berry (2004) Internet Ethics: Privacy, Ethics and Alienation — An Open Source Approach. (http://opensource.mit.edu/papers/berry2.pdf) (PDF file)

[45] El-Emam, K (2001). Ethics and Open Source. Empirical Software Engineering 6(4). (http://springerlink.metapress.com/app/home/contribution.asp?wasp=hf0bld3qlk0unn8f8x2m&referrer=parent&backto=issue,2,12;journal,14,33;linkingpublicationresults,1:100262,1#ContactOfAuthor1)
[46] Elephantsdream.org (http://www.elephantsdream.org/)
[47] http://www.lcmedia.com/americanrevolution.pdf
[48] "The American Revolution (http://www.lcmedia.com/americanrevolution.pdf)
[49] http://www.opensourcecinema.org
[50] http://www.nfb.ca
[51] Open Source Pharmaceuticals http://www.farmavita.net/content/view/336/84/
[52] ISCA — International Sport and Culture Association — Youth — Youth corner — Racism in football (http://www.isca-web.org/english/youth/yource/thenetwork)
[53] Eclipse.org (http://www.eclipse.org/org/foundation/membersminutes/20070920MembersMeeting/07.09.12-Eclipse-Open-Innovation.pdf)
[54] Open Source Yoga Unity — Home (http://www.yogaunity.org)
[55] http://www.amazon.com/Copy-Rip-Burn-Politics-Source/dp/0745324142
[56] http://producingoss.com
[57] http://dreamsongs.com./IHE/IHE.html
[58] http://www.chandospublishing.com/chandos_publishing_record_detail.php?ID=98
[59] http://www.amazon.com/Success-Open-Source-Steven-Weber/dp/0674018583/ref=ed_oe_p
[60] http://cec.concordia.ca/econtact/11_3/Nettingsmeier_dont_hack.html
[61] http://shop.fsf.org/product/free-software-free-society
[62] http://electroacoustic.ca/econtact/11_3
[63] http://cecpublic.pbworks.com/OpenSource
[64] http://flet.netcipia.net/xwiki/bin/download/Main/publications%2Dfr/GEM2008%2DFLetellier%2DSubmittedPaper.pdf
[65] http://www.benkler.org/CoasesPenguin.PDF
[66] http://www.archive.org/details/LibreCultureMeditationsOnFreeCulture
[67] http://ideas.repec.org/p/wpa/wuwpio/0512001.html
[68] http://ideas.repec.org/p/jrp/jrpwrp/2008-045.html
[69] http://ideas.repec.org/p/jrp/jrpwrp/2008-047.html
[70] http://ideas.repec.org/p/diw/diwwpp/dp799.html
[71] http://ec.europa.eu/enterprise/ict/policy/doc/2006-11-20-flossimpact.pdf
[72] http://www.people.hbs.edu/jlerner/simple.pdf
[73] http://papers.ssrn.com/sol3/papers.cfm?abstract_id=1114371
[74] http://www.crema-research.ch/papers/2005-08.pdf
[75] http://www.riehle.org/computer-science/research/2007/computer-2007-article.html
[76] http://ideas.repec.org/p/usi/wpaper/424.html
[77] http://www.rnejournal.com/articles/schiff_software_mar02.pdf
[78] http://economist.com/displaystory.cfm?story_id=E1_NSNQQND
[79] http://www.askmar.com/open.html
[80] http://www.sdforum.org/index.cfm?fuseaction=Calendar.eventDetail&eventID=13068
[81] http://mloss.org
[82] http://code.google.com/opensource/osa-hall-of-fame.html
[83] http://www.qualipso.org
[84] http://www.iist.unu.edu
[85] http://opencert.iist.unu.edu
[86] http://news.bbc.co.uk/1/hi/technology/7841486.stm
[87] http://www.focus.com/fyi/information-technology/open-source-open-world/
[88] http://www.granneman.com/techinfo/linux/contributewithoutcoding.htm

Cross-platform

In computing, **cross-platform**, or **multi-platform**, is an attribute conferred to computer software or computing methods and concepts that are implemented and inter-operate on multiple computer platforms[1] [2] . Cross-platform software may be divided into two types; one requires individual building or compilation for each platform that it supports, and the other one can be directly run on any platform without special preparation, e.g., software written in an interpreted language or pre-compiled portable bytecode for which the interpreters or run-time packages are common or standard components of all platforms.

For example, a cross-platform application may run on Microsoft Windows on the x86 architecture, Linux on the x86 architecture and Mac OS X on either the PowerPC or x86 based Apple Macintosh systems. A cross-platform application may run on as many as all existing platforms, or on as few as two platforms.

Platforms

A platform is a combination of hardware and software used to run software applications. A platform can be described simply as an operating system or computer architecture, or it could be the combination of both. Probably the most familiar platform is Microsoft Windows running on the x86 architecture. Other well-known desktop computer platforms include Linux/Unix and Mac OS X (both of which are themselves cross-platform). There are, however, many devices such as cellular telephones that are also effectively computer platforms but less commonly thought about in that way. Application software can be written to depend on the features of a particular platform—either the hardware, operating system, or virtual machine it runs on. The Java platform is a virtual machine platform which runs on many operating systems and hardware types, and is a common platform for software to be written for.

Hardware platforms

A **hardware platform** can refer to a computer's architecture or processor architecture. For example, the x86 and x86-64 CPUs make up one of the most common computer architectures in use in general-purpose home computers today. These machines commonly run Microsoft Windows, though they can run other operating systems as well, including Linux, OpenBSD, NetBSD, Mac OS X and FreeBSD.

Software platforms

Software platforms can either be an operating system or programming environment, though more commonly it is a combination of both. A notable exception to this is Java, which uses an operating system independent virtual machine for its compiled code, known in the world of Java as bytecode. Examples of software platforms include:

- AmigaOS (m68k), AmigaOS 4 (PowerPC), AROS (x86, PowerPC, m68k), MorphOS (PowerPC)
- BSD, very cross platform (see NetBSD, for example)
- Java
- Linux (x86, x86-64, PowerPC, and other architectures)
- Mac OS X (PowerPC, x86, x86-64)
- Microsoft Windows (x86, x86-64)
- MS-DOS and compatibles on the x86: MS-DOS, DR-DOS, FreeDOS, etc.
- OS/2, eComStation
- Solaris (SPARC, x86, x86-64)
- The CLI, also known by the implementation names .NET Framework (from Microsoft) and Mono (from Novell)

Java platform

As previously noted, the Java platform is an exception to the general rule that an operating system is a software platform. The Java language provides a virtual machine, or a "virtual CPU" which runs all of the code that is written for the language. This enables the same executable binary to run on all systems which support the Java software, through the Java Virtual Machine. Java executables do not run directly on the operating system; that is, neither Windows nor Linux execute Java programs directly.

Because of this, however, Java is limited in that it does not directly support system-specific functionality. JNI can be used to access system specific functions, but then the code is likely no longer portable. Java programs can run on at least the Microsoft Windows, Mac OS X, Linux, and Solaris operating systems, and so the language is limited to functionality that exists on all these systems. This includes things such as computer networking, Internet sockets, but not necessarily raw hardware input/output.

Cross-platform software

In order for software to be considered **cross-platform**, it must be able to function on more than one computer architecture or operating system. This can be a time-consuming task given that different operating systems have different application programming interfaces or APIs (for example, Linux uses a different API for application software than Windows does).

Just because a particular operating system may run on different computer architectures, that does not mean that the software written for that operating system will automatically work on all architectures that the operating system supports. One example as of August, 2006 was OpenOffice.org, which did not natively run on the AMD64 or Intel 64 lines of processors implementing the x86-64 64-bit standards for computers; this has since been changed, and the OpenOffice.org suite of software is "mostly" ported to these 64-bit systems [3]. This also means that just because a program is written in a popular programming language such as C or C++, it does not mean it will run on all operating systems that support that programming language—or even on the same operating system on a different architecture.

Web applications

Web applications are typically described as cross-platform because, ideally, they are accessible from any of various web browsers within different operating systems. Such applications generally employ a client–server system architecture, and vary widely in complexity and functionality. This wide variability significantly complicates the goal of cross-platform capability, which is routinely at odds with the goal of advanced functionality.

Basic applications

Basic web applications perform all or most processing from a stateless web server, and pass the result to the client web browser. All user interaction with the application consists of simple exchanges of data requests and server responses. These types of applications were the norm in the early phases of World Wide Web application development. Such applications follow a simple transaction model, identical to that of serving static web pages. Today, they are still relatively common, especially where cross-platform compatibility and simplicity are deemed more critical than advanced functionalities. hence this is basic application

Advanced applications

Prominent examples of advanced web applications include the Web interface to Gmail, A9.com, and the maps.live.com website, part of the Live Search service from Microsoft. Such advanced applications routinely depend on additional features found only in the more recent versions of popular web browsers. These dependencies include Ajax, JavaScript, "Dynamic" HTML, SVG, and other components of rich internet applications. Older versions of popular browsers tend to lack support for certain features.

Design strategies

Because of the competing interests of cross-platform compatibility and advanced functionality, numerous alternative web application design strategies have emerged.

Such strategies include:

Graceful degradation

Graceful degradation attempts to provide the same or similar functionality to all users and platforms, while diminishing that functionality to a 'least common denominator' for more limited client browsers. For example, a user attempting to use a limited-feature browser to access Gmail may notice that Gmail switches to "Basic Mode," with reduced functionality. Some view this strategy as a lesser form of cross-platform capability.

Separation of functionality

Separation of functionality attempts to simply omit those subsets of functionality that are not capable from within certain client browsers or operating systems, while still delivering a 'complete' application to the user. (see also Separation of concerns).

Multiple codebase

Multiple codebase applications present different versions of an application depending on the specific client in use. This strategy is arguably the most complicated and expensive way to fulfill cross-platform capability, since even different versions of the same client browser (within the same operating system) can differ dramatically between each other. This is further complicated by the support for "plugins" which may or may not be present for any given installation of a particular browser version.

Third party libraries

Third party libraries attempt to simplify cross-platform capability by 'hiding' the complexities of client differentiation behind a single, unified API.

Testing strategies

One complicated aspect of cross-platform web application design is the need for software testing. In addition to the complications mentioned previously, there is the additional restriction that some browsers prohibit installation of different versions of the same browser on the same operating system. Techniques such as full virtualization are sometimes used as a workaround for this problem.

Traditional applications

Although web applications are becoming increasingly popular, many computer users still use traditional application software which does not rely on a client/web-server architecture. The distinction between "traditional" and "web" applications is not always unambiguous, however, because applications have many different features, installation methods and architectures; and some of these can overlap and occur in ways that blur the distinction. Nevertheless, this simplifying distinction is a common and useful generalization.

Binary software

Traditionally in modern computing, application software has been distributed to end-users as **binary images**, which are stored in executables, a specific type of binary file. Such executables only support the operating system and computer architecture that they were built for—which means that making a "cross-platform executable" would be something of a massive task, and is generally not done.

For software that is distributed as a binary executable, such as software written in C or C++, the programmer must build the software for each different operating system and computer architecture. For example, Mozilla Firefox, an open-source web browser, is available on Microsoft Windows, Mac OS X (both PowerPC and x86 through something Apple calls a **Universal binary**), and Linux on multiple computer architectures. The three platforms (in this case, Windows, Mac OS X, and Linux) are separate executable distributions, although they come from the same source code.

In the context of binary software, cross-platform programs are written in the source code and then "translated" to each system that it runs on through compiling it on different platforms. Also, software can be ported to a new computer architecture or operating system so that the program becomes more cross-platform than it already is. For example, a program such as Firefox, which already runs on Windows on the x86 family, can be modified and re-built to run on Linux on the x86 (and potentially other architectures) as well.

As an alternative to porting, cross-platform virtualization allows applications compiled for one CPU and operating system to run on a system with a different CPU and/or operating system, without modification to the source code or binaries. As an example, Apple's Rosetta software, which is built into Intel-based Apple Macintosh computers, runs applications compiled for the previous generation of Macs that used PowerPC CPUs. Another example is IBM PowerVM Lx86, which allows Linux/x86 applications to run unmodified on the Linux/Power operating system.

Scripts and interpreted languages

A script can be considered to be cross-platform if the scripting language is available on multiple platforms and the script only uses the facilities provided by the language. That is, a script written in Python for a Unix-like system will likely run with little or no modification on Windows, because Python also runs on Windows; there is also more than one implementation of Python that will run the same scripts (e.g., IronPython for .NET). The same goes for many of the open source programming languages that are available and are scripting languages.

Unlike binary executables, the same script can be used on all computers that have software to interpret the script. This is because the script is generally stored in plain text in a text file. There may be some issues, however, such as the type of new line character that sits between the lines. Generally, however, little or no work has to be done to make a script written for one system, run on another.

Some quite popular cross-platform scripting or interpreted languages are:

- bash—A Unix shell commonly run on Linux and other modern Unix-like systems, as well as on Windows via the Cygwin POSIX compatibility layer.
- Perl—A scripting language first released in 1987. Used for CGI WWW programming, small system administration tasks, and more.
- PHP—A scripting language most popular in use on the WWW for web applications.
- Python—A modern scripting language where the focus is on rapid application development and ease-of-writing, instead of program run-time efficiency.
- Ruby—A scripting language whose purpose is to be object-oriented and easy to read. Can also be used on the web through Ruby on Rails.
- Tcl - A dynamic programming language, suitable for a wide range of uses, including web and desktop applications, networking, administration, testing and many more.

Video games

Cross-platform is a term that can also apply to video games released on a range of video game consoles, specialized computers dedicated to the task of playing games. Examples of cross-platform games include:

- *Miner 2049er*
- *Phantasy Star Online*
- *Lara Croft Tomb Raider: Legend*
- *FIFA Series*

Each has been released across a variety of gaming platforms, such as the Nintendo Wii, PlayStation 3, Xbox 360, personal computers (PCs), and mobile devices.

The characteristics of a particular system may lengthen the time taken to implement a video game across multiple platforms. So, a video game may initially be released on a few platforms and then later released on remaining platforms. Typically, this situation occurs when a new gaming system is released, because video game developers need to acquaint themselves with the hardware and software associated with the new console.

Some games may not become cross-platform because of licensing agreements between developers and video game console manufacturers that limit development of a game to one particular console. As an example, Disney could create a game with the intention of release on the latest Nintendo and Sony game consoles. Should Disney license the game with Sony first, Disney may in exchange be required to release the game solely on Sony's console for a short time or indefinitely — effectively prohibiting a cross-platform release for the duration.

Several developers have implemented means to play games online while using different platforms. Epic Games, Microsoft, and Valve Software all possess technology that allows Xbox 360 and PlayStation 3 gamers to play with PC gamers, leaving the decision of which platform to use to consumers. The first game to allow this level of interactivity between PC and console games was *Quake 3*.

Games that feature cross-platform online play include:

- *DC Universe Online* (future release)
- *Kane & Lynch: Dead Men*
- *Lost Planet: Colonies*
- *Phantasy Star Online*
- *Shadowrun*
- *Uno*
- *Final Fantasy XI Online*
- *Universe at War: Earth Assault*
- *Game Room*
- *Portal 2* (future release)

Platform-independent software

Software that is platform independent does not rely on any special features of any single platform, or, if it does, handles those special features such that it can deal with multiple platforms.

Cross-platform programming

Cross-platform programming is the practice of actively writing software that will work on more than one platform.

Approaches to cross-platform programming

There are different ways of approaching the problem of writing a cross-platform application program. One such approach is simply to create multiple versions of the same program in different *source trees*—in other words, the

Windows version of a program might have one set of source code files and the Macintosh version might have another, while a FOSS *nix system might have another. While this is a straightforward approach to the problem, it has the potential to be considerably more expensive in development cost, development time, or both, especially for the corporate entities. The idea behind this is to create more than two different programs that have the ability to behave similarly to each other. It is also possible that this means of developing a cross-platform application will result in more problems with bug tracking and fixing, because the two different *source trees* would have different programmers, and thus different defects in each version. The smaller the programming team, the quicker the bug fixes tend to be.

Another approach that is used is to depend on pre-existing software that hides the differences between the platforms—called abstraction of the platform—such that the program itself is unaware of the platform it is running on. It could be said that such programs are *platform agnostic*. Programs that run on the Java Virtual Machine (JVM) are built in this fashion.

Some applications mix various methods of cross-platform programming to create the final application. An example of this is the Firefox web browser, which uses abstraction to build some of the lower-level components, separate source subtrees for implementing platform-specific features (like the GUI), and the implementation of more than one scripting language to help facilitate ease of portability. Firefox implements XUL, CSS and JavaScript for extending the browser, in addition to classic Netscape-style browser plugins. Much of the browser itself is written in XUL, CSS, and JavaScript, as well.

Cross-platform programming toolkits and environments

There are a number of tools[4] [5] which are available to help facilitate the process of cross-platform programming:

- Cairo: A free software library used to provide a vector graphics-based, device-independent API. It is designed to provide primitives for 2-dimensional drawing across a number of different backends. Cairo is written in C and has bindings for many programming languages.
- FLTK: Another open source cross platform toolkit, but more lightweight because it restricts itself to the GUI.
- fpGUI: An open source widget toolkit that is completely implemented in Object Pascal. It currently supports Linux, Windows and a bit of Windows CE.
- GTK+: An open source widget toolkit for Unix-like systems with X11 and Microsoft Windows.
- Mono (an open source version of Microsoft .NET): A cross-platform framework for applications and programming languages.
- Mozilla: An open source platform for building Mac, Windows and Linux applications.
- OpenGL: A cross-platform 3D graphics library.
- Qt—An application framework and widget toolkit for Unix-like systems with X11, Microsoft Windows, Mac OS X, and other systems—available under both open source and proprietary licenses.
- Simple and Fast Multimedia Library—A multimedia C++ API that provides low and high level access to graphics, input, audio, etc.
- Simple DirectMedia Layer—An open source cross-platform multimedia library written in C that creates an abstraction over various platforms' graphics, sound, and input APIs. It runs on many operating systems including Linux, Windows and Mac OS X and is aimed at games and multimedia applications.
- Tcl/Tk
- wxWidgets: An open source widget toolkit that is also an application framework[6] . It runs on Unix-like systems with X11, Microsoft Windows and Mac OS X. It permits applications written to use it to run on all of the systems that it supports, if the application does not use any operating system-specific programming in addition to it.
- XVT: A cross-platform toolkit for creating desktop applications in C/C++ on Windows, Linux and Unix (Solaris, HPUX, AIX), and Mac.

- Juce: An application framework written in in C++, used to write native software on numerous systems (Microsoft Windows, POSIX, Mac OS X), with no change to the code.

Challenges to cross-platform development

There are certain issues associated with cross-platform development. Some of these include:

- Testing cross-platform applications may be considerably more complicated, since different platforms can exhibit slightly different behaviors or subtle bugs. This problem has led some developers to deride cross-platform development as "Write Once, Debug Everywhere", a take on Sun's "Write Once, Run Anywhere" marketing slogan.
- Developers are often restricted to using the lowest common denominator subset of features which are available on all platforms. This may hinder the application's performance or prohibit developers from using platforms' most advanced features.
- Different platforms often have different user interface conventions, which cross-platform applications do not always accommodate. For example, applications developed for Mac OS X and GNOME are supposed to place the most important button on the right-hand side of windows and dialogs, whereas Microsoft Windows and KDE have the opposite convention. Though many of these differences are subtle, a cross-platform application which does not conform appropriately to these conventions may feel clunky or alien to the user. When working quickly, such opposing conventions may even result in data loss, such as in a dialog box confirming whether the user wants to save or discard changes to a file.
- Scripting languages and virtual machines must be translated into native executable code each time the application is executed, imposing a performance penalty. This performance hit can be alleviated using advanced techniques like just-in-time compilation; but even using such techniques, some performance overhead may be unavoidable.
- Different platforms require the use of native package formats such as RPM and MSI. Multiplatform installers such as InstallBuilder and IzPack address this need.
- Cross-platform execution environments may suffer cross-platform security flaws, creating a fertile environment for cross-platform malware.

See also

- List of widget toolkits
- Platform virtualization
- Java Platform
- Programming languages

References

[1] Design Guidelines: Glossary (http://java.sun.com/products/jlf/ed1/dg/higq.htm)
[2] Magenta Technology – Glossary (http://www.magenta-technology.com/en/technology/glossary/)
[3] http://wiki.services.openoffice.org/wiki/Porting_to_x86-64_(AMD64,_EM64T)
[4] The GUI Toolkit, Framework Page (http://www.oocities.com/SiliconValley/Vista/7184/guitool.html)
[5] Platform Independent FAQ (http://www.zeta.org.au/~rosko/pigui.htm)
[6] WxWidgets Description (http://wxwidgets.org/)

Software test

Software testing is an investigation conducted to provide stakeholders with information about the quality of the product or service under test.[1] Software testing also provides an objective, independent view of the software to allow the business to appreciate and understand the risks at implementation of the software. Test techniques include, but are not limited to, the process of executing a program or application with the intent of finding software bugs.

Software testing can also be stated as the process of validating and verifying that a software program/application/product:

1. meets the business and technical requirements that guided its design and development;
2. works as expected; and
3. can be implemented with the same characteristics.

Software testing, depending on the testing method employed, can be implemented at any time in the development process. However, most of the test effort occurs after the requirements have been defined and the coding process has been completed. As such, the methodology of the test is governed by the software development methodology adopted.

Different software development models will focus the test effort at different points in the development process. Newer development models, such as Agile, often employ test driven development and place an increased portion of the testing in the hands of the developer, before it reaches a formal team of testers. In a more traditional model, most of the test execution occurs after the requirements have been defined and the coding process has been completed.

Overview

Testing can never completely identify all the defects within software. Instead, it furnishes a *criticism* or *comparison* that compares the state and behavior of the product against oracles—principles or mechanisms by which someone might recognize a problem. These oracles may include (but are not limited to) specifications, contracts,[2] comparable products, past versions of the same product, inferences about intended or expected purpose, user or customer expectations, relevant standards, applicable laws, or other criteria.

Every software product has a target audience. For example, the audience for video game software is completely different from banking software. Therefore, when an organization develops or otherwise invests in a software product, it can assess whether the software product will be acceptable to its end users, its target audience, its purchasers, and other stakeholders. **Software testing** is the process of attempting to make this assessment.

A study conducted by NIST in 2002 reports that software bugs cost the U.S. economy $59.5 billion annually. More than a third of this cost could be avoided if better software testing was performed.[3]

History

The separation of debugging from testing was initially introduced by Glenford J. Myers in 1979.[4] Although his attention was on breakage testing ("a successful test is one that finds a bug"[4] [5]) it illustrated the desire of the software engineering community to separate fundamental development activities, such as debugging, from that of verification. Dave Gelperin and William C. Hetzel classified in 1988 the phases and goals in software testing in the following stages:[6]

- Until 1956 - Debugging oriented[7]
- 1957–1978 - Demonstration oriented[8]
- 1979–1982 - Destruction oriented[9]
- 1983–1987 - Evaluation oriented[10]
- 1988–2000 - Prevention oriented[11]

Software testing topics

Scope

A primary purpose for testing is to detect software failures so that defects may be discovered and corrected. This is a non-trivial pursuit. Testing cannot establish that a product functions properly under all conditions but can only establish that it does not function properly under specific conditions.[12] The scope of software testing often includes examination of code as well as execution of that code in various environments and conditions as well as examining the aspects of code: does it do what it is supposed to do and do what it needs to do. In the current culture of software development, a testing organization may be separate from the development team. There are various roles for testing team members. Information derived from software testing may be used to correct the process by which software is developed.[13]

Functional vs non-functional testing

Functional testing refers to tests that verify a specific action or function of the code. These are usually found in the code requirements documentation, although some development methodologies work from use cases or user stories. Functional tests tend to answer the question of "can the user do this" or "does this particular feature work".

Non-functional testing refers to aspects of the software that may not be related to a specific function or user action, such as scalability or security. Non-functional testing tends to answer such questions as "how many people can log in at once".

Defects and failures

Not all software defects are caused by coding errors. One common source of expensive defects is caused by requirement gaps, e.g., unrecognized requirements, that result in errors of omission by the program designer.[14] A common source of requirements gaps is non-functional requirements such as testability, scalability, maintainability, usability, performance, and security.

Software faults occur through the following processes. A programmer makes an error (mistake), which results in a defect (fault, bug) in the software source code. If this defect is executed, in certain situations the system will produce wrong results, causing a failure.[15] Not all defects will necessarily result in failures. For example, defects in dead code will never result in failures. A defect can turn into a failure when the environment is changed. Examples of these changes in environment include the software being run on a new hardware platform, alterations in source data or interacting with different software.[15] A single defect may result in a wide range of failure symptoms.

Finding faults early

It is commonly believed that the earlier a defect is found the cheaper it is to fix it.[16] The following table shows the cost of fixing the defect depending on the stage it was found.[17] For example, if a problem in the requirements is found only post-release, then it would cost 10–100 times more to fix than if it had already been found by the requirements review.

		Time detected				
		Requirements	Architecture	Construction	System test	Post-release
Time introduced	**Requirements**	1×	3×	5–10×	10×	10–100×
	Architecture	-	1×	10×	15×	25–100×
	Construction	-	-	1×	10×	10–25×

Compatibility

A common cause of software failure (real or perceived) is a lack of compatibility with other application software, operating systems (or operating system versions, old or new), or target environments that differ greatly from the original (such as a terminal or GUI application intended to be run on the desktop now being required to become a web application, which must render in a web browser). For example, in the case of a lack of backward compatibility, this can occur because the programmers develop and test software only on the latest version of the target environment, which not all users may be running. This results in the unintended consequence that the latest work may not function on earlier versions of the target environment, or on older hardware that earlier versions of the target environment was capable of using. Sometimes such issues can be fixed by proactively abstracting operating system functionality into a separate program module or library.

Input combinations and preconditions

A very fundamental problem with software testing is that testing under *all* combinations of inputs and preconditions (initial state) is not feasible, even with a simple product.[12] [18] This means that the number of defects in a software product can be very large and defects that occur infrequently are difficult to find in testing. More significantly, non-functional dimensions of quality (how it is supposed to *be* versus what it is supposed to *do*)—usability, scalability, performance, compatibility, reliability—can be highly subjective; something that constitutes sufficient value to one person may be intolerable to another.

Static vs. dynamic testing

There are many approaches to software testing. Reviews, walkthroughs, or inspections are considered as static testing, whereas actually executing programmed code with a given set of test cases is referred to as dynamic testing. Static testing can be (and unfortunately in practice often is) omitted. Dynamic testing takes place when the program itself is used for the first time (which is generally considered the beginning of the testing stage). Dynamic testing may begin before the program is 100% complete in order to test particular sections of code (modules or discrete functions). Typical techniques for this are either using stubs/drivers or execution from a debugger environment. For example, spreadsheet programs are, by their very nature, tested to a large extent interactively ("on the fly"), with results displayed immediately after each calculation or text manipulation.

Software verification and validation

Software testing is used in association with verification and validation:[19]

- Verification: Have we built the software right? (i.e., does it match the specification).
- Validation: Have we built the right software? (i.e., is this what the customer wants).

The terms verification and validation are commonly used interchangeably in the industry; it is also common to see these two terms incorrectly defined. According to the IEEE Standard Glossary of Software Engineering Terminology:

> Verification is the process of evaluating a system or component to determine whether the products of a given development phase satisfy the conditions imposed at the start of that phase.
>
> Validation is the process of evaluating a system or component during or at the end of the development process to determine whether it satisfies specified requirements.

The software testing team

Software testing can be done by software testers. Until the 1980s the term "software tester" was used generally, but later it was also seen as a separate profession. Regarding the periods and the different goals in software testing,[20] different roles have been established: *manager*, *test lead*, *test designer*, *tester*, *automation developer*, and *test administrator*.

Software quality assurance (SQA)

Though controversial, software testing may be viewed as an important part of the software quality assurance (SQA) process.[12] In SQA, software process specialists and auditors take a broader view on software and its development. They examine and change the software engineering process itself to reduce the amount of faults that end up in the delivered software: the so-called *defect rate*.

What constitutes an "acceptable defect rate" depends on the nature of the software; A flight simulator video game would have much higher defect tolerance than software for an actual airplane.

Although there are close links with SQA, testing departments often exist independently, and there may be no SQA function in some companies.

Software testing is a task intended to detect defects in software by contrasting a computer program's expected results with its actual results for a given set of inputs. By contrast, QA (quality assurance) is the implementation of policies and procedures intended to prevent defects from occurring in the first place.

Testing methods

The box approach

Software testing methods are traditionally divided into white- and black-box testing. These two approaches are used to describe the point of view that a test engineer takes when designing test cases.

White box testing

White box testing is when the tester has access to the internal data structures and algorithms including the code that implement these.

Types of white box testing

> The following types of white box testing exist:

- API testing (application programming interface) - testing of the application using public and private APIs

- Code coverage - creating tests to satisfy some criteria of code coverage (e.g., the test designer can create tests to cause all statements in the program to be executed at least once)
- Fault injection methods - improving the coverage of a test by introducing faults to test code paths
- Mutation testing methods
- Static testing - White box testing includes all static testing

Test coverage

White box testing methods can also be used to evaluate the completeness of a test suite that was created with black box testing methods. This allows the software team to examine parts of a system that are rarely tested and ensures that the most important function points have been tested.[21]

Two common forms of code coverage are:

- *Function coverage*, which reports on functions executed
- *Statement coverage*, which reports on the number of lines executed to complete the test

They both return a code coverage metric, measured as a percentage.

Black box testing

Black box testing treats the software as a "black box"—without any knowledge of internal implementation. Black box testing methods include: equivalence partitioning, boundary value analysis, all-pairs testing, fuzz testing, model-based testing, traceability matrix, exploratory testing and specification-based testing.

Specification-based testing: Specification-based testing aims to test the functionality of software according to the applicable requirements.[22] Thus, the tester inputs data into, and only sees the output from, the test object. This level of testing usually requires thorough test cases to be provided to the tester, who then can simply verify that for a given input, the output value (or behavior), either "is" or "is not" the same as the expected value specified in the test case.

Specification-based testing is necessary, but it is insufficient to guard against certain risks.[23]

Advantages and disadvantages: The black box tester has no "bonds" with the code, and a tester's perception is very simple: a code *must* have bugs. Using the principle, "Ask and you shall receive," black box testers find bugs where programmers do not. On the other hand, black box testing has been said to be "like a walk in a dark labyrinth without a flashlight," because the tester doesn't know how the software being tested was actually constructed. As a result, there are situations when (1) a tester writes many test cases to check something that could have been tested by only one test case, and/or (2) some parts of the back-end are not tested at all.

Therefore, black box testing has the advantage of "an unaffiliated opinion", on the one hand, and the disadvantage of "blind exploring", on the other. [24]

Grey box testing

Grey box testing (American spelling: **gray box testing**) involves having knowledge of internal data structures and algorithms for purposes of designing the test cases, but testing at the user, or black-box level. Manipulating input data and formatting output do not qualify as grey box, because the input and output are clearly outside of the "black-box" that we are calling the system under test. This distinction is particularly important when conducting integration testing between two modules of code written by two different developers, where only the interfaces are exposed for test. However, modifying a data repository does qualify as grey box, as the user would not normally be able to change the data outside of the system under test. Grey box testing may also include reverse engineering to determine, for instance, boundary values or error messages.

Testing levels

Tests are frequently grouped by where they are added in the software development process, or by the level of specificity of the test.

Unit testing

Unit testing refers to tests that verify the functionality of a specific section of code, usually at the function level. In an object-oriented environment, this is usually at the class level, and the minimal unit tests include the constructors and destructors.[25]

These type of tests are usually written by developers as they work on code (white-box style), to ensure that the specific function is working as expected. One function might have multiple tests, to catch corner cases or other branches in the code. Unit testing alone cannot verify the functionality of a piece of software, but rather is used to assure that the building blocks the software uses work independently of each other.

Unit testing is also called *component testing*.

Integration testing

Integration testing is any type of software testing that seeks to verify the interfaces between components against a software design. Software components may be integrated in an iterative way or all together ("big bang"). Normally the former is considered a better practice since it allows interface issues to be localised more quickly and fixed.

Integration testing works to expose defects in the interfaces and interaction between integrated components (modules). Progressively larger groups of tested software components corresponding to elements of the architectural design are integrated and tested until the software works as a system.[26]

System testing

System testing tests a completely integrated system to verify that it meets its requirements.[27]

System integration testing

System integration testing verifies that a system is integrated to any external or third party systems defined in the system requirements.

Regression testing

Regression testing focuses on finding defects after a major code change has occurred. Specifically, it seeks to uncover software regressions, or old bugs that have come back. Such regressions occur whenever software functionality that was previously working correctly stops working as intended. Typically, regressions occur as an unintended consequence of program changes, when the newly developed part of the software collides with the previously existing code. Common methods of regression testing include re-running previously run tests and checking whether previously fixed faults have re-emerged. The depth of testing depends on the phase in the release process and the risk of the added features. They can either be complete, for changes added late in the release or deemed to be risky, to very shallow, consisting of positive tests on each feature, if the changes are early in the release or deemed to be of low risk.

Acceptance testing

Acceptance testing can mean one of two things:

1. A smoke test is used as an acceptance test prior to introducing a new build to the main testing process, i.e. before integration or regression.
2. Acceptance testing performed by the customer, often in their lab environment on their own hardware, is known as user acceptance testing (UAT). Acceptance testing may be performed as part of the hand-off process between any two phases of development.

Alpha testing

Alpha testing is simulated or actual operational testing by potential users/customers or an independent test team at the developers' site. Alpha testing is often employed for off-the-shelf software as a form of internal acceptance testing, before the software goes to beta testing. van Veenendaal, Erik. "Standard glossary of terms used in Software Testing" [28]. Retrieved 17 June 2010.

Beta testing

Beta testing comes after alpha testing. Versions of the software, known as beta versions, are released to a limited audience outside of the programming team. The software is released to groups of people so that further testing can ensure the product has few faults or bugs. Sometimes, beta versions are made available to the open public to increase the feedback field to a maximal number of future users.

Non-functional testing

Special methods exist to test non-functional aspects of software. In contrast to functional testing, which establishes the correct operation of the software (correct in that it matches the expected behavior defined in the design requirements), non-functional testing verifies that the software functions properly even when it receives invalid or unexpected inputs. Software fault injection, in the form of fuzzing, is an example of non-functional testing. Non-functional testing, especially for software, is designed to establish whether the device under test can tolerate invalid or unexpected inputs, thereby establishing the robustness of input validation routines as well as error-handling routines. Various commercial non-functional testing tools are linked from the software fault injection page; there are also numerous open-source and free software tools available that perform non-functional testing.

Software performance testing and load testing

Performance testing is executed to determine how fast a system or sub-system performs under a particular workload. It can also serve to validate and verify other quality attributes of the system, such as scalability, reliability and resource usage. Load testing is primarily concerned with testing that can continue to operate under a specific load, whether that be large quantities of data or a large number of users. This is generally referred to as software scalability. The related load testing activity of when performed as a non-functional activity is often referred to as *endurance testing*.

Volume testing is a way to test functionality. *Stress testing* is a way to test reliability. *Load testing* is a way to test performance. There is little agreement on what the specific goals of load testing are. The terms load testing, performance testing, reliability testing, and volume testing, are often used interchangeably.

Stability testing

Stability testing checks to see if the software can continuously function well in or above an acceptable period. This activity of non-functional software testing is often referred to as load (or endurance) testing.

Usability testing

Usability testing is needed to check if the user interface is easy to use and understand.

Security testing

Security testing is essential for software that processes confidential data to prevent system intrusion by hackers.

Internationalization and localization

Internationalization and localization is needed to test these aspects of software, for which a pseudolocalization method can be used. It will verify that the application still works, even after it has been translated into a new language or adapted for a new culture (such as different currencies or time zones).

Destructive testing

Destructive testing attempts to cause the software or a sub-system to fail, in order to test its robustness.

The testing process

Traditional CMMI or waterfall development model

A common practice of software testing is that testing is performed by an independent group of testers after the functionality is developed, before it is shipped to the customer.[29] This practice often results in the testing phase being used as a project buffer to compensate for project delays, thereby compromising the time devoted to testing.[30]

Another practice is to start software testing at the same moment the project starts and it is a continuous process until the project finishes.[31]

Agile or Extreme development model

In counterpoint, some emerging software disciplines such as extreme programming and the agile software development movement, adhere to a "test-driven software development" model. In this process, unit tests are written first, by the software engineers (often with pair programming in the extreme programming methodology). Of course these tests fail initially; as they are expected to. Then as code is written it passes incrementally larger portions of the test suites. The test suites are continuously updated as new failure conditions and corner cases are discovered, and they are integrated with any regression tests that are developed. Unit tests are maintained along with the rest of the software source code and generally integrated into the build process (with inherently interactive tests being relegated to a partially manual build acceptance process). The ultimate goal of this test process is to achieve continuous deployment where software updates can be published to the public frequently. [32] [33]

A sample testing cycle

Although variations exist between organizations, there is a typical cycle for testing[34] . The sample below is common among organizations employing the Waterfall development model.

- **Requirements analysis**: Testing should begin in the requirements phase of the software development life cycle. During the design phase, testers work with developers in determining what aspects of a design are testable and with what parameters those tests work.
- **Test planning**: Test strategy, test plan, testbed creation. Since many activities will be carried out during testing, a plan is needed.
- **Test development**: Test procedures, test scenarios, test cases, test datasets, test scripts to use in testing software.
- **Test execution**: Testers execute the software based on the plans and test documents then report any errors found to the development team.
- **Test reporting**: Once testing is completed, testers generate metrics and make final reports on their test effort and whether or not the software tested is ready for release.
- **Test result analysis**: Or Defect Analysis, is done by the development team usually along with the client, in order to decide what defects should be treated, fixed, rejected (i.e. found software working properly) or deferred to be dealt with later.
- **Defect Retesting**: Once a defect has been dealt with by the development team, it is retested by the testing team. AKA Resolution testing.
- **Regression testing**: It is common to have a small test program built of a subset of tests, for each integration of new, modified, or fixed software, in order to ensure that the latest delivery has not ruined anything, and that the software product as a whole is still working correctly.
- **Test Closure**: Once the test meets the exit criteria, the activities such as capturing the key outputs, lessons learned, results, logs, documents related to the project are archived and used as a reference for future projects.

Automated testing

Many programming groups are relying more and more on automated testing, especially groups that use test-driven development. There are many frameworks to write tests in, and continuous integration software will run tests automatically every time code is checked into a version control system.

While automation cannot reproduce everything that a human can do (and all the ways they think of doing it), it can be very useful for regression testing. However, it does require a well-developed test suite of testing scripts in order to be truly useful.

Testing tools

Program testing and fault detection can be aided significantly by testing tools and debuggers. Testing/debug tools include features such as:

- Program monitors, permitting full or partial monitoring of program code including:
  - Instruction set simulator, permitting complete instruction level monitoring and trace facilities
  - Program animation, permitting step-by-step execution and conditional breakpoint at source level or in machine code
  - Code coverage reports
- Formatted dump or symbolic debugging, tools allowing inspection of program variables on error or at chosen points
- Automated functional GUI testing tools are used to repeat system-level tests through the GUI
- Benchmarks, allowing run-time performance comparisons to be made
- Performance analysis (or profiling tools) that can help to highlight hot spots and resource usage

Some of these features may be incorporated into an Integrated Development Environment (IDE).

Measurement in software testing

Usually, quality is constrained to such topics as correctness, completeness, security, but can also include more technical requirements as described under the ISO standard ISO/IEC 9126, such as capability, reliability, efficiency, portability, maintainability, compatibility, and usability.

There are a number of frequently-used software measures, often called *metrics*, which are used to assist in determining the state of the software or the adequacy of the testing.

Testing artifacts

Software testing process can produce several artifacts.

Test plan

A test specification is called a test plan. The developers are well aware what test plans will be executed and this information is made available to management and the developers. The idea is to make them more cautious when developing their code or making additional changes. Some companies have a higher-level document called a test strategy.

Traceability matrix

A traceability matrix is a table that correlates requirements or design documents to test documents. It is used to change tests when the source documents are changed, or to verify that the test results are correct.

Test case

A test case normally consists of a unique identifier, requirement references from a design specification, preconditions, events, a series of steps (also known as actions) to follow, input, output, expected result, and actual result. Clinically defined a test case is an input and an expected result.[35] This can be as pragmatic as 'for condition x your derived result is y', whereas other test cases described in more detail the input scenario and what results might be expected. It can occasionally be a series of steps (but often steps are contained in a separate test procedure that can be exercised against multiple test cases, as a matter of economy) but with one expected result or expected outcome. The optional fields are a test case ID, test step, or order of execution number, related requirement(s), depth, test category, author, and check boxes for whether the test is automatable and has been automated. Larger test cases may also contain prerequisite states or steps, and descriptions. A test case should also contain a place for the actual result. These steps can be stored in a word processor document, spreadsheet, database, or other common repository. In a database system, you may also be able to see past test results, who generated the results, and what system configuration was used to generate those results. These past results would usually be stored in a separate table.

Test script

The test script is the combination of a test case, test procedure, and test data. Initially the term was derived from the product of work created by automated regression test tools. Today, test scripts can be manual, automated, or a combination of both.

Test suite

The most common term for a collection of test cases is a test suite. The test suite often also contains more detailed instructions or goals for each collection of test cases. It definitely contains a section where the tester identifies the system configuration used during testing. A group of test cases may also contain prerequisite states or steps, and descriptions of the following tests.

Test data

In most cases, multiple sets of values or data are used to test the same functionality of a particular feature. All the test values and changeable environmental components are collected in separate files and stored as test data. It is also useful to provide this data to the client and with the product or a project.

Test harness

The software, tools, samples of data input and output, and configurations are all referred to collectively as a test harness.

Certifications

Several certification programs exist to support the professional aspirations of software testers and quality assurance specialists. No certification currently offered actually requires the applicant to demonstrate the ability to test software. No certification is based on a widely accepted body of knowledge. This has led some to declare that the testing field is not ready for certification.[36] Certification itself cannot measure an individual's productivity, their skill, or practical knowledge, and cannot guarantee their competence, or professionalism as a tester.[37]

Software testing certification types

- *Exam-based*: Formalized exams, which need to be passed; can also be learned by self-study [e.g., for ISTQB or QAI][38]
- *Education-based*: Instructor-led sessions, where each course has to be passed [e.g., International Institute for Software Testing (IIST)].

Testing certifications

- Certified Associate in Software Testing (CAST) offered by the Quality Assurance Institute (QAI)[39]
- CATe offered by the *International Institute for Software Testing*[40]
- Certified Manager in Software Testing (CMST) offered by the Quality Assurance Institute (QAI)[39]
- Certified Software Tester (CSTE) offered by the Quality Assurance Institute (QAI)[39]
- Certified Software Test Professional (CSTP) offered by the *International Institute for Software Testing*[40]
- CSTP (TM) (Australian Version) offered by *K. J. Ross & Associates*[41]
- ISEB offered by the Information Systems Examinations Board
- ISTQB Certified Tester, Foundation Level (CTFL) offered by the International Software Testing Qualification Board [42] [43]
- ISTQB Certified Tester, Advanced Level (CTAL) offered by the International Software Testing Qualification Board [42] [43]
- TMPF TMap Next Foundation offered by the *Examination Institute for Information Science*[44]

Quality assurance certifications

- CMSQ offered by the *Quality Assurance Institute* (QAI)[39] .
- CSQA offered by the *Quality Assurance Institute* (QAI)[39]
- CSQE offered by the American Society for Quality (ASQ)[45]
- CQIA offered by the American Society for Quality (ASQ)[45]

Controversy

Some of the major software testing controversies include:

What constitutes responsible software testing?

Members of the "context-driven" school of testing[46] believe that there are no "best practices" of testing, but rather that testing is a set of skills that allow the tester to select or invent testing practices to suit each unique situation.[47]

Agile vs. traditional

Should testers learn to work under conditions of uncertainty and constant change or should they aim at process "maturity"? The agile testing movement has received growing popularity since 2006 mainly in commercial circles [48] [49], whereas government and military[50] software providers are slow to embrace this methodology in favour of traditional test-last models (e.g. in the Waterfall model).

Exploratory test vs. scripted[51]

Should tests be designed at the same time as they are executed or should they be designed beforehand?

Manual testing vs. automated

Some writers believe that test automation is so expensive relative to its value that it should be used sparingly.[52] More in particular, test-driven development states that developers should write unit-tests of the XUnit type before coding the functionality. The tests then can be considered as a way to capture and implement the requirements.

Software design vs. software implementation[53]

Should testing be carried out only at the end or throughout the whole process?

Who watches the watchmen?

The idea is that any form of observation is also an interaction—the act of testing can also affect that which is being tested[54].

See also

- All-pairs testing
- Automated testing
- Dynamic program analysis
- Formal verification
- GUI software testing
- Manual testing
- Orthogonal array testing
- Pair Testing
- Reverse semantic traceability
- Software testability
- Static code analysis
- Web testing

External links

- Software testing tools and products [55] at the Open Directory Project
- "Software that makes Software better" Economist.com [56]
- Software QA Testing Glossary [57]

References

[1] Exploratory Testing (http://www.kaner.com/pdfs/ETatQAI.pdf), Cem Kaner, Florida Institute of Technology, *Quality Assurance Institute Worldwide Annual Software Testing Conference*, Orlando, FL, November 2006

[2] Leitner, A., Ciupa, I., Oriol, M., Meyer, B., Fiva, A., "Contract Driven Development = Test Driven Development - Writing Test Cases" (http://se.inf.ethz.ch/people/leitner/publications/cdd_leitner_esec_fse_2007.pdf), Proceedings of ESEC/FSE'07: European Software Engineering Conference and the ACM SIGSOFT Symposium on the Foundations of Software Engineering 2007, (Dubrovnik, Croatia), September 2007

[3] Software errors cost U.S. economy $59.5 billion annually (http://www.nist.gov/public_affairs/releases/n02-10.htm), NIST report

[4] Myers, Glenford J. (1979). *The Art of Software Testing*. John Wiley and Sons. ISBN 0-471-04328-1.

[5] Company, People's Computer (1987). "Dr. Dobb's journal of software tools for the professional programmer" (http://books.google.com/?id=7RoIAAAAIAAJ). *Dr. Dobb's journal of software tools for the professional programmer* (M&T Pub) **12** (1-6): 116. .

[6] Gelperin, D.; B. Hetzel (1988). "The Growth of Software Testing". *CACM* **31** (6). ISSN 0001-0782.

[7] *until 1956 it was the debugging oriented period, when testing was often associated to debugging: there was no clear difference between testing and debugging*. Gelperin, D.; B. Hetzel (1988). "The Growth of Software Testing". *CACM* **31** (6). ISSN 0001-0782.

[8] *From 1957–1978 there was the demonstration oriented period where debugging and testing was distinguished now - in this period it was shown, that software satisfies the requirements*. Gelperin, D.; B. Hetzel (1988). "The Growth of Software Testing". *CACM* **31** (6). ISSN 0001-0782.

[9] *The time between 1979–1982 is announced as the destruction oriented period, where the goal was to find errors*. Gelperin, D.; B. Hetzel (1988). "The Growth of Software Testing". *CACM* **31** (6). ISSN 0001-0782.

[10] *1983–1987 is classified as the evaluation oriented period: intention here is that during the software lifecycle a product evaluation is provided and measuring quality*. Gelperin, D.; B. Hetzel (1988). "The Growth of Software Testing". *CACM* **31** (6). ISSN 0001-0782.

[11] *From 1988 on it was seen as prevention oriented period where tests were to demonstrate that software satisfies its specification, to detect faults and to prevent faults*. Gelperin, D.; B. Hetzel (1988). "The Growth of Software Testing". *CACM* **31** (6). ISSN 0001-0782.

[12] Kaner, Cem; Falk, Jack and Nguyen, Hung Quoc (1999). *Testing Computer Software, 2nd Ed.*. New York, et al: John Wiley and Sons, Inc.. pp. 480 pages. ISBN 0-471-35846-0.

[13] Kolawa, Adam; Huizinga, Dorota (2007). *Automated Defect Prevention: Best Practices in Software Management* (http://www.wiley.com/WileyCDA/WileyTitle/productCd-0470042125.html). Wiley-IEEE Computer Society Press. pp. 41–43. ISBN 0470042125. .

[14] Kolawa, Adam; Huizinga, Dorota (2007). *Automated Defect Prevention: Best Practices in Software Management* (http://www.wiley.com/WileyCDA/WileyTitle/productCd-0470042125.html). Wiley-IEEE Computer Society Press. p. 86. ISBN 0470042125. .

[15] Section 1.1.2, Certified Tester Foundation Level Syllabus (http://www.istqb.org/downloads/syllabi/SyllabusFoundation.pdf), International Software Testing Qualifications Board

[16] Kaner, Cem; James Bach, Bret Pettichord (2001). *Lessons Learned in Software Testing: A Context-Driven Approach*. Wiley. p. 4. ISBN 0-471-08112-4.

[17] McConnell, Steve (2004). *Code Complete* (2nd ed.). Microsoft Press. pp. 960. ISBN 0-7356-1967-0.

[18] Principle 2, Section 1.3, Certified Tester Foundation Level Syllabus (http://www.bcs.org/upload/pdf/istqbsyll.pdf), International Software Testing Qualifications Board

[19] Tran, Eushiuan (1999). "Verification/Validation/Certification" (http://www.ece.cmu.edu/~koopman/des_s99/verification/index.html). in Koopman, P.. *Topics in Dependable Embedded Systems*. USA: Carnegie Mellon University. . Retrieved 2008-01-13.

[20] see D. Gelperin and W.C. Hetzel

[21] Introduction (http://www.bullseye.com/coverage.html#intro), Code Coverage Analysis, Steve Cornett

[22] Laycock, G. T. (1993) (PostScript). *The Theory and Practice of Specification Based Software Testing* (http://www.mcs.le.ac.uk/people/gtl1/thesis.ps.gz). Dept of Computer Science, Sheffield University, UK. . Retrieved 2008-02-13.

[23] Bach, James (June 1999). "Risk and Requirements-Based Testing" (http://www.satisfice.com/articles/requirements_based_testing.pdf) (PDF). *Computer* **32** (6): 113–114. . Retrieved 2008-08-19.

[24] Savenkov, Roman (2008). *How to Become a Software Tester*. Roman Savenkov Consulting. p. 159. ISBN 978-0-615-23372-7.

[25] Binder, Robert V. (1999). *Testing Object-Oriented Systems: Objects, Patterns, and Tools*. Addison-Wesley Professional. p. 45. ISBN 0-201-80938-9.

[26] Beizer, Boris (1990). *Software Testing Techniques* (Second ed.). New York: Van Nostrand Reinhold. pp. 21,430. ISBN 0-442-20672-0.

[27] IEEE (1990). *IEEE Standard Computer Dictionary: A Compilation of IEEE Standard Computer Glossaries*. New York: IEEE. ISBN 1559370793.

[28] http://www.astqb.org/educational-resources/glossary.php#A

[29] e)Testing Phase in Software Testing:- (http://www.etestinghub.com/testing_lifecycles.php#2)
[30] Myers, Glenford J. (1979). *The Art of Software Testing*. John Wiley and Sons. pp. 145–146. ISBN 0-471-04328-1.
[31] Dustin, Elfriede (2002). *Effective Software Testing*. Addison Wesley. p. 3. ISBN 0-20179-429-2.
[32] Marchenko, Artem (November 16, 2007). "XP Practice: Continuous Integration" (http://agilesoftwaredevelopment.com/xp/practices/continuous-integration). . Retrieved 2009-11-16.
[33] Gurses, Levent (February 19, 2007). "Agile 101: What is Continuous Integration?" (http://www.jacoozi.com/blog/?p=18). . Retrieved 2009-11-16.
[34] Pan, Jiantao (Spring 1999). "Software Testing (18-849b Dependable Embedded Systems)" (http://www.ece.cmu.edu/~koopman/des_s99/sw_testing/). *Topics in Dependable Embedded Systems*. Electrical and Computer Engineering Department, Carnegie Mellon University. .
[35] IEEE (1998). *IEEE standard for software test documentation*. New York: IEEE. ISBN 0-7381-1443-X.
[36] Kaner, Cem (2001). "NSF grant proposal to "lay a foundation for significant improvements in the quality of academic and commercial courses in software testing"" (http://www.testingeducation.org/general/nsf_grant.pdf) (pdf). .
[37] Kaner, Cem (2003). "Measuring the Effectiveness of Software Testers" (http://www.testingeducation.org/a/mest.pdf) (pdf). .
[38] Black, Rex (December 2008). *Advanced Software Testing- Vol. 2: Guide to the ISTQB Advanced Certification as an Advanced Test Manager*. Santa Barbara: Rocky Nook Publisher. ISBN 1933952369.
[39] Quality Assurance Institute (http://www.qaiglobalinstitute.com/)
[40] International Institute for Software Testing (http://www.testinginstitute.com/)
[41] K. J. Ross & Associates (http://www.kjross.com.au/cstp/)
[42] "ISTQB" (http://www.istqb.org/). .
[43] "ISTQB in the U.S." (http://www.astqb.org/). .
[44] EXIN: Examination Institute for Information Science (http://www.exin-exams.com)
[45] American Society for Quality (http://www.asq.org/)
[46] context-driven-testing.com (http://www.context-driven-testing.com)
[47] Article on taking agile traits without the agile method. (http://www.technicat.com/writing/process.html)
[48] "We're all part of the story" (http://stpcollaborative.com/knowledge/272-were-all-part-of-the-story) by David Strom, July 1, 2009
[49] IEEE article about differences in adoption of agile trends between experienced managers vs. young students of the Project Management Institute (http://ieeexplore.ieee.org/Xplore/login.jsp?url=/iel5/10705/33795/01609838.pdf?temp=x). See also Agile adoption study from 2007 (http://www.ambysoft.com/downloads/surveys/AgileAdoption2007.ppt)
[50] Agile software development practices slowly entering the military (http://www.stsc.hill.af.mil/crosstalk/2004/04/0404willison.html)
[51] IEEE article on Exploratory vs. Non Exploratory testing (http://ieeexplore.ieee.org/iel5/10351/32923/01541817.pdf?arnumber=1541817)
[52] An example is Mark Fewster, Dorothy Graham: *Software Test Automation*. Addison Wesley, 1999, ISBN 0-201-33140-3.
[53] Article referring to other links questioning the necessity of unit testing (http://java.dzone.com/news/why-evangelising-unit-testing-)
[54] Microsoft Development Network Discussion on exactly this topic (http://channel9.msdn.com/forums/Coffeehouse/402611-Are-you-a-Test-Driven-Developer/)
[55] http://www.dmoz.org/Computers/Programming/Software_Testing/Products_and_Tools/
[56] http://www.economist.com/science/tq/displaystory.cfm?story_id=10789417
[57] http://www.qatutor.com/glossary.html

Distributed computing

Distributed computing is a field of computer science that studies distributed systems. A **distributed system** consists of multiple autonomous computers that communicate through a computer network. The computers interact with each other in order to achieve a common goal. A computer program that runs in a distributed system is called a **distributed program**, and **distributed programming** is the process of writing such programs.[1]

Distributed computing also refers to the use of distributed systems to solve computational problems. In distributed computing, a problem is divided into many tasks, each of which is solved by one computer.[2]

Introduction

The word *distributed* in terms such as "distributed system", "distributed programming", and "distributed algorithm" originally referred to computer networks where individual computers were physically distributed within some geographical area.[3] The terms are nowadays used in a much wider sense, even referring to autonomous processes that run on the same physical computer and interact with each other by message passing.[4]

While there is no single definition of a distributed system,[5] the following defining properties are commonly used:

- There are several autonomous computational entities, each of which has its own local memory.[6]
- The entities communicate with each other by message passing.[7]

In this article, the computational entities are called *computers* or *nodes*.

A distributed system may have a common goal, such as solving a large computational problem.[8] Alternatively, each computer may have its own user with individual needs, and the purpose of the distributed system is to coordinate the use of shared resources or provide communication services to the users.[9]

Other typical properties of distributed systems include the following:

- The system has to tolerate failures in individual computers.[10]
- The structure of the system (network topology, network latency, number of computers) is not known in advance, the system may consist of different kinds of computers and network links, and the system may change during the execution of a distributed program.[11]
- Each computer has only a limited, incomplete view of the system. Each computer may know only one part of the input.[12]

Parallel or distributed computing?

The terms "concurrent computing", "parallel computing", and "distributed computing" have a lot of overlap, and no clear distinction exists between them.[13] The same system may be characterised both as "parallel" and "distributed"; the processors in a typical distributed system run concurrently in parallel.[14] Parallel computing may be seen as a particular tightly-coupled form of distributed computing,[15] and distributed computing may be seen as a loosely-coupled form of parallel computing.[5] Nevertheless, it is possible to roughly classify concurrent systems as "parallel" or "distributed" using the following criteria:

- In parallel computing, all processors have access to a shared memory. Shared memory can be used to exchange information between processors.[16]
- In distributed computing, each processor has its own private memory (distributed memory). Information is exchanged by passing messages between the processors.[17]

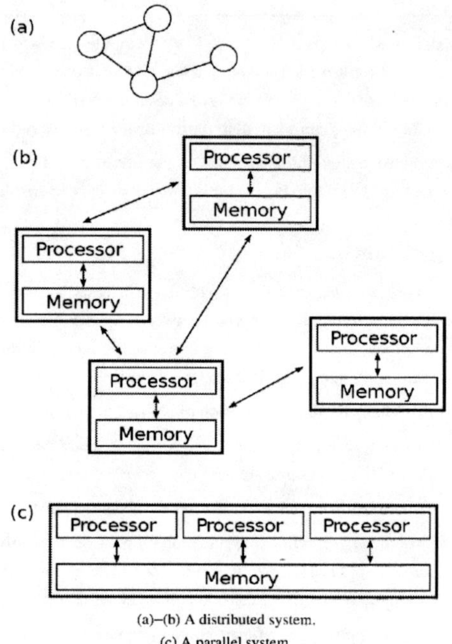

(a)–(b) A distributed system.
(c) A parallel system.

The figure on the right illustrates the difference between distributed and parallel systems. Figure (a) is a schematic view of a typical distributed system; as usual, the system is represented as a graph in which each node (vertex) is a computer and each edge (line between two nodes) is a communication link. Figure (b) shows the same distributed system in more detail: each computer has its own local memory, and information can be exchanged only by passing messages from one node to another by using the available communication links. Figure (c) shows a parallel system in which each processor has a direct access to a shared memory.

The situation is further complicated by the traditional uses of the terms parallel and distributed *algorithm* that do not quite match the above definitions of parallel and distributed *systems*; see the section Theoretical foundations below for more detailed discussion. Nevertheless, as a rule of thumb, high-performance parallel computation in a shared-memory multiprocessor uses parallel algorithms while the coordination of a large-scale distributed system uses distributed algorithms.

History

The use of concurrent processes that communicate by message-passing has its roots in operating system architectures studied in 1960s.[18] The first widespread distributed systems were local-area networks such as Ethernet that was invented in 1970s.[19]

ARPANET, the predecessor of the Internet, was introduced in the late 1960s, and ARPANET e-mail was invented in the early 1970s. E-mail became the most successful application of ARPANET,[20] and it is probably the earliest example of a large-scale distributed application. In addition to ARPANET and its successor Internet, other early worldwide computer networks included Usenet and FidoNet from 1980s, both of which were used to support distributed discussion systems.

The study of distributed computing became its own branch of computer science in the late 1970s and early 1980s. The first conference in the field, Symposium on Principles of Distributed Computing (PODC), dates back to 1982, and its European counterpart International Symposium on Distributed Computing (DISC) was first held in 1985.

Applications

There are two main reasons for using distributed systems and distributed computing. First, the very nature of the application may *require* the use of a communication network that connects several computers. For example, data is produced in one physical location and it is needed in another location.

Second, there are many cases in which the use of a single computer would be possible in principle, but the use of a distributed system is *beneficial* for practical reasons. For example, it may be more cost-efficient to obtain the desired level of performance by using a cluster of several low-end computers, in comparison with a single high-end computer. A distributed system can be more reliable than a non-distributed system, as there is no single point of failure. Moreover, a distributed system may be easier to expand and manage than a monolithic uniprocessor system.[21]

Examples of distributed systems and applications of distributed computing include the following:[22]

- Telecommunication networks:
  - Telephone networks and cellular networks.
  - Computer networks such as the Internet.
  - Wireless sensor networks.
  - Routing algorithms.
- Network applications:
  - World wide web and peer-to-peer networks.
  - Massively multiplayer online games and virtual reality communities.
  - Distributed databases and distributed database management systems.
  - Network file systems.
  - Distributed information processing systems such as banking systems and airline reservation systems.
- Real-time process control:
  - Aircraft control systems.
  - Industrial control systems.
- Parallel computation:
  - Scientific computing, including cluster computing and grid computing and various volunteer computing projects; see the list of distributed computing projects.
  - Distributed rendering in computer graphics.

Theoretical foundations

Models

Many tasks that we would like to automate by using a computer are of question–answer type: we would like to ask a question and the computer should produce an answer. In theoretical computer science, such tasks are called computational problems. Formally, a computational problem consists of *instances* together with a *solution* for each instance. Instances are questions that we can ask, and solutions are desired answers to these questions.

Theoretical computer science seeks to understand which computational problems can be solved by using a computer (computability theory) and how efficiently (computational complexity theory). Traditionally, it is said that a problem can be solved by using a computer if we can design an algorithm that produces a correct solution for any given instance. Such an algorithm can be implemented as a computer program that runs on a general-purpose computer:

the program reads a problem instance from input, performs some computation, and produces the solution as output. Formalisms such as random access machines or universal Turing machines can be used as abstract models of a sequential general-purpose computer executing such an algorithm.

The field of concurrent and distributed computing studies similar questions in the case of either multiple computers, or a computer that executes a network of interacting processes: which computational problems can be solved in such a network and how efficiently? However, it is not at all obvious what is meant by "solving a problem" in the case of a concurrent or distributed system: for example, what is the task of the algorithm designer, and what is the concurrent and/or distributed equivalent of a sequential general-purpose computer?

The discussion below focusses on the case of multiple computers, although many of the issues are the same for concurrent processes running on a single computer.

Three viewpoints are commonly used:

Parallel algorithms in shared-memory model

- All computers have access to a shared memory. The algorithm designer chooses the program executed by each computer.
- One theoretical model is the parallel random access machines (PRAM) are used.[23] However, the classical PRAM model assumes synchronous access to the shared memory.
- A model that is closer to the behavior of real-world multiprocessor machines and takes into account the use of machine instructions such as Compare-and-swap (CAS) is that of *asynchronous shared memory*. There is a wide body of work on this model, a summary of which can be found in the literature.[24] [25]

Parallel algorithms in message-passing model

- The algorithm designer chooses the structure of the network, as well as the program executed by each computer.
- Models such as Boolean circuits and sorting networks are used.[26] A Boolean circuit can be seen as a computer network: each gate is a computer that runs an extremely simple computer program. Similarly, a sorting network can be seen as a computer network: each comparator is a computer.

Distributed algorithms in message-passing model

- The algorithm designer only chooses the computer program. All computers run the same program. The system must work correctly regardless of the structure of the network.
- A commonly used model is a graph with one finite-state machine per node.

In the case of distributed algorithms, computational problems are typically related to graphs. Often the graph that describes the structure of the computer network *is* the problem instance. This is illustrated in the following example.

An example

Consider the computational problem of finding a coloring of a given graph *G*. Different fields might take the following approaches:

Centralized algorithms

- The graph *G* is encoded as a string, and the string is given as input to a computer. The computer program finds a coloring of the graph, encodes the coloring as a string, and outputs the result.

Parallel algorithms

- Again, the graph *G* is encoded as a string. However, multiple computers can access the same string in parallel. Each computer might focus on one part of the graph and produce a colouring for that part.
- The main focus is on high-performance computation that exploits the processing power of multiple computers in parallel.

Distributed algorithms

- The graph G is the structure of the computer network. There is one computer for each node of G and one communication link for each edge of G. Initially, each computer only knows about its immediate neighbours in the graph G; the computers must exchange messages with each other to discover more about the structure of G. Each computer must produce its own colour as output.
- The main focus is on coordinating the operation of an arbitrary distributed system.

While the field of parallel algorithms has a different focus than the field of distributed algorithms, there is a lot of interaction between the two fields. For example, the Cole–Vishkin algorithm for graph colouring[27] was originally presented as a parallel algorithm, but the same technique can also be used directly as a distributed algorithm.

Moreover, a parallel algorithm can be implemented either in a parallel system (using shared memory) or in a distributed system (using message passing).[28] The traditional boundary between parallel and distributed algorithms (choose a suitable network vs. run in any given network) does not lie in the same place as the boundary between parallel and distributed systems (shared memory vs. message passing).

Complexity measures

A centralised algorithm is efficient if it does not require much time (number of computational steps) or space (amount of memory). These complexity measures give rise to complexity classes such as P (decision problems solvable in polynomial time) and PSPACE (decision problems solvable in polynomial space).

In parallel algorithms, yet another resource in addition to time and space is the number of computers. Indeed, often there is a trade-off between the running time and the number of computers: the problem can be solved faster if there are more computers running in parallel (see speedup). If a decision problem can be solved in polylogarithmic time by using a polynomial number of processors, then the problem is said to be in the class NC.[29] The class NC can be defined equally well by using the PRAM formalism or Boolean circuits – PRAM machines can simulate Boolean circuits efficiently and vice versa.[30]

In the analysis of distributed algorithms, more attention is usually paid on communication operations than computational steps. Perhaps the simplest model of distributed computing is a synchronous system where all nodes operate in a lockstep fashion. During each *communication round*, all nodes in parallel (1) receive the latest messages from their neighbours, (2) perform arbitrary local computation, and (3) send new messages to their neighbours. In such systems, a central complexity measure is the number of synchronous communication rounds required to complete the task.[31]

This complexity measure is closely related to the diameter of the network. Let D be the diameter of the network. On the one hand, any computable problem can be solved trivially in a synchronous distributed system in approximately $2D$ communication rounds: simply gather all information in one location (D rounds), solve the problem, and inform each node about the solution (D rounds).

On the other hand, if the running time of the algorithm is much smaller than D communication rounds, then the nodes in the network must produce their output without having the possibility to obtain information about distant parts of the network. In other words, the nodes must make globally consistent decisions based on information that is available in their *local neighbourhood*. Many distributed algorithms are known with the running time much smaller than D rounds, and understanding which problems can be solved by such algorithms is one of the central research questions of the field.[32]

Other commonly used measures are the total number of bits transmitted in the network (cf. communication complexity).

Other problems

Traditional computational problems take the perspective that we ask a question, a computer (or a distributed system) processes the question for a while, and then produces an answer and stops. However, there are also problems where we do not want the system to ever stop. Examples of such problems include the dining philosophers problem and other similar mutual exclusion problems. In these problems, the distributed system is supposed to continuously coordinate the use of shared resources so that no conflicts or deadlocks occur.

There are also fundamental challenges that are unique to distributed computing. The first example is challenges that are related to *fault-tolerance*. Examples of related problems include consensus problems,[33] Byzantine fault tolerance,[34] and self-stabilisation.[35]

A lot of research is also focused on understanding the *asynchronous* nature of distributed systems:

- Synchronizers can be used to run synchronous algorithms in asynchronous systems.[36]
- Logical clocks provide a causal happened-before ordering of events.[37]
- Clock synchronization algorithms provide globally consistent physical time stamps.[38]

Properties of distributed systems

So far the focus has been on *designing* a distributed system that solves a given problem. A complementary research problem is *studying* the properties of a given distributed system.

The halting problem is an analogous example from the field of centralised computation: we are given a computer program and the task is to decide whether it halts or runs forever. The halting problem is undecidable in the general case, and naturally understanding the behaviour of a computer network is at least as hard as understanding the behaviour of one computer.

However, there are many interesting special cases that are decidable. In particular, it is possible to reason about the behaviour of a network of finite-state machines. One example is telling whether a given network of interacting (asynchronous and non-deterministic) finite-state machines can reach a deadlock. This problem is PSPACE-complete,[39] i.e., it is decidable, but it is not likely that there is an efficient (centralised, parallel or distributed) algorithm that solves the problem in the case of large networks.

Architectures

Various hardware and software architectures are used for distributed computing. At a lower level, it is necessary to interconnect multiple CPUs with some sort of network, regardless of whether that network is printed onto a circuit board or made up of loosely-coupled devices and cables. At a higher level, it is necessary to interconnect processes running on those CPUs with some sort of communication system.

Distributed programming typically falls into one of several basic architectures or categories: client–server, 3-tier architecture, *n*-tier architecture, distributed objects, loose coupling, or tight coupling.

- Client–server: Smart client code contacts the server for data then formats and displays it to the user. Input at the client is committed back to the server when it represents a permanent change.
- 3-tier architecture: Three tier systems move the client intelligence to a middle tier so that stateless clients can be used. This simplifies application deployment. Most web applications are 3-Tier.
- *n*-tier architecture: *n*-tier refers typically to web applications which further forward their requests to other enterprise services. This type of application is the one most responsible for the success of application servers.
- Tightly coupled (clustered): refers typically to a cluster of machines that closely work together, running a shared process in parallel. The task is subdivided in parts that are made individually by each one and then put back together to make the final result.
- Peer-to-peer: an architecture where there is no special machine or machines that provide a service or manage the network resources. Instead all responsibilities are uniformly divided among all machines, known as peers. Peers

can serve both as clients and servers.

- Space based: refers to an infrastructure that creates the illusion (virtualization) of one single address-space. Data are transparently replicated according to application needs. Decoupling in time, space and reference is achieved.

Another basic aspect of distributed computing architecture is the method of communicating and coordinating work among concurrent processes. Through various message passing protocols, processes may communicate directly with one another, typically in a master/slave relationship. Alternatively, a "database-centric" architecture can enable distributed computing to be done without any form of direct inter-process communication, by utilizing a shared database.[40]

See also

- List of important publications in concurrent, parallel, and distributed computing
- Edsger W. Dijkstra Prize in Distributed Computing
- List of distributed computing conferences
- List of distributed computing projects
- Parallel programming model
- Parallel distributed processing

References

Books

- Andrews, Gregory R. (2000), *Foundations of Multithreaded, Parallel, and Distributed Programming*, Addison–Wesley, ISBN 0-201-35752-6.
- Arora, Sanjeev; Barak, Boaz (2009), *Computational Complexity – A Modern Approach*, Cambridge, ISBN 978-0-521-42426-4.
- Cormen, Thomas H.; Leiserson, Charles E.; Rivest, Ronald L. (1990), *Introduction to Algorithms* (1st ed.), MIT Press, ISBN 0-262-03141-8.
- Dolev, Shlomi (2000), *Self-Stabilization*, MIT Press, ISBN 0-262-04178-2.
- Elmasri, Ramez; Navathe, Shamkant B. (2000), *Fundamentals of Database Systems* (3rd ed.), Addison–Wesley, ISBN 0-201-54263-3.
- Ghosh, Sukumar (2007), *Distributed Systems – An Algorithmic Approach*, Chapman & Hall/CRC, ISBN 978-1-58488-564-1.
- Lynch, Nancy A. (1996), *Distributed Algorithms*, Morgan Kaufmann, ISBN 1-55860-348-4.
- Herlihy, Maurice P.; Shavit, Nir N. (2008), *The Art of Multiprocessor Programming*, Morgan Kaufmann, ISBN 0-12-370591-6.
- Papadimitriou, Christos H. (1994), *Computational Complexity*, Addison–Wesley, ISBN 0-201-53082-1.
- Peleg, David (2000), *Distributed Computing: A Locality-Sensitive Approach* [41], SIAM, ISBN 0-89871-464-8.

Articles

- Cole, Richard; Vishkin, Uzi (1986), "Deterministic coin tossing with applications to optimal parallel list ranking", *Information and Control* **70** (1): 32–53, doi:10.1016/S0019-9958(86)80023-7.
- Keidar, Idit (2008), "Distributed computing column 32 – The year in review" [42], *ACM SIGACT News* **39** (4): 53–54, doi:10.1145/1466390.1466402.
- Linial, Nathan (1992), "Locality in distributed graph algorithms", *SIAM Journal on Computing* **21** (1): 193–201, doi:10.1137/0221015.
- Naor, Moni; Stockmeyer, Larry (1995), "What can be computed locally?", *SIAM Journal on Computing* **24** (6): 1259–1277, doi:10.1137/S0097539793254571.

Web sites

- Godfrey, Bill (2002). "A primer on distributed computing" [43].
- Peter, Ian (2004). "Ian Peter's History of the Internet" [44]. Retrieved 2009-08-04.

Further reading

Books

- Tel, Gerard (1994), *Introduction to Distributed Algorithms*, Cambridge University Press
- Attiya, Hagit and Welch, Jennifer (2004), *Distributed Computing: Fundamentals, Simulations, and Advanced Topics*, Wiley-Interscience ISBN 0471453242.
- Garg, Vijay K. (2002), *Elements of Distributed Computing*, Wiley-IEEE Press ISBN 0471036005.

Articles

- Keidar, Idit; Rajsbaum, Sergio, eds. (2000–2009), "Distributed computing column" [45], *ACM SIGACT News*.

Conference Papers

- C. Rodríguez, M. Villagra and B. Barán, Asynchronous team algorithms for Boolean Satisfiability (doi:10.1109/BIMNICS.2007.4610083), Bionetics2007, pp. 66–69, 2007.

External links

- Distributed computing [46] at the Open Directory Project
- Distributed computing journals [47] at the Open Directory Project

References

[1] Andrews (2000). Dolev (2000). Ghosh (2007), p. 10.
[2] Godfrey (2002).
[3] Lynch (1996), p. 1.
[4] Andrews (2000), p. 291–292. Dolev (2000), p. 5.
[5] Ghosh (2007), p. 10.
[6] Andrews (2000), p. 8–9, 291. Dolev (2000), p. 5. Ghosh (2007), p. 3. Lynch (1996), p. xix, 1. Peleg (2000), p. xv.
[7] Andrews (2000), p. 291. Ghosh (2007), p. 3. Peleg (2000), p. 4.
[8] Ghosh (2007), p. 3–4. Peleg (2000), p. 1.
[9] Ghosh (2007), p. 4. Peleg (2000), p. 2.
[10] Ghosh (2007), p. 4, 8. Lynch (1996), p. 2–3. Peleg (2000), p. 4.
[11] Lynch (1996), p. 2. Peleg (2000), p. 1.
[12] Ghosh (2007), p. 7. Lynch (1996), p. xix, 2. Peleg (2000), p. 4.
[13] Ghosh (2007), p. 10. Keidar (2008).
[14] Lynch (1996), p. xix, 1–2. Peleg (2000), p. 1.
[15] Peleg (2000), p. 1.
[16] Papadimitriou (1994), Chapter 15. Keidar (2008).
[17] See references in Introduction.
[18] Andrews (2000), p. 348.
[19] Andrews (2000), p. 32.
[20] Peter (2004), The history of email (http://www.nethistory.info/History of the Internet/email.html).
[21] Elmasri & Navathe (2000), Section 24.1.2.
[22] Andrews (2000), p. 10–11. Ghosh (2007), p. 4–6. Lynch (1996), p. xix, 1. Peleg (2000), p. xv. Elmasri & Navathe (2000), Section 24.
[23] Cormen, Leiserson & Rivest (1990), Section 30.
[24] Herlihy & Shavit (2008), Chapters 2-6.
[25] Lynch (1996)
[26] Cormen, Leiserson & Rivest (1990), Sections 28 and 29.
[27] Cole & Vishkin (1986). Cormen, Leiserson & Rivest (1990), Section 30.5.
[28] Andrews (2000), p. ix.
[29] Arora & Barak (2009), Section 6.7. Papadimitriou (1994), Section 15.3.
[30] Papadimitriou (1994), Section 15.2.
[31] Lynch (1996), p. 17–23.

[32] Peleg (2000), Sections 2.3 and 7. Linial (1992). Naor & Stockmeyer (1995).
[33] Lynch (1996), Sections 5–7. Ghosh (2007), Chapter 13.
[34] Lynch (1996), p. 99–102. Ghosh (2007), p. 192–193.
[35] Dolev (2000). Ghosh (2007), Chapter 17.
[36] Lynch (1996), Section 16. Peleg (2000), Section 6.
[37] Lynch (1996), Section 18. Ghosh (2007), Sections 6.2–6.3.
[38] Ghosh (2007), Section 6.4.
[39] Papadimitriou (1994), Section 19.3.
[40] A database-centric virtual chemistry system, J Chem Inf Model. 2006 May-Jun;46(3):1034-9 (http://www.ncbi.nlm.nih.gov/sites/entrez?db=pubmed&list_uids=16711722&cmd=Retrieve)
[41] http://www.ec-securehost.com/SIAM/DT05.html
[42] http://webee.technion.ac.il/~idish/sigactNews/#column%2032
[43] http://www.bacchae.co.uk/docs/dist.html
[44] http://www.nethistory.info/History%20of%20the%20Internet/
[45] http://webee.technion.ac.il/~idish/sigactNews/
[46] http://www.dmoz.org/Computers/Computer_Science/Distributed_Computing//
[47] http://www.dmoz.org/Computers/Computer_Science/Distributed_Computing/Publications//

STAX

Stax can refer to:

- StAX, (Computer Programming) Streaming API for XML. An API for reading and writing XML in Java.
- Stax Earspeakers, a Japanese brand of electrostatic earspeakers
- Stax Records, an American record company
- STAf eXecution engine (STAX), a service available with Software Testing Automation Framework
- Lay's Stax, a brand of potato snack chips sold by Lay's
- Stax Inc., a management consulting firm

HTML

Filename extension	.html, .htm
Internet media type	text/html
Type code	TEXT
Uniform Type Identifier	public.html
Developed by	World Wide Web Consortium & WHATWG
Type of format	Markup language
Extended from	SGML
Extended to	XHTML
Standard(s)	ISO/IEC 15445 W3C HTML 4.01 [1] W3C HTML 5 [2] (draft)

HTML, which stands for **HyperText Markup Language**, is the predominant markup language for web pages. It is written in the form of HTML elements consisting of "tags" surrounded by angle brackets within the web page content.

It allows images and objects to be embedded and can be used to create interactive forms. It provides a means to create structured documents by denoting structural semantics for text such as headings, paragraphs, lists, links, quotes and other items. It can embed scripts in languages such as JavaScript which affect the behavior of HTML webpages.

HTML can also be used to include Cascading Style Sheets (CSS) to define the appearance and layout of text and other material. The W3C, maintainer of both HTML and CSS standards, encourages the use of CSS over explicit presentational markup.[3]

History

The historic logo made by the W3C.

Origins

Tim Berners-Lee

In 1980, physicist Tim Berners-Lee, who was a contractor at CERN, proposed and prototyped ENQUIRE, a system for CERN researchers to use and share documents. In 1989, Berners-Lee wrote a memo proposing an Internet-based hypertext system.[4] Berners-Lee specified HTML and wrote the browser and server software in the last part of 1990. In that year, Berners-Lee and CERN data systems engineer Robert Cailliau collaborated on a joint request for funding, but the project was not formally adopted by CERN. In his personal notes[5] from 1990 he lists[6] "*some of the many areas in which hypertext is used*" and puts an encyclopedia first.

First specifications

The first publicly available description of HTML was a document called *HTML Tags*, first mentioned on the Internet by Berners-Lee in late 1991.[7] [8] It describes 20 elements comprising the initial, relatively simple design of HTML. Except for the hyperlink tag, these were strongly influenced by SGMLguid, an in-house SGML based documentation format at CERN. Thirteen of these elements still exist in HTML 4.[9]

HTML is a text and image formatting language used by web browsers to dynamically format web pages. Many of the text elements are found in the 1988 ISO technical report TR 9537 *Techniques for using SGML*, which in turn covers the features of early text formatting languages such as that used by the RUNOFF command developed in the early 1960s for the CTSS (Compatible Time-Sharing System) operating system: these formatting commands were derived from the commands used by typesetters to manually format documents. However, the SGML concept of generalized markup is based on elements (nested annotated ranges with attributes) rather than merely print effects, with also the separation of structure and processing; HTML has been progressively moved in this direction with CSS.

Berners-Lee considered HTML to be an application of SGML. It was formally defined as such by the Internet Engineering Task Force (IETF) with the mid-1993 publication of the first proposal for an HTML specification: "Hypertext Markup Language (HTML)" Internet-Draft [10] by Berners-Lee and Dan Connolly, which included an SGML Document Type Definition to define the grammar.[11] The draft expired after six months, but was notable for its acknowledgment of the NCSA Mosaic browser's custom tag for embedding in-line images, reflecting the IETF's philosophy of basing standards on successful prototypes.[12] Similarly, Dave Raggett's competing Internet-Draft, "HTML+ (Hypertext Markup Format)", from late 1993, suggested standardizing already-implemented features like tables and fill-out forms.[13]

After the HTML and HTML+ drafts expired in early 1994, the IETF created an HTML Working Group, which in 1995 completed "HTML 2.0", the first HTML specification intended to be treated as a standard against which future implementations should be based.[12] Published as Request for Comments 1866, HTML 2.0 included ideas from the HTML and HTML+ drafts.[14] The 2.0 designation was intended to distinguish the new edition from previous drafts.[15]

Further development under the auspices of the IETF was stalled by competing interests. Since 1996, the HTML specifications have been maintained, with input from commercial software vendors, by the World Wide Web Consortium (W3C).[16] However, in 2000, HTML also became an international standard (ISO/IEC 15445:2000). The last HTML specification published by the W3C is the HTML 4.01 Recommendation, published in late 1999. Its issues and errors were last acknowledged by errata published in 2001.

Version history of the standard

HTML

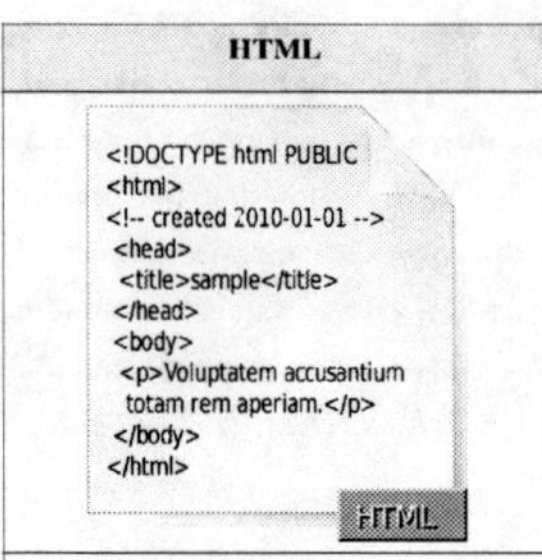

- HTML and HTML5
- Dynamic HTML
- XHTML
- XHTML Mobile Profile and C-HTML
- Canvas element
- Character encodings
- Document Object Model
- Font family
- HTML editor
- HTML element
- HTML Frames
- HTML5 video
- HTML scripting
- Web browser engine
- Quirks mode
- Style sheets
- Unicode and HTML
- W3C and WHATWG
- Web colors
- WebGL
- Web Storage
- Comparison of
  - document markup languages
  - web browsers
  - layout engines for
    - HTML
    - HTML5
      - HTML5 Canvas
      - HTML5 Media
    - Non-standard HTML
    - XHTML

HTML version timeline

November 24, 1995

HTML 2.0 was published as IETF RFC 1866. Supplemental RFCs added capabilities:

- November 25, 1995: RFC 1867 (form-based file upload)
- May 1996: RFC 1942 (tables)
- August 1996: RFC 1980 (client-side image maps)
- January 1997: RFC 2070 (internationalization)

In June 2000, all of these were declared obsolete/historic by RFC 2854.

January 1997

HTML 3.2[17] was published as a W3C Recommendation. It was the first version developed and standardized exclusively by the W3C, as the IETF had closed its HTML Working Group in September 1996.[18]

HTML 3.2 dropped math formulas entirely, reconciled overlap among various proprietary extensions and adopted most of Netscape's visual markup tags. Netscape's blink element and Microsoft's marquee element were omitted due to a mutual agreement between the two companies.[16] A markup for mathematical formulas similar to that in HTML wasn't standardized until 14 months later in MathML.

December 1997

HTML 4.0[19] was published as a W3C Recommendation. It offers three variations:

- Strict, in which deprecated elements are forbidden,
- Transitional, in which deprecated elements are allowed,
- Frameset, in which mostly only frame related elements are allowed;

Initially code-named "Cougar",[20] HTML 4.0 adopted many browser-specific element types and attributes, but at the same time sought to phase out Netscape's visual markup features by marking them as deprecated in favor of style sheets. HTML 4 is an SGML application conforming to ISO 8879 - SGML.[21]

April 1998

HTML 4.0[22] was reissued with minor edits without incrementing the version number.

December 1999

HTML 4.01[23] was published as a W3C Recommendation. It offers the same three variations as HTML 4.0 and its last errata [24] were published May 12, 2001.

May 2000

ISO/IEC 15445:2000[25] [26] ("ISO HTML", based on HTML 4.01 Strict) was published as an ISO/IEC international standard. In the ISO this standard falls in the domain of the ISO/IEC JTC1/SC34 (ISO/IEC Joint Technical Committee 1, Subcommittee 34 - Document description and processing languages).[25]

As of mid-2008, HTML 4.01 and ISO/IEC 15445:2000 are the most recent versions of HTML. Development of the parallel, XML-based language XHTML occupied the W3C's HTML Working Group through the early and mid-2000s.

HTML draft version timeline

October 1991

HTML Tags,[7] an informal CERN document listing twelve HTML tags, was first mentioned in public.

June 1992

First informal draft of the HTML DTD [27], with seven subsequent revisions

November 1992

HTML DTD 1.1 (the first with a version number, based on RCS revisions, which start with 1.1 rather than 1.0), an informal draft

June 1993

Hypertext Markup Language[28] was published by the IETF IIIR Working Group as an Internet-Draft (a rough proposal for a standard). It was replaced by a second version [10] one month later, followed by six further drafts published by IETF itself [29] that finally led to HTML 2.0 in RFC1866

November 1993

HTML+ was published by the IETF as an Internet-Draft and was a competing proposal to the Hypertext Markup Language draft. It expired in May 1994.

April 1995 (authored March 1995)

HTML 3.0[30] was proposed as a standard to the IETF, but the proposal expired five months later without further action. It included many of the capabilities that were in Raggett's HTML+ proposal, such as support for tables, text flow around figures and the display of complex mathematical formulas.[31]

W3C began development of its own Arena browser for testing support for HTML 3 and Cascading Style Sheets, but HTML 3.0 did not succeed for several reasons. The draft was considered very large at 150 pages and the pace of browser development, as well as the number of interested parties, had outstripped the resources of the IETF.[16] Browser vendors, including Microsoft and Netscape at the time, chose to implement different subsets of HTML 3's draft features as well as to introduce their own extensions to it.[16] (See Browser wars) These included extensions to control stylistic aspects of documents, contrary to the "belief [of the academic engineering community] that such things as text color, background texture, font size and font face were definitely outside the scope of a language when their only intent was to specify how a document would be organized."[16] Dave Raggett, who has been a W3C Fellow for many years has commented for example, "To a certain extent, Microsoft built its business on the Web by extending HTML features."[16]

January 2008

HTML 5 was published as a Working Draft (link [32]) by the W3C.[33]

Although its syntax closely resembles that of SGML, HTML 5 has abandoned any attempt to be an SGML application and has explicitly defined its own "html" serialization, in addition to an alternative XML-based XHTML 5 serialization.[34]

XHTML versions

XHTML is a separate language that began as a reformulation of HTML 4.01 using XML 1.0. It continues to be developed:

- XHTML 1.0,[35] published January 26, 2000 as a W3C Recommendation, later revised and republished August 1, 2002. It offers the same three variations as HTML 4.0 and 4.01, reformulated in XML, with minor restrictions.
- XHTML 1.1,[36] published May 31, 2001 as a W3C Recommendation. It is based on XHTML 1.0 Strict, but includes minor changes, can be customized, is reformulated using modules from Modularization of XHTML [37], which was published April 10, 2001 as a W3C Recommendation.
- XHTML 2.0,[38] . There is no XHTML 2.0 standard. XHTML 2.0 is incompatible with XHTML 1.x and, therefore, would be more accurate to characterize as an XHTML-inspired new language than an update to XHTML 1.x.
- XHTML 5, which is an update to XHTML 1.x, is being defined alongside HTML 5 in the HTML 5 draft.[39]

Markup

HTML markup consists of several key components, including *elements* (and their *attributes*), character-based *data types*, *character references* and *entity references*. Another important component is the *document type declaration*, which specifies the Document Type Definition. As of HTML 5, no Document Type Definition will need to be specified and will only determine the layout mode [40].

The Hello world program, a common computer program employed for comparing programming languages, scripting languages and markup languages is made of 9 lines of code in HTML, albeit Newlines are optional:

```
<!doctype html>
<html>
  <head>
    <title>Hello HTML</title>
  </head>
  <body>
    <p>Hello World!</p>
  </body>
</html>
```

This Document Type Declaration is for HTML 5.

If the <!doctype html> declaration is not included, Windows Internet Explorer will render using "quirks mode".[41]

Elements

HTML documents are composed entirely of **HTML elements** that, in their most general form have three components: a pair of element ***tags*** with a "start tag" and "end tag"; some element ***attributes*** given to the element within the tags; and finally, all the actual textual and graphical information *content* that will be rendered on the display. An **HTML element** is everything between and including the tags. A **tag** is a keyword enclosed in angle brackets.

A common form of an **HTML element** is:

```
<tag>content to be rendered</tag>
```

The name of the HTML element is also the name of the tag. Note that the end tag's name starts with a slash character, "/".

The most general form of an **HTML element** is:

```
<tag attribute1="value1" attribute2="value2">content to be rendered</tag>
```

By not assigning attributes most start tags default their attribute values.

There are some basic types of tags: Heading of the HTML:<head>...</head>. Usually the title should be included in the head, for example:

```
<head>
<title>The title</title>
</head>
```

Headings:

```
<h1>Heading1</h1>
<h2>Heading2</h2>
<h3>Heading3</h3>
<h4>Heading4</h4>
<h5>Heading5</h5>
<h6>Heading6</h6>
```

Paragraph Partition:

```
<p>Paragraph 1</p>  <p>Paragraph 2</p>
```

Newline:
. The difference between <br> and <p> is that 'br' breaks a line without altering the semantic structure of the page, whereas 'p' sections the page into paragraphs. Here is an example:

```
<code><p>This <br> is a paragraph <br> with <br> line breaks</p></code>
```

Annotation:

```
<!--..Explain!..-->
```

Annotations can help to understand the coding and do not display in the webpage.

There are several types of markup elements used in HTML.

- **Structural** markup describes the purpose of text. For example, <h2>Golf</h2> establishes "Golf" as a second-level heading, which would be rendered in a browser in a manner similar to the "HTML markup" title at the start of this section. Structural markup does not denote any specific rendering, but most Web browsers have standardized default styles for element formatting. Text may be further styled with Cascading Style Sheets (CSS).
- **Presentational** markup describes the appearance of the text, regardless of its function. For example <b>boldface</b> indicates that visual output devices should render "boldface" in bold text, but gives no indication what devices which are unable to do this (such as aural devices that read the text aloud) should do. In the case of both <b>bold</b> and <i>italic</i>, there are elements which usually have an equivalent visual rendering but are more semantic in nature, namely <strong>strong emphasis</strong> and <em>emphasis</em> respectively. It is easier to see how an aural user agent should interpret the latter two elements. However, they are not equivalent to their presentational counterparts: it would be undesirable for a screen-reader to emphasize the name of a book, for instance, but on a screen such a name would be italicized. Most presentational markup elements have become deprecated under the HTML 4.0 specification, in favor of CSS based style design.
- **Hypertext** markup makes parts of a document into links to other documents. HTML up through version XHTML 1.1 requires the use of an anchor element to create a hyperlink in the flow of text: <a>Wikipedia</a>. In addition, the href attribute must be set to a valid URL. For example, the HTML markup, <a href="http://en.wikipedia.org/">Wikipedia</a>, will render the word "Wikipedia [42]" as a hyperlink. An example to render an image as a hyperlink is: <a href="http://example.org"><img src="image.gif" alt="alternative

text" width="50" height="50"></a>.

Attributes

Most of the attributes of an element are name-value pairs, separated by "=" and written within the start tag of an element after the element's name. The value may be enclosed in single or double quotes, although values consisting of certain characters can be left unquoted in HTML (but not XHTML).[43] [44] Leaving attribute values unquoted is considered unsafe.[45] In contrast with name-value pair attributes, there are some attributes that affect the element simply by their presence in the start tag of the element[7] (like the ismap attribute for the img element[46]).

Most elements can take any of several common attributes:

- The id attribute provides a document-wide unique identifier for an element. This can be used by stylesheets to provide presentational properties: by browsers that focus attention on the specific element, or by scripts to alter the contents or presentation of an element. Appended to the URL of the page, it provides a globally unique identifier for an element, typically a sub-section of the page. For example, the ID "Attributes" in http://en.wikipedia.org/wiki/HTML#Attributes
- The class attribute provides a way of classifying similar elements. This can be used for semantic or presentation purposes. For example, an HTML document might semantically use the designation class="notation" to indicate that all elements with this class value are subordinate to the main text of the document. Presentationally, such elements might be gathered together and presented as footnotes on a page instead of appearing in the place where they occur in the HTML source. Another semantic use of class attributes is in microformats.
- An author may use the style attribute to assign presentational properties to a particular element. It is considered better practice to use an element's id or class attributes to select the element from within a stylesheet, though sometimes this can be too cumbersome for a simple and specific or ad hoc application of styled properties.
- The title attribute is used to attach subtextual explanation to an element. In most browsers this attribute is displayed as what is often referred to as a tooltip.
- The lang attribute identifies the natural language of the element's contents, if different from that of the rest of the document. For example, in an English-language document:

```
<p>Oh well, <span lang="fr">c'est la vie</span>, as they say in France.</p>
```

The abbreviation element, abbr, can be used to demonstrate some of these attributes:

```
<abbr id="anId" class="jargon" style="color:blue;" title="Hypertext Markup Language">HTML</abbr>
```

This example displays as HTML; in most browsers, pointing the cursor at the abbreviation should display the title text "Hypertext Markup Language."

Most elements also take the language-related attribute dir.

Character and entity references

As of version 4.0, HTML defines a set of 252 character entity references and a set of 1,114,050 numeric character references, both of which allow individual characters to be written via simple markup, rather than literally. A literal character and its markup counterpart are considered equivalent and are rendered identically.

The ability to "escape" characters in this way allows for the characters < and & (when written as < and &, respectively) to be interpreted as character data, rather than markup. For example, a literal < normally indicates the start of a tag, and & normally indicates the start of a character entity reference or numeric character reference; writing it as & or & or & allows & to be included in the content of elements or the values of attributes. The double-quote character ("), when used to quote an attribute value, must also be escaped as " or " or " when it appears within the attribute value itself. The single-quote character ('), when used to quote an attribute value, must also be escaped as ' or ' (should NOT be escaped as ' except in XHTML documents[47]) when it appears within the attribute value itself. However, since document authors often overlook the need to escape these characters, browsers tend to be very forgiving, treating them as markup only when subsequent text appears to confirm that intent.

Escaping also allows for characters that are not easily typed or that aren't even available in the document's character encoding to be represented within the element and attribute content. For example, the acute-accented e (é), a character typically found only on Western European keyboards, can be written in any HTML document as the entity reference é or as the numeric references é or é. The characters comprising those references (that is, the &, the ;, the letters in eacute, and so on) are available on all keyboards and are supported in all character encodings, whereas the literal é is not.

Data types

HTML defines several data types for element content, such as script data and stylesheet data, and a plethora of types for attribute values, including IDs, names, URIs, numbers, units of length, languages, media descriptors, colors, character encodings, dates and times, and so on. All of these data types are specializations of character data.

Document type declaration

HTML documents are required to start with a Document Type Declaration (informally, a "doctype"). In browsers, the function of the doctype is to indicate the rendering mode—particularly to avoid quirks mode.

The original purpose of the doctype was to enable parsing and validation of HTML documents by SGML tools based on the Document Type Definition (DTD). The DTD to which the DOCTYPE refers contains machine-readable grammar specifying the permitted and prohibited content for a document conforming to such a DTD. Browsers, on the other hand, do not implement HTML as an application of SGML and by consequence do not read the DTD. HTML 5 does not define a DTD, because of the technology's inherent limitations, so in HTML 5 the doctype declaration, <!doctype html>, does not refer to a DTD.

An example of an HTML 4 doctype is

```
<!DOCTYPE HTML PUBLIC "-//W3C//DTD HTML 4.01//EN" "http://www.w3.org/TR/html4/strict.dtd">
```

This declaration references the DTD for the Strict version of HTML 4.01, which does not include presentational elements like font, leaving formatting to Cascading Style Sheets and the span and div element. SGML-based validators read the DTD in order to properly parse the document and to perform validation. In modern browsers, this doctype activates standards mode as opposed to quirks mode.

In addition, HTML 4.01 provides Transitional and Frameset DTDs, as explained below.

Semantic HTML

Semantic HTML is a way of writing HTML that emphasizes the meaning of the encoded information over its presentation (look). HTML has included semantic markup from its inception,[48] but has also included presentational markup such as <font>, <i> and <center> tags. There are also the semantically neutral span and div tags. Since the late 1990s when Cascading Style Sheets were beginning to work in most browsers, web authors have been encouraged to avoid the use of presentational HTML markup with a view to the separation of presentation and content.[49]

In a 2001 discussion of the Semantic Web, Tim Berners-Lee and others gave examples of ways in which intelligent software 'agents' may one day automatically trawl the Web and find, filter and correlate previously unrelated, published facts for the benefit of human users.[50] Such agents are not commonplace even now, but some of the ideas of Web 2.0, mashups and price comparison websites may be coming close. The main difference between these web application hybrids and Berners-Lee's semantic agents lies in the fact that the current aggregation and hybridisation of information is usually designed in by web developers, who already know the web locations and the API semantics of the specific data they wish to mash, compare and combine.

An important type of web agent that does trawl and read web pages automatically, without prior knowledge of what it might find, is the Web crawler or search-engine spider. These software agents are dependent on the semantic clarity of web pages they find as they use various techniques and algorithms to read and index millions of web pages a day and provide web users with search facilities without which the World Wide Web would be only a fraction of its current usefulness.

In order for search-engine spiders to be able to rate the significance of pieces of text they find in HTML documents, and also for those creating mashups and other hybrids as well as for more automated agents as they are developed, the semantic structures that exist in HTML need to be widely and uniformly applied to bring out the meaning of published text.[51]

Presentational markup tags are deprecated in current HTML and XHTML recommendations and are illegal in HTML 5.

Good semantic HTML also improves the accessibility of web documents (see also Web Content Accessibility Guidelines). For example, when a screen reader or audio browser can correctly ascertain the structure of a document, it will not waste the visually impaired user's time by reading out repeated or irrelevant information when it has been marked up correctly.

Delivery

HTML documents can be delivered by the same means as any other computer file. However, they are most often delivered either by HTTP from a Web server or by e-mail.

HTTP

The World Wide Web is composed primarily of HTML documents transmitted from Web servers to Web browsers using the Hypertext Transfer Protocol (HTTP). However, HTTP is used to serve images, sound, and other content, in addition to HTML. To allow the Web browser to know how to handle each document it receives, other information is transmitted along with the document. This meta data usually includes the MIME type (e.g. `text/html` or `application/xhtml+xml`) and the character encoding (see Character encoding in HTML).

In modern browsers, the MIME type that is sent with the HTML document may affect how the document is initially interpreted. A document sent with the XHTML MIME type is expected to be well-formed XML; syntax errors may cause the browser to fail to render it. The same document sent with the HTML MIME type might be displayed successfully, since some browsers are more lenient with HTML.

The W3C recommendations state that XHTML 1.0 documents that follow guidelines set forth in the recommendation's Appendix C may be labeled with either MIME Type.[52] The current XHTML 1.1 Working Draft also states that XHTML 1.1 documents should[53] be labeled with either MIME type.[54]

HTML e-mail

Most graphical e-mail clients allow the use of a subset of HTML (often ill-defined) to provide formatting and semantic markup not available with plain text. This may include typographic information like coloured headings, emphasized and quoted text, inline images and diagrams. Many such clients include both a GUI editor for composing HTML e-mail messages and a rendering engine for displaying them. Use of HTML in e-mail is controversial because of compatibility issues, because it can help disguise phishing attacks, because it can confuse spam filters and because the message size is larger than plain text.

Naming conventions

The most common filename extension for files containing HTML is `.html`. A common abbreviation of this is `.htm`, which originated because some early operating systems and file systems, such as DOS and FAT, limited file extensions to three letters.

HTML Application

An HTML Application (HTA; file extension ".hta") is a Microsoft Windows application that uses HTML and Dynamic HTML in a browser to provide the application's graphical interface. A regular HTML file is confined to the security model of the web browser, communicating only to web servers and manipulating only webpage objects and site cookies. An HTA runs as a fully trusted application and therefore has more privileges, like creation/editing/removal of files and Windows Registry entries. Because they operate outside the browser's security model, HTAs cannot be executed via HTTP, but must be downloaded (just like an EXE file) and executed from local file system.

Current variations

HTML is precisely what we were trying to PREVENT— ever-breaking links, links going outward only, quotes you can't follow to their origins, no version management, no rights management.

Ted Nelson[55]

Since its inception, HTML and its associated protocols gained acceptance relatively quickly. However, no clear standards existed in the early years of the language. Though its creators originally conceived of HTML as a semantic language devoid of presentation details,[56] practical uses pushed many presentational elements and attributes into the language, driven largely by the various browser vendors. The latest standards surrounding HTML reflect efforts to overcome the sometimes chaotic development of the language[57] and to create a rational foundation for building both meaningful and well-presented documents. To return HTML to its role as a semantic language, the W3C has developed style languages such as CSS and XSL to shoulder the burden of presentation. In conjunction, the HTML specification has slowly reined in the presentational elements.

There are two axes differentiating various variations of HTML as currently specified: SGML-based HTML versus XML-based HTML (referred to as XHTML) on one axis, and strict versus transitional (loose) versus frameset on the other axis.

SGML-based versus XML-based HTML

One difference in the latest HTML specifications lies in the distinction between the SGML-based specification and the XML-based specification. The XML-based specification is usually called XHTML to distinguish it clearly from the more traditional definition. However, the root element name continues to be 'html' even in the XHTML-specified HTML. The W3C intended XHTML 1.0 to be identical to HTML 4.01 except where limitations of XML over the more complex SGML require workarounds. Because XHTML and HTML are closely related, they are sometimes documented in parallel. In such circumstances, some authors conflate the two names as (X)HTML or X(HTML).

Like HTML 4.01, XHTML 1.0 has three sub-specifications: strict, loose and frameset.

Aside from the different opening declarations for a document, the differences between an HTML 4.01 and XHTML 1.0 document—in each of the corresponding DTDs—are largely syntactic. The underlying syntax of HTML allows many shortcuts that XHTML does not, such as elements with optional opening or closing tags, and even EMPTY elements which must not have an end tag. By contrast, XHTML requires all elements to have an opening tag and a closing tag. XHTML, however, also introduces a new shortcut: an XHTML tag may be opened and closed within the same tag, by including a slash before the end of the tag like this: <br/>. The introduction of this shorthand, which is not used in the SGML declaration for HTML 4.01, may confuse earlier software unfamiliar with this new convention. A fix for this is to include a space before closing the tag, as such: <br />.[58]

To understand the subtle differences between HTML and XHTML, consider the transformation of a valid and well-formed XHTML 1.0 document that adheres to Appendix C (see below) into a valid HTML 4.01 document. To make this translation requires the following steps:

1. **The language for an element should be specified with a lang attribute rather than the XHTML xml:lang attribute.** XHTML uses XML's built in language-defining functionality attribute.
2. **Remove the XML namespace (xmlns=URI).** HTML has no facilities for namespaces.
3. **Change the document type declaration** from XHTML 1.0 to HTML 4.01. (see DTD section for further explanation).
4. If present, **remove the XML declaration.** (Typically this is: <?xml version="1.0" encoding="utf-8"?>).
5. **Ensure that the document's MIME type is set to text/html.** For both HTML and XHTML, this comes from the HTTP Content-Type header sent by the server.
6. **Change the XML empty-element syntax to an HTML style empty element** (
 to <br>).

Those are the main changes necessary to translate a document from XHTML 1.0 to HTML 4.01. To translate from HTML to XHTML would also require the addition of any omitted opening or closing tags. Whether coding in HTML or XHTML it may just be best to always include the optional tags within an HTML document rather than remembering which tags can be omitted.

A well-formed XHTML document adheres to all the syntax requirements of XML. A valid document adheres to the content specification for XHTML, which describes the document structure.

The W3C recommends several conventions to ensure an easy migration between HTML and XHTML (see HTML Compatibility Guidelines [59]). The following steps can be applied to XHTML 1.0 documents only:

- Include both xml:lang and lang attributes on any elements assigning language.
- Use the empty-element syntax only for elements specified as empty in HTML.
- Include an extra space in empty-element tags: for example <br /> instead of <br/>.
- Include explicit close tags for elements that permit content but are left empty (for example, <div></div>, not <div />).
- Omit the XML declaration.

By carefully following the W3C's compatibility guidelines, a user agent should be able to interpret the document equally as HTML or XHTML. For documents that are XHTML 1.0 and have been made compatible in this way, the W3C permits them to be served either as HTML (with a text/html MIME type), or as XHTML (with an application/xhtml+xml or application/xml MIME type). When delivered as XHTML, browsers should use an XML parser, which adheres strictly to the XML specifications for parsing the document's contents.

Transitional versus strict

HTML 4 defined three different versions of the language: Strict, Transitional (once called Loose) and Frameset. The Strict version is intended for new documents and is considered best practice, while the Transitional and Frameset versions were developed to make it easier to transition documents that conformed to older HTML specification or didn't conform to any specification to a version of HTML 4. The Transitional and Frameset versions allow for presentational markup, which is omitted in the Strict version. Instead, cascading style sheets are encouraged to improve the presentation of HTML documents.

Because XHTML 1 only defines an XML syntax for the language defined by HTML 4, the same differences apply to XHTML 1 as well.

The Transitional version allows the following parts of the vocabulary, which are not included in the Strict version:

- **A looser content model**
  - Inline elements and plain text are allowed directly in: body, blockquote, form, noscript and noframes

- **Presentation related elements**
  - underline (u)
  - strike-through (s)
  - center
  - font
  - basefont
- **Presentation related attributes**
  - background and bgcolor attributes for body element.
  - align attribute on div, form, paragraph (p) and heading (h1...h6) elements
  - align, noshade, size and width attributes on hr element
  - align, border, vspace and hspace attributes on img and object elements
  - align attribute on legend and caption elements
  - align and bgcolor on table element
  - nowrap, bgcolor, width, height on td and th elements
  - bgcolor attribute on tr element
  - clear attribute on br element
  - compact attribute on dl, dir and menu elements
  - type, compact and start attributes on ol and ul elements
  - type and value attributes on li element
  - width attribute on pre element
- **Additional elements in Transitional specification**
  - menu list (no substitute, though unordered list is recommended)
  - dir list (no substitute, though unordered list is recommended)
  - isindex (element requires server-side support and is typically added to documents server-side, form and input elements can be used as a substitute)
  - applet (deprecated in favor of object element)
- **The language attribute on script element** (redundant with the type attribute).
- **Frame related entities**
  - iframe
  - noframes
  - target attribute on anchor, client-side image-map (imagemap), link, form and base elements

The Frameset version includes everything in the Transitional version, as well as the frameset element (used instead of body) and the frame element.

Frameset versus transitional

In addition to the above transitional differences, the frameset specifications (whether XHTML 1.0 or HTML 4.01) specifies a different content model, with frameset replacing body, that contains either frame elements, or optionally noframes with a body.

Summary of specification versions

As this list demonstrates, the loose versions of the specification are maintained for legacy support. However, contrary to popular misconceptions, the move to XHTML does not imply a removal of this legacy support. Rather the X in XML stands for extensible and the W3C is modularizing the entire specification and opening it up to independent extensions. The primary achievement in the move from XHTML 1.0 to XHTML 1.1 is the modularization of the entire specification. The strict version of HTML is deployed in XHTML 1.1 through a set of modular extensions to the base XHTML 1.1 specification. Likewise, someone looking for the loose (transitional) or frameset specifications will find similar extended XHTML 1.1 support (much of it is contained in the legacy or frame modules). The modularization also allows for separate features to develop on their own timetable. So for example, XHTML 1.1 will allow quicker migration to emerging XML standards such as MathML (a presentational and semantic math language based on XML) and XForms—a new highly advanced web-form technology to replace the existing HTML forms.

In summary, the HTML 4.01 specification primarily reined in all the various HTML implementations into a single clearly written specification based on SGML. XHTML 1.0, ported this specification, as is, to the new XML defined specification. Next, XHTML 1.1 takes advantage of the extensible nature of XML and modularizes the whole specification. XHTML 2.0 will be the first step in adding new features to the specification in a standards-body-based approach.

Hypertext features not in HTML

HTML lacks some of the features found in earlier hypertext systems, such as typed links, source tracking, fat links and others.[60] Even some hypertext features that were in early versions of HTML have been ignored by most popular web browsers until recently, such as the link element and in-browser Web page editing.

Sometimes Web services or browser manufacturers remedy these shortcomings. For instance, wikis and content management systems allow surfers to edit the Web pages they visit.

WYSIWYG Editors

There are some WYSIWYG editors in which the user lays out everything as it is to appear in the HTML document using a graphical user interface, where the editor renders this as an HTML document, no longer requiring the author to have extensive knowledge of HTML.

The WYSIWYG editing model has been criticized,[61] [62] primarily because of the low quality of the generated code; there are voices advocating a change to the WYSIWYM model.

WYSIWYG editors remains a controversial topic because of their perceived flaws such as:

- Relying mainly on layout as opposed to meaning, often using markup that does not convey the intended meaning but simply copies the layout.[63]
- Often producing extremely verbose and redundant code that fails to make use of the cascading nature of HTML and CSS.
- Often producing ungrammatical markup often called tag soup.
- As a great deal of information of HTML documents is not in the layout, the model has been criticized for its 'what you see is all you get'-nature.[64]

Nevertheless, since WYSIWYG editors offer convenience over hand-coded pages as well as not requiring the author to know the finer details of HTML, they still dominate web authoring.

See also

- Breadcrumb (navigation)
- HTML decimal character rendering
- HTML element
- JHTML
- XHTML
- List of document markup languages
- Microformat
- *The HTML Sourcebook: The Complete Guide to HTML* (historical reference from 1995)

External links

- HTML 4.01, the most recent finished specification (1999) [65]
- HTML 5, the upcoming version of HTML [66]
- Dave Raggett's Introduction to HTML [67]
- Empty elements in SGML, HTML, XML and XHTML [68]

Tutorials

- HTML Dog [69]
- HTML Tutorials [70]
- HTML.net [71]
- Your HTML Source [72]
- HTML tutorial [73]
- The How To Guide To Learning HTML [74]
- HTML CSS Developer [75]

References

[1] http://www.w3.org/TR/1999/REC-html401-19991224/

[2] http://dev.w3.org/html5/spec/

[3] HTML 4 — Conformance: requirements and recommendations (http://www.w3.org/TR/html401/conform.html#deprecated)

[4] Tim Berners-Lee, "Information Management: A Proposal." CERN (March 1989, May 1990). W3.org (http://www.w3.org/History/1989/proposal.html)

[5] Tim Berners-Lee, "Design Issues" (http://www.w3.org/DesignIssues/)

[6] Tim Berners-Lee, "Design Issues" (http://www.w3.org/DesignIssues/Uses.html)

[7] "Tags used in HTML" (http://www.w3.org/History/19921103-hypertext/hypertext/WWW/MarkUp/Tags.html). World Wide Web Consortium. November 3, 1992. . Retrieved November 16, 2008.

[8] "First mention of HTML Tags on the www-talk mailing list" (http://lists.w3.org/Archives/Public/www-talk/1991SepOct/0003.html). World Wide Web Consortium. October 29, 1991. . Retrieved April 8, 2007.

[9] "Index of elements in HTML 4" (http://www.w3.org/TR/1999/REC-html401-19991224/index/elements). World Wide Web Consortium. December 24, 1999. . Retrieved April 8, 2007.

[10] http://www.w3.org/MarkUp/draft-ietf-iiir-html-01.txt

[11] Tim Berners-Lee (December 9, 1991). "Re: SGML/HTML docs, X Browser (archived www-talk mailing list post)" (http://lists.w3.org/Archives/Public/www-talk/1991NovDec/0020.html). . Retrieved June 16, 2007. "SGML is very general. HTML is a specific application of the SGML basic syntax applied to hypertext documents with simple structure."

[12] Raymond, Eric. "IETF and the RFC Standards Process" (http://www.faqs.org/docs/artu/ietf_process.html). *[[The Art of Unix Programming* (http://www.faqs.org/docs/artu/)*]]*. . *"In IETF tradition, standards have to arise from experience with a working prototype implementation — but once they become standards, code that does not conform to them is considered broken and mercilessly scrapped. ...Internet-Drafts are not specifications; software implementers and vendors are specifically barred from claiming compliance with them as if they were specifications. Internet-Drafts are focal points for discussion, usually in a working group... Once an Internet-Draft has been published with an RFC number, it is a specification to which implementers may claim conformance. It is expected that the authors of the RFC and the community at large will begin correcting the specification with field experience."*

[13] "HTML+ Internet-Draft - Abstract" (https://datatracker.ietf.org/public/idindex.cgi?command=id_detail&id=789). . "Browser writers are experimenting with extensions to HTML and it is now appropriate to draw these ideas together into a revised document format. The new

format is designed to allow a gradual roll over from HTML, adding features like tables, captioned figures and fill-out forms for querying remote databases or mailing questionnaires."

[14] "RFC 1866: Hypertext Markup Language - 2.0 - Acknowledgments" (http://www.ietf.org/rfc/rfc1866.txt). Internet Engineering Task Force. September 22, 2005. . Retrieved June 16, 2007. "Since 1993, a wide variety of Internet participants have contributed to the evolution of HTML, which has included the addition of in-line images introduced by the NCSA Mosaic software for WWW. Dave Raggett played an important role in deriving the forms material from the HTML+ specification. Dan Connolly and Karen Olson Muldrow rewrote the HTML Specification in 1994. The document was then edited by the HTML working group as a whole, with updates being made by Eric Schieler, Mike Knezovich and Eric W. Sink at Spyglass, Inc. Finally, Roy Fielding restructured the entire draft into its current form."

[15] "RFC 1866: Hypertext Markup Language - 2.0 - Introduction" (http://www.ietf.org/rfc/rfc1866.txt). Internet Engineering Task Force. September 22, 2005. . Retrieved June 16, 2007. "This document thus defines an HTML 2.0 (to distinguish it from the previous informal specifications). Future (generally upwardly compatible) versions of HTML with new features will be released with higher version numbers."

[16] Raggett, Dave (1998). *Raggett on HTML 4* (http://www.w3.org/People/Raggett/book4/ch02.html). . Retrieved July 9, 2007.

[17] "HTML 3.2 Reference Specification" (http://www.w3.org/TR/REC-html32). World Wide Web Consortium. January 14, 1997. . Retrieved November 16, 2008.

[18] "IETF HTML WG" (http://www.w3.org/MarkUp/HTML-WG/). . Retrieved June 16, 2007. "Note: This working group is closed"

[19] "HTML 4.0 Specification" (http://www.w3.org/TR/REC-html40-971218/). World Wide Web Consortium. December 18, 1997. . Retrieved November 16, 2008.

[20] Arnoud Engelfriet. "Introduction to Wilbur" (http://htmlhelp.com/reference/wilbur/intro.html). Web Design Group. . Retrieved June 16, 2007.

[21] "HTML 4 - 4 Conformance: requirements and recommendations" (http://www.w3.org/TR/html4/conform.html#h-4.2). . Retrieved December 30, 2009.

[22] "HTML 4.0 Specification" (http://www.w3.org/TR/1998/REC-html40-19980424/). World Wide Web Consortium. April 24, 1998. . Retrieved November 16, 2008.

[23] "HTML 4.01 Specification" (http://www.w3.org/TR/html401/). World Wide Web Consortium. December 24, 1999. . Retrieved November 16, 2008.

[24] http://www.w3.org/MarkUp/html4-updates/errata

[25] ISO (2000). "ISO/IEC 15445:2000 - Information technology -- Document description and processing languages -- HyperText Markup Language (HTML)" (http://www.iso.org/iso/iso_catalogue/catalogue_tc/catalogue_detail.htm?csnumber=27688). . Retrieved December 26, 2009.

[26] CS.TCD.ie (https://www.cs.tcd.ie/15445/15445.HTML)

[27] http://lists.w3.org/Archives/Public/www-talk/1992MayJun/0020.html

[28] Hypertext Markup Language: A Representation of Textual Information and MetaInformation for Retrieval and Interchange (http://tools.ietf.org/html/draft-ietf-iiir-html-00)

[29] http://tools.ietf.org/html/draft-ietf-html-spec-00

[30] "HTML 3.0 Draft (Expired!) Materials" (http://www.w3.org/MarkUp/html3/). World Wide Web Consortium. December 21, 1995. . Retrieved November 16, 2008.

[31] "HyperText Markup Language Specification Version 3.0" (http://www.w3.org/MarkUp/html3/CoverPage). . Retrieved June 16, 2007.

[32] http://www.w3.org/TR/html5/

[33] "HTML 5" (http://www.w3.org/TR/html5/). World Wide Web Consortium. June 10, 2008. . Retrieved November 16, 2008.

[34] "HTML 5, one vocabulary, two serializations" (http://www.w3.org/QA/2008/01/html5-is-html-and-xml.html). . Retrieved February 25, 2009.

[35] "XHTML 1.0: The Extensible HyperText Markup Language (Second Edition)" (http://www.w3.org/TR/xhtml1/). World Wide Web Consortium. January 26, 2000. . Retrieved November 16, 2008.

[36] "XHTML 1.1 - Module-based XHTML - Second Edition" (http://www.w3.org/TR/xhtml11/). World Wide Web Consortium. February 16, 2007. . Retrieved November 16, 2008.

[37] http://www.w3.org/TR/xhtml-modularization/

[38] "XHTM 2.0" (http://www.w3.org/TR/xhtml2/). World Wide Web Consortium. July 26, 2006. . Retrieved November 16, 2008. "XHTML 2 Working Group Expected to Stop Work End of 2009, W3C to Increase Resources on HTML 5" (http://www.w3.org/News/2009#item119). World Wide Web Consortium. July 17, 2009. . Retrieved November 16, 2008.

[39] "HTML 5" (http://www.w3.org/html/wg/html5/). World Wide Web Consortium. October 24, 2008. . Retrieved November 16, 2008.

[40] http://www.w3.org/2008/Talks/04-24-smith/index.html

[41] Activating Browser Modes with Doctype (http://hsivonen.iki.fi/doctype/)

[42] http://en.wikipedia.org/

[43] "On SGML and HTML" (http://www.w3.org/TR/html401/intro/sgmltut.html#h-3.2.2). World Wide Web Consortium. . Retrieved November 16, 2008.

[44] "XHTML 1.0 - Differences with HTML 4" (http://www.w3.org/TR/xhtml1/diffs.html#h-4.4). World Wide Web Consortium. . Retrieved November 16, 2008.

[45] Korpela, Jukka (July 6, 1998). "Why attribute values should always be quoted in HTML" (http://www.cs.tut.fi/~jkorpela/qattr.html). Cs.tut.fi. . Retrieved November 16, 2008.

[46] "Objects, Images, and Applets in HTML documents" (http://www.w3.org/TR/1999/REC-html401-19991224/struct/objects.html#adef-ismap). World Wide Web Consortium. December 24, 1999. . Retrieved November 16, 2008.
[47] "The Named Character Reference '" (http://www.w3.org/TR/xhtml1/#C_16). World Wide Web Consortium. January 26, 2000. .
[48] Berners-Lee, Tim; Fischetti, Mark (2000). *Weaving the Web: The Original Design and Ultimate Destiny of the World Wide Web by Its Inventor*. San Francisco: Harper. ISBN 978-0-06-251587-X.
[49] Raggett, Dave (2002). "Adding a touch of style" (http://www.w3.org/MarkUp/Guide/Style.html). W3C. . Retrieved October 2, 2009. This article notes that presentational HTML markup may be useful when targeting browsers "before Netscape 4.0 and Internet Explorer 4.0". See the list of web browsers to confirm that these were both released in 1997.
[50] Tim Berners-Lee, James Hendler and Ora Lassila (2001). "The Semantic Web" (http://www.scientificamerican.com/article.cfm?id=the-semantic-web). Scientific American. . Retrieved October 2, 2009.
[51] Nigel Shadbolt, Wendy Hall and Tim Berners-Lee (2006). "The Semantic Web Revisited" (http://eprints.ecs.soton.ac.uk/12614/1/Semantic_Web_Revisted.pdf). IEEE Intelligent Systems. . Retrieved October 2, 2009.
[52] "XHTML 1.0 The Extensible HyperText Markup Language (Second Edition)" (http://www.w3.org/TR/xhtml1/#media). World Wide Web Consortium. 2000, revised 2002. . Retrieved December 7, 2008. "XHTML Documents which follow the guidelines set forth in Appendix C, "HTML Compatibility Guidelines" may be labeled with the Internet Media Type "text/html" [RFC2854], as they are compatible with most HTML browsers. Those documents, and any other document conforming to this specification, may also be labeled with the Internet Media Type "application/xhtml+xml" as defined in [RFC3236]."
[53] "RFC 2119: Key words for use in RFCs to Indicate Requirement Levels" (http://www.ietf.org/rfc/rfc2119.txt). Harvard University. 1997. . Retrieved December 7, 2008. "3. SHOULD This word, or the adjective "RECOMMENDED", mean that there may exist valid reasons in particular circumstances to ignore a particular item, but the full implications must be understood and carefully weighed before choosing a different course."
[54] "XHTML 1.1 - Module-based XHTML - Second Edition" (http://www.w3.org/TR/xhtml11/conformance.html#strict). World Wide Web Consortium. 2007. . Retrieved December 7, 2008. "XHTML 1.1 documents SHOULD be labeled with the Internet Media Type text/html as defined in [RFC2854] or application/xhtml+xml as defined in [RFC3236]."
[55] Ted Nelson (29 January 1999). "Ted Nelson's Computer Paradigm, Expressed as One-Liners" (http://xanadu.com.au/ted/TN/WRITINGS/TCOMPARADIGM/tedCompOneLiners.html). Xanadu. . Retrieved 26 July 2010.
[56] HTML Design Constraints (http://www.w3.org/History/19921103-hypertext/hypertext/WWW/MarkUp/HTMLConstraints.html), W3C Archives
[57] WWW:BTB – HTML (http://ei.cs.vt.edu/~wwwbtb/book/chap13/who.html), Pris Sears
[58] Freeman, E (2005). Head First HTML. O'Reilly.
[59] http://www.w3.org/TR/xhtml1/#guidelines
[60] Jakob Nielsen (January 3, 2005). "Reviving Advanced Hypertext" (http://www.useit.com/alertbox/20050103.html). . Retrieved June 16, 2007.
[61] Sauer, C.: WYSIWIKI - Questioning WYSIWYG in the Internet Age. In: Wikimania (2006)
[62] Spiesser, J., Kitchen, L.: Optimization of html automatically generated by WYSIWYG programs. In: 13th International Conference on World Wide Web, pp. 355--364. WWW '04. ACM, New York, NY (New York, NY, USA, May 17–20, 2004)
[63] http://xhtml.com/en/xhtml/reference/blockquote/
[64] http://www.invisiblerevolution.net/
[65] http://www.w3.org/TR/html401/
[66] http://dev.w3.org/html5/spec/spec.html
[67] http://www.w3.org/MarkUp/Guide/
[68] http://www.cs.tut.fi/~jkorpela/html/empty.html
[69] http://htmldog.com/guides/
[70] http://phpforms.net/tutorial/tutorial.html
[71] http://www.html.net/tutorials/html/introduction.asp
[72] http://www.yourhtmlsource.com/
[73] http://programming-guides.com/html
[74] http://www.pdfconverter.com/resources/articles/HTMLtutorial/
[75] http://www.htmlcssdeveloper.com/tutorial/

E-mail

The at sign, a part of every e-mail address[1]

Electronic mail, commonly called **email** or **e-mail**, is a method of exchanging digital messages across the Internet or other computer networks. Originally, email was transmitted directly from one user to another computer. This required both computers to be online at the same time, a la instant messenger. Today's email systems are based on a store-and-forward model. Email servers accept, forward, deliver and store messages. Users no longer need be online simultaneously and need only connect briefly, typically to an email server, for as long as it takes to send or receive messages.

An email message consists of two components, the message *header*, and the message *body*, which is the email's content. The message header contains control information, including, minimally, an originator's email address and one or more recipient addresses. Usually additional information is added, such as a subject header field.

Originally a text-only communications medium, email was extended to carry multi-media content attachments, a process standardized in RFC 2045 through 2049. Collectively, these RFCs have come to be called Multipurpose Internet Mail Extensions (MIME).

The history of modern, global Internet email services reaches back to the early ARPANET. Standards for encoding email messages were proposed as early as 1973 (RFC 561). Conversion from ARPANET to the Internet in the early 1980s produced the core of the current services. An email sent in the early 1970s looks quite similar to one sent on the Internet today.

Network-based email was initially exchanged on the ARPANET in extensions to the File Transfer Protocol (FTP), but is now carried by the Simple Mail Transfer Protocol (SMTP), first published as Internet standard 10 (RFC 821) in 1982. In the process of transporting email messages between systems, SMTP communicates delivery parameters using a message *envelope* separate from the message (header and body) itself.

Spelling

There are several spelling variations that occasionally prove cause for surprisingly vehement disagreement.[2] [3]

- *email* is the form required by IETF Requests for Comment and working groups[4] This spelling also appears in most dictionaries.[5] [6] [7] [8] [9] [10]
- *e-mail* is a form recommended by some prominent journalistic and technical style guides.[11] [12]
- *mail* was the form used in the original RFC. The service is referred to as *mail* and a single piece of electronic mail is called a *message*.[13] [14] [15]
- *eMail*, capitalizing only the letter *M*, was common among ARPANET users and the early developers of Unix, CMS, AppleLink, eWorld, AOL, GEnie, and Hotmail.
- *EMail* is a traditional form that has been used in RFCs for the "Author's Address",[14] [15] and is expressly required *"...for historical reasons..."*.[16]

Origin

Electronic mail predates the inception of the Internet, and was in fact a crucial tool in creating it.

MIT first demonstrated the Compatible Time-Sharing System (CTSS) in 1961.[17] It allowed multiple users to log into the IBM 7094[18] from remote dial-up terminals, and to store files online on disk. This new ability encouraged users to share information in new ways. Email started in 1965 as a way for multiple users of a time-sharing mainframe computer to communicate. Among the first systems to have such a facility were SDC's Q32 and MIT's CTSS.

Host-based mail systems

The original email systems allowed communication only between users who logged into the same host or "mainframe". This could be hundreds or even thousands of users within an organization.

By 1966 (or earlier, it is possible that the SAGE system had something similar some time before), such systems allowed email between different organizations, so long as they ran compatible operating systems.

Examples include BITNET, IBM PROFS, Digital Equipment Corporation ALL-IN-1 and the original Unix mail.

LAN-based mail systems

From the early 1980s, networked personal computers on LANs became increasingly important. Server-based systems similar to the earlier mainframe systems were developed. Again these systems initially allowed communication only between users logged into the same server infrastructure. Eventually these systems could also be linked between different organizations, as long as they ran the same email system and proprietary protocol.

Examples include cc:Mail, Lantastic, WordPerfect Office, Microsoft Mail, Banyan VINES and Lotus Notes - with various vendors supplying gateway software to link these incompatible systems.

Attempts at interoperability

- Novell briefly championed the open MHS protocol but abandoned it after purchasing the non-MHS WordPerfect Office (renamed Groupwise)
- uucp was used as an open "glue" between differing mail systems
- The Coloured Book protocols on UK academic networks until 1992
- X.400 in the early 1990s was mandated for government use under GOSIP but almost immediately abandoned by all but a few — in favour of Internet SMTP

From SNDMSG to MSG

In the early 1970s, Ray Tomlinson updated an existing utility called *SNDMSG* so that it could copy files over the network. Lawrence Roberts, the project manager for the ARPANET development, updated *READMAIL* and called the program *RD*. Barry Wessler then updated *RD* and called it *NRD*.

Marty Yonke combined *SNDMSG* and *NRD* to include reading, sending, and a help system, and called the utility *WRD*. John Vittal then updated this version to include message forwarding and an *Answer* command to create replies with the correct address, and called it *MSG*. With inclusion of these features, *MSG* is considered to be the first modern email program, from which many other applications have descended.[19]

The rise of ARPANET mail

The ARPANET computer network made a large contribution to the development of e-mail. There is one report that indicates experimental inter-system e-mail transfers began shortly after its creation in 1969.[20] Ray Tomlinson is credited by some as having sent the first email, initiating the use of the "@" sign to separate the names of the user and the user's machine in 1971, when he sent a message from one Digital Equipment Corporation DEC-10 computer to another DEC-10. The two machines were placed next to each other.[21] [22] The ARPANET significantly increased the popularity of e-mail, and it became the killer app of the ARPANET.

Most other networks had their own email protocols and address formats; as the influence of the ARPANET and later the Internet grew, central sites often hosted email gateways that passed mail between the Internet and these other networks. Internet email addressing is still complicated by the need to handle mail destined for these older networks. Some well-known examples of these were UUCP (mostly Unix computers), BITNET (mostly IBM and VAX mainframes at universities), FidoNet (personal computers), DECNET (various networks) and CSNET a forerunner of NSFNet.

An example of an Internet email address that routed mail to a user at a UUCP host:

```
hubhost!middlehost!edgehost!user@uucpgateway.somedomain.example.com
```

This was necessary because in early years UUCP computers did not maintain (or consult servers for) information about the location of all hosts they exchanged mail with, but rather only knew how to communicate with a few network neighbors; email messages (and other data such as Usenet News) were passed along in a chain among hosts who had explicitly agreed to share data with each other.

Operation overview

The diagram to the right shows a typical sequence of events[23] that takes place when Alice composes a message using her mail user agent (MUA). She enters the e-mail address of her correspondent, and hits the "send" button.

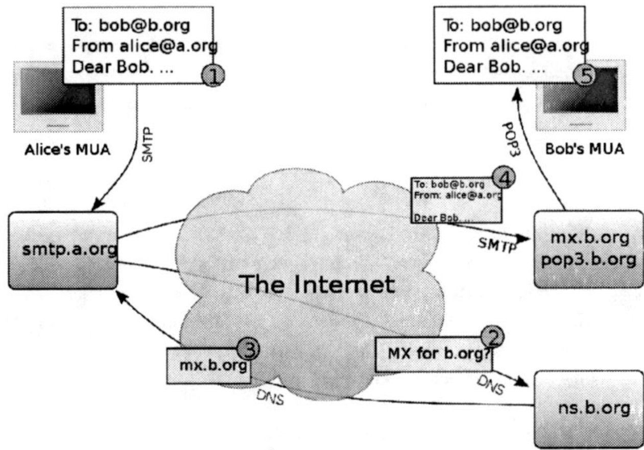

1. Her MUA formats the message in e-mail format and uses the Simple Mail Transfer Protocol (SMTP) to send the message to the local mail transfer agent (MTA), in this case `smtp.a.org`, run by Alice's internet service provider (ISP).
2. The MTA looks at the destination address provided in the SMTP protocol (not from the message header), in this case `bob@b.org`. An Internet e-mail address is a string of the form `localpart@exampledomain`. The part

before the @ sign is the *local part* of the address, often the username of the recipient, and the part after the @ sign is a domain name or a fully qualified domain name. The MTA resolves a domain name to determine the fully qualified domain name of the mail exchange server in the Domain Name System (DNS).

3. The DNS server for the `b.org` domain, `ns.b.org`, responds with any MX records listing the mail exchange servers for that domain, in this case `mx.b.org`, a server run by Bob's ISP.
4. `smtp.a.org` sends the message to `mx.b.org` using SMTP, which delivers it to the mailbox of the user `bob`.
5. Bob presses the "get mail" button in his MUA, which picks up the message using the Post Office Protocol (POP3).

That sequence of events applies to the majority of e-mail users. However, there are many alternative possibilities and complications to the e-mail system:

- Alice or Bob may use a client connected to a corporate e-mail system, such as IBM Lotus Notes or Microsoft Exchange. These systems often have their own internal e-mail format and their clients typically communicate with the e-mail server using a vendor-specific, proprietary protocol. The server sends or receives e-mail via the Internet through the product's Internet mail gateway which also does any necessary reformatting. If Alice and Bob work for the same company, the entire transaction may happen completely within a single corporate e-mail system.
- Alice may not have a MUA on her computer but instead may connect to a webmail service.
- Alice's computer may run its own MTA, so avoiding the transfer at step 1.
- Bob may pick up his e-mail in many ways, for example using the Internet Message Access Protocol, by logging into `mx.b.org` and reading it directly, or by using a webmail service.
- Domains usually have several mail exchange servers so that they can continue to accept mail when the main mail exchange server is not available.
- E-mail messages are not secure if e-mail encryption is not used correctly.

Many MTAs used to accept messages for any recipient on the Internet and do their best to deliver them. Such MTAs are called *open mail relays*. This was very important in the early days of the Internet when network connections were unreliable. If an MTA couldn't reach the destination, it could at least deliver it to a relay closer to the destination. The relay stood a better chance of delivering the message at a later time. However, this mechanism proved to be exploitable by people sending unsolicited bulk e-mail and as a consequence very few modern MTAs are open mail relays, and many MTAs don't accept messages from open mail relays because such messages are very likely to be spam.

Message format

The Internet e-mail message format is defined in RFC 5322 and a series of RFCs, RFC 2045 through RFC 2049, collectively called, *Multipurpose Internet Mail Extensions*, or *MIME*. Although as of July 13, 2005, RFC 2822 is technically a proposed IETF standard and the MIME RFCs are draft IETF standards,[24] these documents are the standards for the format of Internet e-mail. Prior to the introduction of RFC 2822 in 2001, the format described by RFC 822 was the standard for Internet e-mail for nearly 20 years; it is still the official IETF standard. The IETF reserved the numbers 5321 and 5322 for the updated versions of RFC 2821 (SMTP) and RFC 2822, as it previously did with RFC 821 and RFC 822, honoring the extreme importance of these two RFCs. RFC 822 was published in 1982 and based on the earlier RFC 733 (see [25]).

Internet e-mail messages consist of two major sections:

- *Header* — Structured into fields such as summary, sender, receiver, and other information about the e-mail.
- *Body* — The message itself as unstructured text; sometimes containing a signature block at the end. This is exactly the same as the body of a regular letter.

The header is separated from the body by a blank line.

Message header

Each message has exactly one header, which is structured into fields. Each field has a name and a value. RFC 5322 specifies the precise syntax.

Informally, each line of text in the header that begins with a printable character begins a separate field. The field name starts in the first character of the line and ends before the separator character ":". The separator is then followed by the field value (the "body" of the field). The value is continued onto subsequent lines if those lines have a space or tab as their first character. Field names and values are restricted to 7-bit ASCII characters. Non-ASCII values may be represented using MIME encoded words.

Header fields

The message header should include at least the following fields:

- *From*: The e-mail address, and optionally the name of the author(s). In many e-mail clients not changeable except through changing account settings.
- *To*: The e-mail address(es), and optionally name(s) of the message's recipient(s). Indicates primary recipients (multiple allowed), for secondary recipients see Cc: and Bcc: below.
- *Subject*: A brief summary of the topic of the message. Certain abbreviations are commonly used in the subject, including "RE:" and "FW:".
- *Date*: The local time and date when the message was written. Like the *From:* field, many email clients fill this in automatically when sending. The recipient's client may then display the time in the format and time zone local to him/her.
- *Message-ID*: Also an automatically generated field; used to prevent multiple delivery and for reference in In-Reply-To: (see below).

Note that the *To:* field is not necessarily related to the addresses to which the message is delivered. The actual delivery list is supplied separately to the transport protocol, SMTP, which may or may not originally have been extracted from the header content. The "To:" field is similar to the addressing at the top of a conventional letter which is delivered according to the address on the outer envelope. Also note that the "From:" field does not have to be the real sender of the e-mail message. One reason is that it is very easy to fake the "From:" field and let a message seem to be from any mail address. It is possible to digitally sign e-mail, which is much harder to fake, but such signatures require extra programming and often external programs to verify. Some ISPs do not relay e-mail claiming to come from a domain not hosted by them, but very few (if any) check to make sure that the person or even e-mail address named in the "From:" field is the one associated with the connection. Some ISPs apply e-mail authentication systems to e-mail being sent through their MTA to allow other MTAs to detect forged spam that might appear to come from them.

RFC 3864 describes registration procedures for message header fields at the IANA; it provides for permanent [26] and provisional [27] message header field names, including also fields defined for MIME, netnews, and http, and referencing relevant RFCs. Common header fields for email include:

- Bcc: Blind Carbon Copy; addresses added to the SMTP delivery list but not (usually) listed in the message data, remaining invisible to other recipients.
- Cc: Carbon copy; Many e-mail clients will mark e-mail in your inbox differently depending on whether you are in the To: or Cc: list.
- Content-Type: Information about how the message is to be displayed, usually a MIME type.
- In-Reply-To: Message-ID of the message that this is a reply to. Used to link related messages together.
- Precedence: commonly with values "bulk", "junk", or "list"; used to indicate that automated "vacation" or "out of office" responses should not be returned for this mail, e.g. to prevent vacation notices from being sent to all other subscribers of a mailinglist.

- Received: Tracking information generated by mail servers that have previously handled a message, in reverse order (last handler first).
- References: Message-ID of the message that this is a reply to, and the message-id of the message the previous was reply a reply to, etc.
- Reply-To: Address that should be used to reply to the message.
- Sender: Address of the actual sender acting on behalf of the author listed in the From: field (secretary, list manager, etc.).

Message body

Content encoding

E-mail was originally designed for 7-bit ASCII.[28] Much e-mail software is 8-bit clean but must assume it will communicate with 7-bit servers and mail readers. The MIME standard introduced character set specifiers and two content transfer encodings to enable transmission of non-ASCII data: quoted printable for mostly 7 bit content with a few characters outside that range and base64 for arbitrary binary data. The 8BITMIME extension was introduced to allow transmission of mail without the need for these encodings but many mail transport agents still do not support it fully. In some countries, several encoding schemes coexist; as the result, by default, the message in a non-Latin alphabet language appears in non-readable form (the only exception is coincidence, when the sender and receiver use the same encoding scheme). Therefore, for international character sets, Unicode is growing in popularity.

Plain text and HTML

Most modern graphic e-mail clients allow the use of either plain text or HTML for the message body at the option of the user. HTML e-mail messages often include an automatically-generated plain text copy as well, for compatibility reasons.

Advantages of HTML include the ability to include in-line links and images, set apart previous messages in block quotes, wrap naturally on any display, use emphasis such as underlines and italics, and change font styles. Disadvantages include the increased size of the email, privacy concerns about web bugs, abuse of HTML email as a vector for phishing attacks and the spread of malicious software.[29]

Some web based Mailing lists recommend that all posts be made in plain-text[30] [31] for all the above reasons, but also because they have a significant number of readers using text-based e-mail clients such as Mutt.

Some Microsoft e-mail clients allow rich formatting using RTF, but unless the recipient is guaranteed to have a compatible e-mail client this should be avoided.[32]

In order to ensure that HTML sent in an email is rendered properly by the recipient's client software, an additional header must be specified when sending: "Content-type: text/html". Most email programs send this header automatically.

Servers and client applications

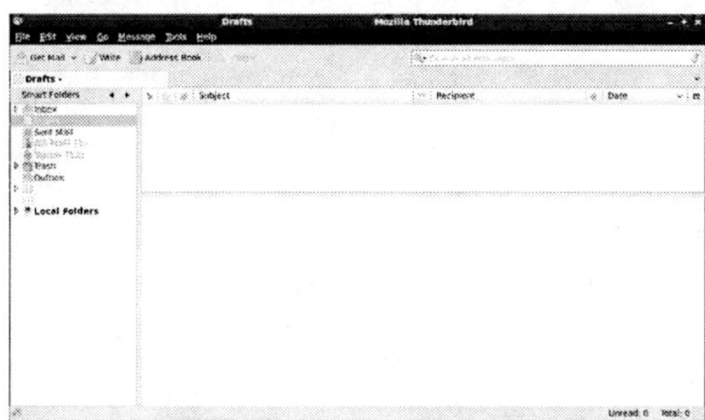

The interface of an e-mail client, Thunderbird.

Messages are exchanged between hosts using the Simple Mail Transfer Protocol with software programs called mail transfer agents. Users can retrieve their messages from servers using standard protocols such as POP or IMAP, or, as is more likely in a large corporate environment, with a proprietary protocol specific to Lotus Notes or Microsoft Exchange Servers. Webmail interfaces allow users to access their mail with any standard web browser, from any computer, rather than relying on an e-mail client.

Mail can be stored on the client, on the server side, or in both places. Standard formats for mailboxes include Maildir and mbox. Several prominent e-mail clients use their own proprietary format and require conversion software to transfer e-mail between them.

Accepting a message obliges an MTA to deliver it, and when a message cannot be delivered, that MTA must send a bounce message back to the sender, indicating the problem.

Filename extensions

Upon reception of e-mail messages, e-mail client applications save message in operating system files in the file-system. Some clients save individual messages as separate files, while others use various database formats, often proprietary, for collective storage. A historical standard of storage is the *mbox* format. The specific format used is often indicated by special filename extensions:

`eml`
: Used by many e-mail clients including Microsoft Outlook Express, Windows Mail and Mozilla Thunderbird.[33] The files are plain text in MIME format, containing the e-mail header as well as the message contents and attachments in one or more of several formats.

`emlx`
: Used by Apple Mail.

`msg`
: Used by Microsoft Office Outlook and OfficeLogic Groupware.

`mbx`
: Used by Opera Mail, KMail, and Apple Mail based on the mbox format.

Some applications (like Apple Mail) leave attachments encoded in messages for searching while also saving separate copies of the attachments. Others separate attachments from messages and save them in a specific directory.

URI scheme *mailto:*

The URI scheme, as registered with the IANA, defines the `mailto:` scheme for SMTP email addresses. Though its use is not strictly defined, URLs of this form are intended to be used to open the new message window of the user's mail client when the URL is activated, with the address as defined by the URL in the *To:* field.[34]

Use

In society

There are numerous ways in which people have changed the way they communicate in the last 50 years; e-mail is certainly one of them. Traditionally, social interaction in the local community was the basis for communication – face to face. Yet, today face-to-face meetings are no longer the primary way to communicate as one can use a landline telephone, mobile phones, fax services, or any number of the computer mediated communications such as e-mail.

Research has shown that people actively use e-mail to maintain core social networks, particularly when others live at a distance. However, contradictory to previous research, the results suggest that increases in Internet usage are associated with decreases in other modes of communication, with proficiency of Internet and e-mail use serving as a mediating factor in this relationship.[35] With the introduction of chat messengers and video conference, there are more ways to communicate.

Flaming

Flaming occurs when a person sends a message with angry or antagonistic content. Flaming is assumed to be more common today because of the ease and impersonality of e-mail communications: confrontations in person or via telephone require direct interaction, where social norms encourage civility, whereas typing a message to another person is an indirect interaction, so civility may be forgotten. Flaming is generally looked down upon by Internet communities as it is considered rude and non-productive.

E-mail bankruptcy

Also known as "e-mail fatigue", e-mail bankruptcy is when a user ignores a large number of e-mail messages after falling behind in reading and answering them. The reason for falling behind is often due to information overload and a general sense there is so much information that it is not possible to read it all. As a solution, people occasionally send a boilerplate message explaining that the e-mail inbox is being cleared out. Stanford University law professor Lawrence Lessig is credited with coining this term, but he may only have popularized it.[36]

In business

E-mail was widely accepted by the business community as the first broad electronic communication medium and was the first 'e-revolution' in business communication. E-mail is very simple to understand and like postal mail, e-mail solves two basic problems of communication: logistics and synchronization (see below).

LAN based email is also an emerging form of usage for business. It not only allows the business user to download mail when *offline*, it also provides the small business user to have multiple users e-mail ID's with just *one e-mail connection*.

Pros

- *The problem of logistics*: Much of the business world relies upon communications between people who are not physically in the same building, area or even country; setting up and attending an in-person meeting, telephone call, or conference call can be inconvenient, time-consuming, and costly. E-mail provides a way to exchange information between two or more people with no set-up costs and that is generally far less expensive than physical meetings or phone calls.
- *The problem of synchronisation*: With real time communication by meetings or phone calls, participants have to work on the same schedule, and each participant must spend the same amount of time in the meeting or call. E-mail allows asynchrony: each participant may control their schedule independently.

Cons

Most business workers today spend from one to two hours of their working day on e-mail: reading, ordering, sorting, 're-contextualizing' fragmented information, and writing e-mail.[37] The use of e-mail is increasing due to increasing levels of globalisation—labour division and outsourcing amongst other things. E-mail can lead to some well-known problems:

- *Loss of context*: which means that the context is lost forever; there is no way to get the text back. Information in context (as in a newspaper) is much easier and faster to understand than unedited and sometimes unrelated fragments of information. Communicating in context can only be achieved when both parties have a full understanding of the context and issue in question.
- *Information overload*: E-mail is a push technology—the sender controls who receives the information. Convenient availability of mailing lists and use of "copy all" can lead to people receiving unwanted or irrelevant information of no use to them.
- *Inconsistency*: E-mail can duplicate information. This can be a problem when a large team is working on documents and information while not in constant contact with the other members of their team.

Despite these disadvantages, e-mail has become the most widely used medium of communication within the business world.

Problems

Attachment size limitation

Email messages may have one or more attachments. Attachments serve the purpose of delivering binary or text files of unspecified size. In principle there is no technical intrinsic restriction in the SMTP protocol limiting the size or number of attachments. In practice, however, email service providers implement various limitations on the permissible size of files or the size of an entire message.

Furthermore, due to technical reasons, often a small attachment can increase in size when sent,[38] which can be confusing to senders when trying to assess whether they can or cannot send a file by e-mail, and this can result in their message being rejected.

As larger and larger file sizes are being created and traded, many users are either forced to upload and download their files using an FTP server, or more popularly, use online file sharing facilities or services, usually over web-friendly HTTP, in order to send and receive them.

Information overload

A December 2007 New York Times blog post described information overload as "a $650 Billion Drag on the Economy",[39] and the New York Times reported in April 2008 that "E-MAIL has become the bane of some people's professional lives" due to information overload, yet "none of the current wave of high-profile Internet start-ups focused on e-mail really eliminates the problem of e-mail overload because none helps us prepare replies".[40] Technology investors reflect similar concerns.[41]

The email services are trying to provide maximum email inbox space to save the large size documents(attachments).

Spamming and computer viruses

The usefulness of e-mail is being threatened by four phenomena: e-mail bombardment, spamming, phishing, and e-mail worms.

Spamming is unsolicited commercial (or bulk) e-mail. Because of the very low cost of sending e-mail, spammers can send hundreds of millions of e-mail messages each day over an inexpensive Internet connection. Hundreds of active spammers sending this volume of mail results in information overload for many computer users who receive voluminous unsolicited e-mail each day.[42] [43]

E-mail worms use e-mail as a way of replicating themselves into vulnerable computers. Although the first e-mail worm affected UNIX computers, the problem is most common today on the more popular Microsoft Windows operating system.

The combination of spam and worm programs results in users receiving a constant drizzle of junk e-mail, which reduces the usefulness of e-mail as a practical tool.

A number of anti-spam techniques mitigate the impact of spam. In the United States, U.S. Congress has also passed a law, the Can Spam Act of 2003, attempting to regulate such e-mail. Australia also has very strict spam laws restricting the sending of spam from an Australian ISP,[44] but its impact has been minimal since most spam comes from regimes that seem reluctant to regulate the sending of spam.

E-mail spoofing

E-mail spoofing occurs when the header information of an email is altered to make the message appear to come from a known or trusted source. It is often used as a ruse to collect personal information.

E-mail bombing

E-mail bombing is the intentional sending of large volumes of messages to a target address. The overloading of the target email address can render it unusable and can even cause the mail server to crash.

Privacy concerns

E-mail privacy, without some security precautions, can be compromised because:

- e-mail messages are generally not encrypted.
- e-mail messages have to go through intermediate computers before reaching their destination, meaning it is relatively easy for others to intercept and read messages.
- many Internet Service Providers (ISP) store copies of e-mail messages on their mail servers before they are delivered. The backups of these can remain for up to several months on their server, despite deletion from the mailbox.
- the "Received:"-fields and other information in the e-mail can often identify the sender, preventing anonymous communication.

There are cryptography applications that can serve as a remedy to one or more of the above. For example, Virtual Private Networks or the Tor anonymity network can be used to encrypt traffic from the user machine to a safer network while GPG, PGP, SMEmail,[45] or S/MIME can be used for end-to-end message encryption, and SMTP STARTTLS or SMTP over Transport Layer Security/Secure Sockets Layer can be used to encrypt communications for a single mail hop between the SMTP client and the SMTP server.

Additionally, many mail user agents do not protect logins and passwords, making them easy to intercept by an attacker. Encrypted authentication schemes such as SASL prevent this.

Finally, attached files share many of the same hazards as those found in peer-to-peer filesharing. Attached files may contain trojans or viruses.

Tracking of sent mail

The original SMTP mail service provides limited mechanisms for tracking a transmitted message, and none for verifying that it has been delivered or read. It requires that each mail server must either deliver it onward or return a failure notice (bounce message), but both software bugs and system failures can cause messages to be lost. To remedy this, the IETF introduced Delivery Status Notifications (delivery receipts) and Message Disposition Notifications (return receipts); however, these are not universally deployed in production.

Many ISPs now deliberately disable non-delivery report (NDRs) and delivery receipts due to the activities of spammers:

- Delivery Reports can be used to verify whether an address exists and so is available to be spammed
- If the spammer uses a forged sender Email address (E-mail spoofing), then the innocent E-mail address that was used can be flooded with NDRs from the many invalid E-mail addresses the spammer may have attempted to mail. These NDRs then constitute spam from the ISP to the innocent user

There are a number of systems that allow the sender to see if messages have been opened.[46] [47] [48]

US Government

The US Government has been involved in e-mail in several different ways.

Starting in 1977, the US Postal Service (USPS) recognized that electronic mail and electronic transactions posed a significant threat to First Class mail volumes and revenue. Therefore, the USPS initiated an experimental e-mail service known as E-COM. Electronic messages were transmitted to a post office, printed out, and delivered as hard copy. To take advantage of the service, an individual had to transmit at least 200 messages. The delivery time of the messages was the same as First Class mail and cost 26 cents. Both the Postal Regulatory Commission and the Federal Communications Commission opposed E-COM. The FCC concluded that E-COM constituted common carriage under its jurisdiction and the USPS would have to file a tariff.[49] Three years after initiating the service, USPS canceled E-COM and attempted to sell it off.[50] [51] [52] [53] [54] [55] [56]

The early ARPANET dealt with multiple e-mail clients that had various, and at times incompatible, formats. For example, in the system Multics, the "@" sign meant "kill line" and anything after the "@" sign was ignored.[57] The Department of Defense DARPA desired to have uniformity and interoperability for e-mail and therefore funded efforts to drive towards unified inter-operable standards. This led to David Crocker, John Vittal, Kenneth Pogran, and Austin Henderson publishing RFC 733, "Standard for the Format of ARPA Network Text Message" (November 21, 1977), which was apparently not effective. In 1979, a meeting was held at BBN to resolve incompatibility issues. Jon Postel recounted the meeting in RFC 808, "Summary of Computer Mail Services Meeting Held at BBN on 10 January 1979" (March 1, 1982), which includes an appendix listing the varying e-mail systems at the time. This, in turn, lead to the release of David Crocker's RFC 822, "Standard for the Format of ARPA Internet Text Messages" (August 13, 1982).[58]

The National Science Foundation took over operations of the ARPANET and Internet from the Department of Defense, and initiated NSFNet, a new backbone for the network. A part of the NSFNet AUP forbade commercial traffic.[59] In 1988, Vint Cerf arranged for an interconnection of MCI Mail with NSFNET on an experimental basis. The following year Compuserve e-mail interconnected with NSFNET. Within a few years the commercial traffic restriction was removed from NSFNETs AUP, and NSFNET was privatised.

In the late 1990s, the Federal Trade Commission grew concerned with fraud transpiring in e-mail, and initiated a series of procedures on spam, fraud, and phishing.[60] In 2004, FTC jurisdiction over spam was codified into law in the form of the CAN SPAM Act.[61] Several other US Federal Agencies have also exercised jurisdiction including the Department of Justice and the Secret Service.

See also

Enhancements and related services

- E-mail encryption
- Google Wave
- HTML e-mail
- Internet fax
- L- or letter mail, e-mail letter and letter e-mail
- Mule (e-mail)
- Privacy-enhanced Electronic Mail
- Push e-mail

E-mail social issues

- Anti-spam techniques (e-mail)
- Computer virus
- CompuServe (first consumer service)
- E-card
- E-mail art
- E-mail jamming
- E-mail spam
- E-mail spoofing
- E-mail storm
- E-mail subject abbreviations
- Information overload
- Internet humor
- Internet slang
- Netiquette
- Usenet quoting

Clients and servers

- Biff
- E-mail address
- E-mail authentication
- E-mail client, Comparison of e-mail clients
- E-mail hosting service
- Internet mail standards
- Mail transfer agent
- Mail user agent
- Unicode and e-mail
- Webmail

Mailing list

- Anonymous remailer
- Disposable e-mail address
- E-mail encryption
- E-mail tracking
- Electronic mailing list
- Mailer-Daemon
- Mailing list archive

Protocols

- IMAP
- POP3
- SMTP
- UUCP
- X400

Further reading

- Cemil Betanov, *Introduction to X.400*, Artech House, ISBN 0890065977.
- Lawrence Hughes, *Internet e-mail Protocols, Standards and Implementation*, Artech House Publishers, ISBN 0890069395.
- Kevin Johnson, *Internet Email Protocols: A Developer's Guide*, Addison-Wesley Professional, ISBN 0201432889.
- Pete Loshin, *Essential Email Standards: RFCs and Protocols Made Practical*, John Wiley & Sons, ISBN 0471345970.
- Sara Radicati, *Electronic Mail: An Introduction to the X.400 Message Handling Standards*, Mcgraw-Hill, ISBN 0070511047.
- John Rhoton, *Programmer's Guide to Internet Mail: SMTP, POP, IMAP, and LDAP*, Elsevier, ISBN 1555582125.
- John Rhoton, *X.400 and SMTP: Battle of the E-mail Protocols*, Elsevier, ISBN 155558165X.
- David Wood, *Programming Internet Mail*, O'Reilly, ISBN 1565924797.

External links

- E-mail [62] at the Open Directory Project
- IANA's list of standard header fields [26]
- The History of Electronic Mail [63] is a personal memoir by the implementer of an early e-mail system
- Online E-mail Decode [64]

References

[1] Klensin, J. (October 2008). "RFC 5321 - Simple Mail Transfer Protocol" (http://tools.ietf.org/html/rfc5321#section-2.3.11). *Network Working Group.*. Retrieved 2010-02-27.

[2] *"A Matter of (Wired News) Style"*, Tony Long, Wired magazine, 23 October 2000 (http://www.nettime.org/Lists-Archives/nettime-bold-0010/msg00471.html)

[3] *"Readers on (Wired News) Style"*, Wired magazine, 24 October 2000 (http://www.wired.com/culture/lifestyle/news/2000/10/39651)

[4] "RFC Editor Terms List" (http://www.rfc-editor.org/rfc-style-guide/terms-online-03.txt). IETF..

[5] AskOxford Language Query team. "What is the correct way to spell 'e' words such as 'email', 'ecommerce', 'egovernment'?" (http://www.askoxford.com/asktheexperts/faq/aboutspelling/email). *FAQ*. Oxford University Press.. Retrieved 4 September 2009. "We recommend email, as this is now by far the most common form"

[6] Reference.com (http://dictionary.reference.com/browse/email)

[7] Random House Unabridged Dictionary, 2006

[8] The American Heritage Dictionary of the English Language, Fourth Edition

[9] Princeton University WordNet 3.0
[10] The American Heritage Science Dictionary, 2002
[11] Microsoft Corporation Editorial Style Board (November 12, 2003). "Microsoft Manual of Style for Technical Publications Third Edition" (http://safari.oreilly.com/0735617465). .
[12] APStylebook.com (http://www.apstylebook.com/ask_editor.php)
[13] RFC 821 (rfc821) - Simple Mail Transfer Protocol (http://www.faqs.org/rfcs/rfc821.html)
[14] RFC 1939 (rfc1939) - Post Office Protocol - Version 3 (http://www.faqs.org/rfcs/rfc1939.html)
[15] RFC 3501 (rfc3501) - Internet Message Access Protocol - version 4rev1 (http://www.faqs.org/rfcs/rfc3501.html)
[16] *"RFC Style Guide"*, Table of decisions on consistent usage in RFC (http://www.rfc-editor.org/rfc-style-guide/terms-online-03.txt)
[17] "CTSS, Compatible Time-Sharing System" (September 4, 2006), University of South Alabama, USA-CTSS (http://www.cis.usouthal.edu/faculty/daigle/project1/ctss.htm).
[18] Tom Van Vleck, "The IBM 7094 and CTSS" (September 10, 2004), *Multicians.org* (Multics), web: Multicians-7094 (http://www.multicians.org/thvv/7094.html).
[19] Email History (http://www.livinginternet.com/e/ei.htm)
[20] The History of Electronic Mail (http://www.multicians.org/thvv/mail-history.html)
[21] The First Email (http://openmap.bbn.com/~tomlinso/ray/firstemailframe.html)
[22] Wave New World,Time Magazine, October 19, 2009, p.48
[23] *How E-mail Works* (http://www.webcastr.com/videos/informational/how-email-works.html). [internet video]. howstuffworks.com. 2008. .
[24] "RFC Index" (http://www.ietf.org/iesg/1rfc_index.txt). .
[25] Ken Simpson, "An update to the email standards" (October 3, 2008), *blog.mailchannels.com*, web: MailChannels Blog Entry (http://blog.mailchannels.com/2008/10/update-to-email-standards.html).
[26] http://www.iana.org/assignments/message-headers/perm-headers.html
[27] http://www.iana.org/assignments/message-headers/prov-headers.html
[28] Craig Hunt (2002). *TCP/IP Network Administration.* O'Reilly Media. pp. 70. ISBN 978-0596002978.
[29] "Email policies that prevent viruses" (http://advosys.ca/papers/mail-policies.html). .
[30] "When posting to a RootsWeb mailing list..." (http://helpdesk.rootsweb.com/listadmins/plaintext.html)
[31] "...Plain text, 72 characters per line..." (http://www.openbsd.org/mail.html)
[32] How to Prevent the Winmail.dat File from Being Sent to Internet Users (http://support.microsoft.com/kb/138053)
[33] "File Extension .EML Details" (http://filext.com/file-extension/EML). *FILExt - The File Extension Source*. . Retrieved 2009-09-26.
[34] RFC 2368 section 3 : by Paul Hoffman in 1998 discusses operation of the "mailto" URL.
[35] Stern, Michael J.Information, Communication & Society; Oct2008, Vol. 11 Issue 5, p591-616, 26p. CLB Oklahoma State University, Stillwater, OK, USA.
[36] Barrett, Grant (December 23, 2007). "All We Are Saying." (http://www.nytimes.com/2007/12/23/weekinreview/23buzzwords.html?ref=weekinreview). New York Times. . Retrieved 2007-12-24.
[37] "Email Right to Privacy - Why Small Businesses Care" (http://www.smallbiztrends.com/2007/06/email-has-right-to-privacy-why-small-businesses-care.html). Anita Campbell. 2007-06-19. .
[38] "Exchange 2007: Attachment Size Increase,..." (http://technet.microsoft.com/en-us/magazine/2009.01.exchangeqa.aspx?pr=blog). TechNet Magazine, Microsoft.com US. 2010-03-25. .
[39] Lohr, Steve (2007-12-20). "Is Information Overload a $650 Billion Drag on the Economy?" (http://bits.blogs.nytimes.com/2007/12/20/is-information-overload-a-650-billion-drag-on-the-economy). New York Times. . Retrieved May 1, 2010.
[40] Stross, Randall (2008-04-20). "Struggling to Evade the E-Mail Tsunami" (http://www.nytimes.com/2008/04/20/technology/20digi.html?_r=2&oref=slogin&oref=slogin). New York Times. . Retrieved May 1, 2010.
[41] "Did Darwin Skip Over Email?" (http://www.foundrygroup.com/blog/archives/2008/04/did-darwin-skip-over-email.php). Foundry Group. 2008-04-28. .
[42] Rich Kawanagh. The top ten e-mail spam list of 2005. ITVibe news, 2006, january 02, ITvibe.com (http://itvibe.com/news/3837/)
[43] How Microsoft is losing the war on spam Salon.com (http://dir.salon.com/story/tech/feature/2005/01/19/microsoft_spam/index.html)
[44] Spam Bill 2003 (PDF (http://www.aph.gov.au/library/pubs/bd/2003-04/04bd045.pdf))
[45] Mohsen Toorani, SMEmail - A New Protocol for the Secure E-mail in Mobile Environments (http://ieeexplore.ieee.org/xpl/freeabs_all.jsp?arnumber=4783292), Proceedings of the Australian Telecommunications Networks and Applications Conference (ATNAC'08), pp.39-44, Adelaide, Australia, December 2008. (PDF (http://arxiv1.library.cornell.edu/ftp/arxiv/papers/1002/1002.3176.pdf))
[46] About.com (http://email.about.com/od/emailbehindthescenes/a/html_return_rcp.htm)
[47] Webdevelopersnotes.com (http://www.webdevelopersnotes.com/tips/yahoo/notification-when-yahoo-email-is-opened.php)
[48] Microsoft.com (http://support.microsoft.com/kb/222163)
[49] In re Request for declaratory ruling and investigation by Graphnet Systems, Inc., concerning the proposed E-COM service, FCC Docket No. 79-6 (September 4, 1979)
[50] History of the United States Postal Service, USPS (http://www.usps.com/history/history/his1.htm)

[51] Hardy, Ian R; The Evolution of ARPANET Email (http://www.archive.org/web/*/http:/www.ifla.org/documents/internet/hari1.txt); 1996-05-13; History Thesis Paper; University of California at Berkeley
[52] James Bovard, The Law Dinosaur: The US Postal Service, CATO Policy Analysis (February 1985)
[53] Jay Akkad, The History of Email (http://www.cs.ucsb.edu/~almeroth/classes/F04.176A/homework1_good_papers/jay-akkad.html)
[54] Cybertelecom : Email (http://www.cybertelecom.org/notes/email.htm)
[55] US Postal Service: Postal Activities and Laws Related to Electronic Commerce, GAO-00-188 (http://www.gao.gov/archive/2000/gg00188.pdf)
[56] Implications of Electronic Mail and Message Systems for the U.S. Postal Service , Office of Technology Assessment, Congress of the United States, August 1982 (http://govinfo.library.unt.edu/ota/Ota_4/DATA/1982/8214.PDF)
[57] Jay Akkad, The History of Email (http://www.cs.ucsb.edu/~almeroth/classes/F04.176A/homework1_good_papers/jay-akkad.html)
[58] Email History, How Email was Invented, Living Internet (http://www.livinginternet.com/e/ei.htm)
[59] Cybertelecom : Internet History (http://www.cybertelecom.org/notes/internet_history80s.htm)
[60] Cybertelecom : SPAM Reference (http://www.cybertelecom.org/spam/Spamref.htm)
[61] Cybertelecom : Can Spam Act (http://www.cybertelecom.org/spam/canspam.htm)
[62] http://www.dmoz.org/Computers/Internet/E-mail//
[63] http://www.multicians.org/thvv/mail-history.html
[64] http://www.mxcz.net/tools/en-us/emaildecode.aspx

File system

A **file system** (often also written as **filesystem**) is a method of storing and organizing computer files and their data. Essentially, it organizes these files into a database for the storage, organization, manipulation, and retrieval by the computer's operating system.

File systems are used on data storage devices such as hard disks or CD-ROMs to maintain the physical location of the files. Beyond this, they might provide access to data on a file server by acting as clients for a network protocol (e.g., NFS, SMB, or 9P clients), or they may be virtual and exist only as an access method for virtual data (e.g., procfs). It is distinguished from a directory service and registry.

Aspects of file systems

Most file systems make use of an underlying data storage device that offers access to an array of fixed-size physical sectors, generally a power of 2 in size (512 bytes or 1, 2, or 4 KiB are most common). The file system is responsible for organizing these sectors into files and directories, and keeping track of which sectors belong to which file and which are not being used. Most file systems address data in fixed-sized units called "clusters" or "blocks" which contain a certain number of disk sectors (usually 1-64). This is the smallest amount of disk space that can be allocated to hold a file. However, file systems need not make use of a storage device at all. A file system can be used to organize and represent access to any data, whether it is stored or dynamically generated (e.g., procfs).

File names

A **file name** is a name assigned to a file in order to secure storage location in the computer memory. By this file name a file can be further accessed. Whether the file system has an underlying storage device or not, file systems typically have directories which associate **file names** with files, usually by connecting the file name to an index in a file allocation table of some sort, such as the FAT in a DOS file system, or an inode in a Unix-like file system. Directory structures may be flat, or allow hierarchies where directories may contain subdirectories. In some file systems, file names are structured, with special syntax for filename extensions and version numbers. In others, file names are simple strings, and per-file metadata is stored elsewhere.

Metadata

Other bookkeeping information is typically associated with each file within a file system. The length of the data contained in a file may be stored as the number of blocks allocated for the file or as an exact byte count. The time that the file was last modified may be stored as the file's timestamp. Some file systems also store the file creation time, the time it was last accessed, and the time that the file's meta-data was changed. (Note that many early PC operating systems did not keep track of file times.) Other information can include the file's device type (e.g., block, character, socket, subdirectory, etc.), its owner user-ID and group-ID, and its access permission settings (e.g., whether the file is read-only, executable, etc.).

Arbitrary attributes can be associated on advanced file systems, such as NTFS, XFS, ext2/ext3, some versions of UFS, and HFS+, using extended file attributes. This feature is implemented in the kernels of Linux, FreeBSD and Mac OS X operating systems, and allows metadata to be associated with the file at the *file system* level. This, for example, could be the author of a document, the character encoding of a plain-text document, or a checksum.

Hierarchical file systems

The hierarchical file system (not to be confused with Apple's HFS) was an early research interest of Dennis Ritchie of Unix fame; previous implementations were restricted to only a few levels, notably the IBM implementations, even of their early databases like IMS. After the success of Unix, Ritchie extended the file system concept to every object in his later operating system developments, such as Plan 9 and Inferno.

Facilities

Traditional file systems offer facilities to create, move and delete both files and directories. They lack facilities to create additional links to a directory (hard links in Unix), rename parent links (".." in Unix-like OS), and create bidirectional links to files.

Traditional file systems also offer facilities to truncate, append to, create, move, delete and in-place modify files. They do not offer facilities to prepend to or truncate from the beginning of a file, let alone arbitrary insertion into or deletion from a file. The operations provided are highly asymmetric and lack the generality to be useful in unexpected contexts. For example, interprocess pipes in Unix have to be implemented outside of the file system because the pipes concept does not offer truncation from the beginning of files.

Secure access

Secure access to basic file system operations can be based on a scheme of access control lists or capabilities. Research has shown access control lists to be difficult to secure properly, which is why research operating systems tend to use capabilities. Commercial file systems still use access control lists.

Types of file systems

File system types can be classified into disk file systems, network file systems and special purpose file systems.

Disk file systems

A *disk file system* is a file system designed for the storage of files on a data storage device, most commonly a disk drive, which might be directly or indirectly connected to the computer. Examples of disk file systems include FAT (FAT12, FAT16, FAT32, exFAT), NTFS, HFS and HFS+, HPFS, UFS, ext2, ext3, ext4, btrfs, ISO 9660, ODS-5, Veritas File System, ZFS, ReiserFS, Linux SWAP and UDF. Some disk file systems are journaling file systems or versioning file systems.

ISO 9660 and Universal Disk Format are the two most common formats that target Compact Discs and DVDs. Mount Rainier is a newer extension to UDF supported by Linux 2.6 series and Windows Vista that facilitates rewriting to DVDs in the same fashion as has been possible with floppy disks.

Flash file systems

A *flash file system* is a file system designed for storing files on flash memory devices. These are becoming more prevalent as the number of mobile devices is increasing, and the capacity of flash memories increase.

While a disk file system can be used on a flash device, this is suboptimal for several reasons:

- Erasing blocks: Flash memory blocks have to be explicitly erased before they can be rewritten. The time taken to erase blocks can be significant, thus it is beneficial to erase unused blocks while the device is idle.
- Random access: Disk file systems are optimized to avoid disk seeks whenever possible, due to the high cost of seeking. Flash memory devices impose no seek latency.
- Wear levelling: Flash memory devices tend to wear out when a single block is repeatedly overwritten; flash file systems are designed to spread out writes evenly.

Log-structured file systems have many of the desirable properties for a flash file system. Such file systems include JFFS2 and YAFFS.

Tape file systems

A *tape file system* is a file system and tape format designed to store files on tape in a self-describing form. Magnetic tapes are sequential storage media, posing challenges to the creation and efficient management of a general-purpose file system. IBM has recently announced a new file system for tape called the Linear Tape File System. The IBM implementation of this file system has been released as the open-source IBM Long Term File System product.

Database file systems

A new concept for file management is the concept of a database-based file system. Instead of, or in addition to, hierarchical structured management, files are identified by their characteristics, like type of file, topic, author, or similar metadata.

Transactional file systems

Some programs need to update multiple files "all at once." For example, a software installation may write program binaries, libraries, and configuration files. If the software installation fails, the program may be unusable. If the installation is upgrading a key system utility, such as the command shell, the entire system may be left in an unusable state.

Transaction processing introduces the isolation guarantee, which states that operations within a transaction are hidden from other threads on the system until the transaction commits, and that interfering operations on the system will be properly serialized with the transaction. Transactions also provide the atomicity guarantee, that operations inside of a transaction are either all committed, or the transaction can be aborted and the system discards all of its partial results. This means that if there is a crash or power failure, after recovery, the stored state will be consistent. Either the software will be completely installed or the failed installation will be completely rolled back, but an unusable partial install will not be left on the system.

Windows, beginning with Vista, added transaction support to NTFS, abbreviated TxF. TxF is the only commercial implementation of a transactional file system, as transactional file systems are difficult to implement correctly in practice. There are a number of research prototypes of transactional file systems for UNIX systems, including the Valor file system[1] , Amino[2] , LFS [3] , and a transactional ext3 file system on the TxOS kernel[4] , as well as transactional file systems targeting embedded systems, such as TFFS [5] .

Ensuring consistency across multiple file system operations is difficult, if not impossible, without file system transactions. File locking can be used as a concurrency control mechanism for individual files, but it typically does not protect the directory structure or file metadata. For instance, file locking cannot prevent TOCTTOU race conditions on symbolic links. File locking also cannot automatically roll back a failed operation, such as a software upgrade; this requires atomicity.

Journaling file systems are one technique used to introduce transaction-level consistency to file system structures. Journal transactions are not exposed to programs as part of the OS API; they are only used internally to ensure consistency at the granularity of a single system call.

Network file systems

A network file system is a file system that acts as a client for a remote file access protocol, providing access to files on a server. Examples of network file systems include clients for the NFS, AFS, SMB protocols, and file-system-like clients for FTP and WebDAV.

Shared disk file systems

A shared disk file system is one in which a number of machines (usually servers) all have access to the same external disk subsystem (usually a SAN). The file system arbitrates access to that subsystem, preventing write collisions. Examples include GFS from Red Hat, GPFS from IBM, and SFS from DataPlow.

Special purpose file systems

A special purpose file system is basically any file system that is not a disk file system or network file system. This includes systems where the files are arranged dynamically by software, intended for such purposes as communication between computer processes or temporary file space.

Special purpose file systems are most commonly used by file-centric operating systems such as Unix. Examples include the procfs (`/proc`) file system used by some Unix variants, which grants access to information about processes and other operating system features.

Deep space science exploration craft, like Voyager I and II used digital tape-based special file systems. Most modern space exploration craft like Cassini-Huygens used Real-time operating system file systems or RTOS influenced file systems. The Mars Rovers are one such example of an RTOS file system, important in this case because they are implemented in flash memory.

File systems and operating systems

Most operating systems provide a file system, as a file system is an integral part of any modern operating system. Early microcomputer operating systems' only real task was file management — a fact reflected in their names (see DOS). Some early operating systems had a separate component for handling file systems which was called a disk operating system. On some microcomputers, the disk operating system was loaded separately from the rest of the operating system. On early operating systems, there was usually support for only one, native, unnamed file system; for example, CP/M supports only its own file system, which might be called "CP/M file system" if needed, but which didn't bear any official name at all.

Because of this, there needs to be an interface provided by the operating system software between the user and the file system. This interface can be textual (such as provided by a command line interface, such as the Unix shell, or OpenVMS DCL) or graphical (such as provided by a graphical user interface, such as file browsers). If graphical, the metaphor of the *folder*, containing documents, other files, and nested folders is often used (see also: directory and folder).

Flat file systems

In a flat file system, there are no subdirectories—everything is stored at the same (root) level on the media, be it a hard disk, floppy disk, etc. While simple, this system rapidly becomes inefficient as the number of files grows, and makes it difficult for users to organize data into related groups.

Like many small systems before it, the original Apple Macintosh featured a flat file system, called Macintosh File System. Its version of Mac OS was unusual in that the file management software (Macintosh Finder) created the illusion of a partially hierarchical filing system on top of EMFS. This structure meant that every file on a disk had to have a unique name, even if it appeared to be in a separate folder. MFS was quickly replaced with Hierarchical File System, which supported real directories.

A recent addition to the flat file system family is Amazon's S3, a remote storage service, which is intentionally simplistic to allow users the ability to customize how their data is stored. The only constructs are buckets (imagine a disk drive of unlimited size) and objects (similar, but not identical to the standard concept of a file). Advanced file management is allowed by being able to use nearly any character (including '/') in the object's name, and the ability to select subsets of the bucket's content based on identical prefixes.

File systems under Unix-like operating systems

Unix-like operating systems create a virtual file system, which makes all the files on all the devices appear to exist in a single hierarchy. This means, in those systems, there is one root directory, and every file existing on the system is located under it somewhere. Unix-like systems can use a RAM disk or network shared resource as its root directory.

Unix-like systems assign a device name to each device, but this is not how the files on that device are accessed. Instead, to gain access to files on another device, the operating system must first be informed where in the directory tree those files should appear. This process is called mounting a file system. For example, to access the files on a CD-ROM, one must tell the operating system "Take the file system from this CD-ROM and make it appear under such-and-such directory". The directory given to the operating system is called the *mount point* – it might, for example, be `/media`. The `/media` directory exists on many Unix systems (as specified in the Filesystem Hierarchy Standard) and is intended specifically for use as a mount point for removable media such as CDs, DVDs, USB drives or floppy disks. It may be empty, or it may contain subdirectories for mounting individual devices. Generally, only the administrator (i.e. root user) may authorize the mounting of file systems.

Unix-like operating systems often include software and tools that assist in the mounting process and provide it new functionality. Some of these strategies have been coined "auto-mounting" as a reflection of their purpose.

1. In many situations, file systems other than the root need to be available as soon as the operating system has booted. All Unix-like systems therefore provide a facility for mounting file systems at boot time. System administrators define these file systems in the configuration file fstab or vfstab in Solaris Operating Environment, which also indicates options and mount points.
2. In some situations, there is no need to mount certain file systems at boot time, although their use may be desired thereafter. There are some utilities for Unix-like systems that allow the mounting of predefined file systems upon demand.
3. Removable media have become very common with microcomputer platforms. They allow programs and data to be transferred between machines without a physical connection. Common examples include USB flash drives, CD-ROMs, and DVDs. Utilities have therefore been developed to detect the presence and availability of a medium and then mount that medium without any user intervention.

1. Progressive Unix-like systems have also introduced a concept called **supermounting**; see, for example, the Linux supermount-ng project [6]. For example, a floppy disk that has been supermounted can be physically removed from the system. Under normal circumstances, the disk should have been synchronized and then unmounted before its removal. Provided synchronization has occurred, a different disk can be inserted into the drive. The

system automatically notices that the disk has changed and updates the mount point contents to reflect the new medium. Similar functionality is found on Windows machines.

2. A similar innovation preferred by some users is the use of autofs [7], a system that, like supermounting, eliminates the need for manual mounting commands. The difference from supermount, other than compatibility in an apparent greater range of applications such as access to file systems on network servers, is that devices are mounted transparently when requests to their file systems are made, as would be appropriate for file systems on network servers, rather than relying on events such as the insertion of media, as would be appropriate for removable media.

File systems under Linux

Linux supports many different file systems, but common choices for the system disk include the ext* family (such as ext2, ext3 and ext4), XFS, JFS, ReiserFS and btrfs.

File systems under Solaris

The Sun Microsystems Solaris operating system in earlier releases defaulted to (non-journaled or non-logging) UFS for bootable and supplementary file systems. Solaris defaulted to, supported, and extended UFS.

Support for other file systems and significant enhancements were added over time, including Veritas Software Corp. (Journaling) VxFS, Sun Microsystems (Clustering) QFS, Sun Microsystems (Journaling) UFS, and Sun Microsystems (open source, poolable, 128 bit compressible, and error-correcting) ZFS.

Kernel extensions were added to Solaris to allow for bootable Veritas VxFS operation. Logging or Journaling was added to UFS in Sun's Solaris 7. Releases of Solaris 10, Solaris Express, OpenSolaris, and other open source variants of the Solaris operating system later supported bootable ZFS.

Logical Volume Management allows for spanning a file system across multiple devices for the purpose of adding redundancy, capacity, and/or throughput. Legacy environments in Solaris may use Solaris Volume Manager (formerly known as Solstice DiskSuite.) Multiple operating systems (including Solaris) may use Veritas Volume Manager. Modern Solaris based operating systems eclipse the need for Volume Management through leveraging virtual storage pools in ZFS.

File systems under Mac OS X

Mac OS X uses a file system that it inherited from classic Mac OS called HFS Plus, sometimes called *Mac OS Extended*. HFS Plus is a metadata-rich and case preserving file system. Due to the Unix roots of Mac OS X, Unix permissions were added to HFS Plus. Later versions of HFS Plus added journaling to prevent corruption of the file system structure and introduced a number of optimizations to the allocation algorithms in an attempt to defragment files automatically without requiring an external defragmenter.

Filenames can be up to 255 characters. HFS Plus uses Unicode to store filenames. On Mac OS X, the filetype can come from the type code, stored in file's metadata, or the filename.

HFS Plus has three kinds of links: Unix-style hard links, Unix-style symbolic links and aliases. Aliases are designed to maintain a link to their original file even if they are moved or renamed; they are not interpreted by the file system itself, but by the File Manager code in userland.

Mac OS X also supports the UFS file system, derived from the BSD Unix Fast File System via NeXTSTEP. However, as of Mac OS X 10.5 (Leopard), Mac OS X can no longer be installed on a UFS volume, nor can a pre-Leopard system installed on a UFS volume be upgraded to Leopard.[8]

File systems under Plan 9 from Bell Labs

Plan 9 from Bell Labs was originally designed to extend some of Unix's good points, and to introduce some new ideas of its own while fixing the shortcomings of Unix.

With respect to file systems, the Unix system of treating things as files was continued, but in Plan 9, *everything* is treated as a file, and accessed as a file would be (i.e., no ioctl or mmap). Perhaps surprisingly, while the file interface is made universal it is also simplified considerably: symlinks, hard links and suid are made obsolete, and an atomic create/open operation is introduced. More importantly the set of file operations becomes well defined and subversions of this like ioctl are eliminated.

Secondly, the underlying 9P protocol was used to remove the difference between local and remote files (except for a possible difference in latency or in throughput). This has the advantage that a device or devices, represented by files, on a remote computer could be used as though it were the local computer's own device(s). This means that under Plan 9, multiple file servers provide access to devices, classing them as file systems. Servers for "synthetic" file systems can also run in user space bringing many of the advantages of micro kernel systems while maintaining the simplicity of the system.

Everything on a Plan 9 system has an abstraction as a file; networking, graphics, debugging, authentication, capabilities, encryption, and other services are accessed via I-O operations on file descriptors. For example, this allows the use of the IP stack of a gateway machine without need of NAT, or provides a network-transparent window system without the need of any extra code.

Another example: a Plan-9 application receives FTP service by opening an FTP site. The ftpfs server handles the open by essentially mounting the remote FTP site as part of the local file system. With ftpfs as an intermediary, the application can now use the usual file-system operations to access the FTP site as if it were part of the local file system. A further example is the mail system which uses file servers that synthesize virtual files and directories to represent a user mailbox as `/mail/fs/mbox`. The wikifs provides a file system interface to a wiki.

These file systems are organized with the help of private, per-process namespaces, allowing each process to have a different view of the many file systems that provide resources in a distributed system.

The Inferno operating system shares these concepts with Plan 9.

File systems under Microsoft Windows

Windows makes use of the FAT and NTFS file systems.

```
C:\Temp> dir
 Volume in drive C is C
 Volume Serial Number is 74F5-B93C

 Directory of C:\Temp

2009-08-25  11:59    <DIR>          .
2009-08-25  11:59    <DIR>          ..
2007-03-01  11:37         2,321,600 AdobeUpdater12345.exe
2009-04-03  10:01            27,988 dd_depcheckdotnetfx30.txt
2009-04-03  10:01               764 dd_dotnetfx3error.txt
2009-04-03  10:01            32,572 dd_dotnetfx3install.txt
2009-06-09  13:46            35,145 GenProfile.log
2009-08-05  12:11               155 KB969856.log
2009-04-20  08:37               402 MSI29e0b.LOG
2009-04-09  16:34            38,895 offcln11.log
2009-04-03  16:02    <DIR>          OfficePatches
2009-07-14  14:30    <DIR>          OHotfix
2009-08-25  10:52            16,384 Perflib_Perfdata_c30.dat
2009-04-03  10:01             1,744 uxeventlog.txt
2009-08-25  11:42        50,245,632 WFV2F.tmp
2009-04-20  10:07             1,397 {AC76BA86-7AD7-1033-7B44-A81200000003}.ini
2009-04-20  10:13               617 {AC76BA86-7AD7-1033-7B44-A81300000003}.ini
              13 File(s)     52,723,295 bytes
               4 Dir(s)  83,570,208,768 bytes free
```

Directory listing in a Windows command shell

FAT

The File Allocation Table (FAT) filing system, supported by all versions of Microsoft Windows, was an evolution of that used in Microsoft's earlier operating system (MS-DOS which in turn was based on 86-DOS). FAT ultimately traces its roots back to the short-lived M-DOS project and Standalone disk BASIC before it. Over the years various features have been added to it, inspired by similar features found on file systems used by operating systems such as Unix.

Older versions of the FAT file system (FAT12 and FAT16) had file name length limits, a limit on the number of entries in the root directory of the file system and had restrictions on the maximum size of FAT-formatted disks or partitions. Specifically, FAT12 and FAT16 had a limit of 8 characters for the file name, and 3 characters for the extension (such as .exe). This is commonly referred to as the 8.3 filename limit. VFAT, which was an extension to FAT12 and FAT16 introduced in Windows NT 3.5 and subsequently included in Windows 95, allowed long file names (LFN).

FAT32 also addressed many of the limits in FAT12 and FAT16, but remains limited compared to NTFS.

exFAT (also known as FAT64) is the newest iteration of FAT, with certain advantages over NTFS with regards to file system overhead. exFAT is only compatible with newer Windows systems, such as Windows 2003, Windows Vista, Windows 2008, Windows 7 and more recently, support has been added for WinXP[9].

NTFS

NTFS, introduced with the Windows NT operating system, allowed ACL-based permission control. Hard links, multiple file streams, attribute indexing, quota tracking, sparse files, encryption, compression, reparse points (directories working as mount-points for other file systems, symlinks, junctions, remote storage links) are also supported, though not all these features are well-documented.

Unlike many other operating systems, Windows uses a *drive letter* abstraction at the user level to distinguish one disk or partition from another. For example, the path `C:\WINDOWS` represents a directory `WINDOWS` on the partition represented by the letter C. The C drive is most commonly used for the primary hard disk partition, on which Windows is usually installed and from which it boots. This "tradition" has become so firmly ingrained that bugs came about in older applications which made assumptions that the drive that the operating system was installed on was C. The tradition of using "C" for the drive letter can be traced to MS-DOS, where the letters A and B were reserved for up to two floppy disk drives. This in turn derived from CP/M in the 1970s, which however used A: and B: for hard drives, and C: for floppy disks, and ultimately from IBM's CP/CMS of 1967.

Network drives may also be mapped to drive letters.

Other file systems

- The Prospero File System is a file system based on the Virtual System Model. The system was created by Dr. B. Clifford Neuman of the Information Sciences Institute at the University of Southern California.[10]
- RSRE FLEX file system - written in ALGOL 68
- The file system of the Michigan Terminal System (MTS) is interesting because: (i) it provides "line files" where record lengths and line numbers are associated as metadata with each record in the file, lines can be added, replaced, updated with the same or different length records, and deleted anywhere in the file without the need to read and rewrite the entire file; (ii) using program keys files may be shared or permitted to commands and programs in addition to users and groups; and (iii) there is a comprehensive file locking mechanism that protects both the file's data and its metadata.[11] [12]

See also

- Comparison of file systems
- Directory structure
- Disk sharing
- Distributed file system
- Filename extension
- File manager
- File system fragmentation
- Filesystem API
- Physical and logical storage
- List of file systems
- List of Unix programs

- Virtual file system
- Storage efficiency

References

General references

- Jonathan de Boyne Pollard (1996). "Disc and volume size limits" [13]. *Frequently Given Answers*. Retrieved February 9, 2005.
- IBM. "OS/2 corrective service fix JR09427" [14]. Retrieved February 9, 2005.
- "Attribute - $EA_INFORMATION (0xD0)" [15]. *NTFS Information, Linux-NTFS Project*. Retrieved February 9, 2005.
- "Attribute - $EA (0xE0)" [16]. *NTFS Information, Linux-NTFS Project*. Retrieved February 9, 2005.
- "Attribute - $STANDARD_INFORMATION (0x10)" [17]. *NTFS Information, Linux-NTFS Project*. Retrieved February 21, 2005.
- Apple Computer Inc. "Technical Note TN1150: HFS Plus Volume Format" [18]. *Detailed HFS Plus and HFSX description*. Retrieved May 2, 2006.
- File System Forensic Analysis [19], Brian Carrier, Addison Wesley, 2005.

Further reading

Books

- Carrier, Brian (2005). *File System Forensic Analysis*. Addison-Wesley. ISBN 0321268172.
- Custer, Helen (1994). *Inside the Windows NT File System*. Microsoft Press. ISBN 155615660X.
- Giampaolo, Dominic (1999) (PDF). *Practical File System Design with the Be File System* [20]. Morgan Kaufmann Publishers. ISBN 1558604979. Retrieved 2010-01-22.
- McCoy, Kirby (1990). *VMS File System Internals*. VAX - VMS Series. Digital Press. ISBN 1555580564.
- Mitchell, Stan (1997). *Inside the Windows 95 File System*. O'Reilly. ISBN 156592200X.
- Nagar, Rajeev (1997). *Windows NT File System Internals : A Developer's Guide*. O'Reilly. ISBN 9781565922495.
- Pate, Steve D. (2003). *UNIX Filesystems: Evolution, Design, and Implementation*. Wiley. ISBN 0471164836.
- Rosenblum, Mendel (1994). *The Design and Implementation of a Log-Structured File System*. The Springer International Series in Engineering and Computer Science. Springer. ISBN 0792395417.
- Russinovich, Mark; Solomon, David A.; Ionescu, Alex (2009). "File Systems". *Windows Internals* (5th ed.). Microsoft Press. ISBN 0735625301.
- Prabhakaran, Vijayan (2006). *IRON File Systems* [21]. PhD disseration, University of Wisconsin-Madison.
- Silberschatz, Abraham; Galvin, Peter Baer; Gagne, Greg (2004). "Storage Management". *Operating System Concepts* (7th ed.). Wiley. ISBN 0471694665.
- Tanenbaum, Andrew S. (2007). "File Systems". *Modern operating Systems* (3rd ed.). Prentice Hall. ISBN 0136006639.
- Tanenbaum, Andrew S.; Woodhull, Albert S. (2006). "File Systems". *Operating Systems: Design and Implementation* (3rd ed.). Prentice Hall. ISBN 0131429388.

Online articles

- Benchmarking Filesystems (outdated) [22] by Justin Piszcz, Linux Gazette 102, May 2004
- Benchmarking Filesystems Part II [23] using kernel 2.6, by Justin Piszcz, Linux Gazette 122, January 2006
- Filesystems (ext3, ReiserFS, XFS, JFS) comparison on Debian Etch [24]
- Interview With the People Behind JFS, ReiserFS & XFS [25]

- Journal File System Performance (outdated) [26]: ReiserFS, JFS, and Ext3FS show their merits on a fast RAID appliance
- Journaled Filesystem Benchmarks (outdated) [27]: A comparison of ReiserFS, XFS, JFS, ext3 & ext2
- Large List of File System Summaries [28]
- Linux File System Benchmarks [29] v2.6 kernel with a stress on CPU usage
- Linux Filesystem Benchmarks [30]
- Linux large file support (outdated) [31]
- Local Filesystems for Windows [32]
- Overview of some filesystems (outdated) [33]
- Sparse files support (outdated) [34]
- Jeremy Reimer (March 16, 2008). "From BFS to ZFS: past, present, and future of file systems" [35]. arstechnica.com. Retrieved 2008-03-18.

External links

- Filesystem Specifications - Links & Whitepapers [36]
- Interesting File System Projects [37]

References

[1] Spillane, Richard; Gaikwad, Sachin; Chinni, Manjunath; Zadok, Erez and Wright, Charles P.; 2009; "Enabling transactional file access via lightweight kernel extensions" (http://www.fsl.cs.sunysb.edu/docs/valor/valor_fast2009.pdf); Seventh USENIX Conference on File and Storage Technologies (FAST 2009)

[2] Wright, Charles P.; Spillane, Richard; Sivathanu, Gopalan; Zadok, Erez; 2007; "Extending ACID Semantics to the File System (http://www.fsl.cs.sunysb.edu/docs/amino-tos06/amino.pdf); ACM Transactions on Storage

[3] Selzter, Margo I.; 1993; "Transaction Support in a Log-Structured File System" (http://www.eecs.harvard.edu/~margo/papers/icde93/paper.pdf); Proceedings of the Ninth International Conference on Data Engineering

[4] Porter, Donald E.; Hofmann, Owen S.; Rossbach, Christopher J.; Benn, Alexander and Witchel, Emmett; 2009; "Operating System Transactions" (http://www.sigops.org/sosp/sosp09/papers/porter-sosp09.pdf); In the Proceedings of the 22nd ACM Symposium on Operating Systems Principles (SOSP '09), Big Sky, MT, October 2009.

[5] Gal, Eran; Toledo, Sivan; "A Transactional Flash File System for Microcontrollers" (http://www.usenix.org/event/usenix05/tech/general/full_papers/gal/gal.pdf)

[6] http://sourceforge.net/projects/supermount-ng

[7] http://freshmeat.net/projects/autofs/

[8] Mac OS X 10.5 Leopard: Installing on a UFS-formatted volume Newer versions Mac OS X are capable of reading and writing to the legacy FAT file systems(16 & 32). They are capable of reading, but not writing to the NTFS file system. Third party software is still necessary to write to the NTFS file system under Snow Leopard 10.6.2. (http://docs.info.apple.com/article.html?artnum=306516)

[9] Microsoft WinXP exFat patch http://www.microsoft.com/downloads/details.aspx?FamilyID=1cbe3906-ddd1-4ca2-b727-c2dff5e30f61&displaylang=en

[10] http://www.cs.ucsb.edu/~ravenben/papers/fsml/prospero-gfsvsm.ps.gz

[11] "A file system for a general-purpose time-sharing environment" (http://ieeexplore.ieee.org/xpl/freeabs_all.jsp?arnumber=1451786), G. C. Pirkola, *Proceedings of the IEEE*, June 1975, volume 63 no. 6, pp. 918–924, ISSN 0018-9219

[12] "The Protection of Information in a General Purpose Time-Sharing Environment", Gary C. Pirkola and John Sanguinetti, *Proceedings of the IEEE Symposium on Trends and Applications 1977: Computer Security and Integrity*, vol. 10 no. 4, , pp. 106-114

[13] http://homepage.ntlworld.com./jonathan.deboynepollard/FGA/os2-disc-and-volume-size-limits.html

[14] ftp://service.boulder.ibm.com/ps/products/os2/fixes/v4warp/english-us/jr09427/JR09427.TXT

[15] http://linux-ntfs.sourceforge.net/ntfs/attributes/ea_information.html

[16] http://linux-ntfs.sourceforge.net/ntfs/attributes/ea.html

[17] http://linux-ntfs.sourceforge.net/ntfs/attributes/standard_information.html

[18] http://developer.apple.com/technotes/tn/tn1150.html

[19] http://www.digital-evidence.org/fsfa/

[20] http://www.nobius.org/~dbg/practical-file-system-design.pdf

[21] http://www.cs.wisc.edu/~vijayan/vijayan-thesis.pdf

[22] http://linuxgazette.net/102/piszcz.html

[23] http://linuxgazette.net/122/piszcz.html

[24] http://www.debian-administration.org/articles/388
[25] http://www.osnews.com/story.php?news_id=69
[26] http://www.open-mag.com/features/Vol_18/filesystems/filesystems.htm
[27] http://staff.osuosl.org/~kveton/fs/
[28] http://www.osdata.com/system/logical/logical.htm
[29] http://fsbench.netnation.com/
[30] http://www.techyblog.com/linux-news/linux-26-filesystem-benchmarks-older.html
[31] http://www.suse.de/~aj/linux_lfs.html
[32] http://www.microsoft.com/whdc/device/storage/LocFileSys.mspx
[33] http://osdev.berlios.de/osd-fs.html
[34] http://www.lrdev.com/lr/unix/sparsefile.html
[35] http://arstechnica.com/articles/paedia/past-present-future-file-systems.ars
[36] http://www.forensics.nl/filesystems
[37] http://filesystems.org/all-projects.html

cron

Cron is a time-based job scheduler in Unix-like computer operating systems. The name *cron* comes from the word "chronos", Greek for "time". Cron enables users to schedule jobs (commands or shell scripts) to run periodically at certain times or dates. It is commonly used to automate system maintenance or administration, though its general-purpose nature means that it can be used for other purposes, such as connecting to the Internet and downloading email.[1]

Overview

Cron is driven by a *crontab*, a **configuration file** that specifies shell commands to run periodically on a given schedule. The crontab files are stored where the lists of jobs and other instructions to the cron daemon are kept. Users can have their own individual crontab files and often there is a system wide crontab file (usually in /etc or a subdirectory of /etc) which only system administrators can edit.

Each line of a crontab file represents a job and is composed of a CRON expression, followed by a shell command to execute. Some implementations of cron, such as that in the popular 4th BSD edition written by Paul Vixie and included in many Linux distributions, add a sixth field to the format: an account username that the specified job will be run by (subject to user existence and permissions). This is only allowed in the system crontabs, not in others which are each assigned to a single user to configure.

For "day of the week" (field 5), both 0 and 7 are considered Sunday, though some versions of Unix such as AIX do not list "7" as acceptable in the man page. While normally the job is executed when the time/date specification fields *all* match the current time and date, there is one exception: if both "day of month" and "day of week" are restricted (not "*"), then **either** the "day of month" field (3) **or** the "day of week" field (5) must match the current day.

Examples

The following will clear the Apache error log at one minute past midnight (00:01 of every day of the month, of every day of the week).

```
1 0 * * *  echo -n "" > /www/apache/logs/error_log
```

The following will run the script /home/user/test.pl every 5 minutes.

```
*/5 * * * *  /home/user/test.pl
```

```
.---------------- minute (0 - 59)
|   .------------- hour (0 - 23)
```

```
|   |   .---------- day of month (1 - 31)
|   |   |   .------- month (1 - 12) OR jan,feb,mar,apr ...
|   |   |   |   .----- day of week (0 - 7) (Sunday=0 or 7)  OR sun,mon,tue,wed,thu,fri,sat
|   |   |   |   |
*   *   *   *   *  command to be executed
```

Predefined scheduling definitions

There are several special predefined values which can be used to substitute the CRON expression.

Entry	Description	Equivalent To
@yearly (or @annually)	Run once a year	0 0 1 1 *
@monthly	Run once a month	0 0 1 * *
@weekly	Run once a week	0 0 * * 0
@daily (or @midnight)	Run once a day	0 0 * * *
@hourly	Run once an hour	0 * * * *
@reboot	Run at startup	

Also available is @reboot, which allows a job to run once every time the cron daemon is started, which will typically coincide with the server being booted. It can be useful if there is a need to start up a server or daemon under a particular user, or if user does not have access to the rc.d/init.d files.

Cron permissions

The following two files plays an important role:

- **/etc/cron.allow** - If this file exists, then you must be listed therein (your username must be listed) in order to be allowed to use cron jobs.
- **/etc/cron.deny** - If the cron.allow file does not exist but the /etc/cron.deny file does exist, then you must not be listed in the /etc/cron.deny file in order to use cron jobs.

Please note that if neither of these files exists, then depending on site-dependent configuration parameters, only the super user will be allowed to use cron jobs, or all users will be able to use cron jobs.

Timezone handling

Most cron implementations simply interpret crontab entries in the system time zone setting under which the cron daemon itself is run. This can be a source of dispute if a large multiuser machine has users in several time zones, especially if the system default timezone includes the potentially confusing DST. Thus, a cron implementation may special-case any "TZ=<timezone>" environment variable setting lines in user crontabs, interpreting subsequent crontab entries relative to that timezone.[2]

History

Early versions

The cron in Version 7 Unix, written by Brian Kernighan, was a system service (later called daemons) invoked from /etc/inittab when the operating system entered multi-user mode. Its algorithm was straightforward:

1. Read /usr/etc/crontab
2. Determine if any commands are to be run at the current date and time and if so, run them as the Superuser, root.
3. Sleep for one minute
4. Repeat from step 1.

This version of cron was basic and robust but it also consumed resources whether it found any work to do or not. In an experiment at Purdue University in the late 1970s to extend cron's service to all 100 users on a time-shared VAX, it was found to place too much load on the system.

Multi-user capability

The next version of cron, with the release of Unix System V, was created to extend the capabilities of cron to all users of a Unix system, not just the superuser. Though this may seem trivial today with most Unix and Unix-like systems having powerful processors and small numbers of users, at the time it required a new approach on a 1 MIPS system having roughly 100 user accounts.

In the August, 1977 issue of the Communications of the ACM, W. R. Franta and Kurt Maly published an article entitled "An efficient data structure for the simulation event set" describing an event queue data structure for discrete event-driven simulation systems that demonstrated "performance superior to that of commonly used simple linked list algorithms," good behavior given non-uniform time distributions, and worst case complexity $O\left(\sqrt{n}\right)$, "n" being the number of events in the queue.

A graduate student, Robert Brown, reviewing this article, recognized the parallel between cron and discrete event simulators, and created an implementation of the Franta-Maly event list manager (ELM) for experimentation. Discrete event simulators run in "virtual time", peeling events off the event queue as quickly as possible and advancing their notion of "now" to the scheduled time of the next event. By running the event simulator in "real time" instead of virtual time, a version of cron was created that spent most of its time sleeping, waiting for the moment in time when the task at the head of the event list was to be executed.

The following school year brought new students into the graduate program, including Keith Williamson, who joined the systems staff in the Computer Science department. As a "warm up task" Brown asked him to flesh out the prototype cron into a production service, and this multi-user cron went into use at Purdue in late 1979. This version of cron wholly replaced the /etc/cron that was in use on the Computer Science department's VAX 11/780 running 32/V.

The algorithm used by this cron is as follows:

1. On start-up, look for a file named .crontab in the home directories of all account holders.
2. For each crontab file found, determine the next time in the future that each command is to be run.
3. Place those commands on the Franta-Maly event list with their corresponding time and their "five field" time specifier.
4. Enter main loop:
    1. Examine the task entry at the head of the queue, compute how far in the future it is to be run.
    2. Sleep for that period of time.
    3. On awakening and after verifying the correct time, execute the task at the head of the queue (in background) with the privileges of the user who created it.
    4. Determine the next time in the future to run this command and place it back on the event list at that time value.

Additionally, the daemon would respond to SIGHUP signals to rescan modified crontab files and would schedule special "wake up events" on the hour and half hour to look for modified crontab files. Much detail is omitted here concerning the inaccuracies of computer time-of-day tracking, Unix alarm scheduling, explicit time-of-day changes, and process management, all of which account for the majority of the lines of code in this cron. This cron also captured the output of *stdout* and *stderr* and e-mailed any output to the crontab owner.

The resources consumed by this cron scale only with the amount of work it is given and do not inherently increase over time with the exception of periodically checking for changes.

Williamson completed his studies and departed the University with a Masters of Science in Computer Science and joined AT&T Bell Labs in Murray Hill, New Jersey, and took this cron with him. At Bell Labs, he and others incorporated the Unix at command into cron, moved the crontab files out of users' home directories (which were not host-specific) and into a common host-specific spool directory, and of necessity added the crontab command to allow users to copy their crontabs to that spool directory.

This version of cron later appeared largely unchanged in Unix System V and in BSD and their derivatives, the Solaris Operating System from Sun Microsystems, IRIX from Silicon Graphics, HP-UX from Hewlett-Packard, and IBM AIX. Technically, the original license for these implementations should be with the Purdue Research Foundation who funded the work, but this took place at a time when little concern was given to such matters.

Modern versions

With the advent of the GNU Project and Linux, new crons appeared. The most prevalent of these is the Vixie cron, originally coded by Paul Vixie in 1987. Version 3 of **Vixie cron** was released in late 1993. Version 4.1 was renamed to **ISC Cron** and was released in January 2004. Version 3, with some minor bugfixes, is used in most distributions of Linux and BSDs.

In 2007, RedHat forked vixie-cron 4.1 to the cronie project and included anacron 2.3 in 2009.

Other popular implementations include anacron and fcron. However, anacron is not an independent cron program; it relies on another cron program to call it in order to perform.

See also

- CRON expression
- at (Unix)
- Launchd
- List of Unix utilities

External links

- crontab [3]: schedule periodic background work – Commands & Utilities Reference, The Single UNIX® Specification, Issue 7 from The Open Group
- GNU cron [4] (mcron)
- ISC Cron 4.1 [5]
- Fedorahosted.org [6] - a fork of vixie-cron 4.1 and anacron 2.3 from the RedHat project
- ACM Digital library – Franta, Maly, "An efficient data structure for the simulation event set" [7] (requires ACM pubs subscription)
- UNIX / Linux cron tutorial [8] - a quick tutorial for UNIX like operating systems with sample shell scripts.
- All about Cron on one page [9] - a page covering Cron, starting with theory and ending with many practical examples about its usage.

.

References

[1] Newbie Introduction to cron (http://www.unixgeeks.org/security/newbie/unix/cron-1.html)
[2] Sun.com (http://blogs.sun.com/chrisg/entry/timezone_aware_cron_finally_pushed)
[3] http://www.opengroup.org/onlinepubs/9699919799/utilities/crontab.html
[4] http://www.gnu.org/software/mcron/
[5] ftp://ftp.isc.org/isc/cron/cron_4.1.shar
[6] https://fedorahosted.org/cronie
[7] http://portal.acm.org/citation.cfm?id=359763.359801&coll=ACM&dl=ACM&CFID=63647367&CFTOKEN=55814330
[8] http://www.cyberciti.biz/faq/how-do-i-add-jobs-to-cron-under-linux-or-unix-oses/
[9] http://www.markus-gattol.name/ws/time.html#cron

IBM

Type	• Public (NYSE: IBM [1]) • Dow Jones Industrial Average Component
Industry	• Computer Systems • Computer hardware • Computer software • IT consulting • IT services
Founded	Endicott, New York, U.S. June 16, 1911
Headquarters	Armonk, New York, U.S.
Area served	Worldwide
Key people	• **Samuel J. Palmisano** (Chairman, President and CEO) • **Mark Loughridge** (SVP and CFO)
Products	See products listing
Revenue	▲ US$ 103.630 billion (2009)[2]
Operating income	▲ US$ 17.012 billion (2009)
Net income	▲ US$ 12.334 billion (2009)[2]
Total assets	▼ US$ 109.023 billion (2009)
Total equity	▲ US$ 22.637 billion (2009)
Employees	399,409 (2009)[3]
Subsidiaries	• ADSTAR • FileNet • ILOG • Informix • Iris Associates • Lotus Software • Rational Software • Sequent Computer Systems • Telelogic • Tivoli Software • List of mergers and acquisitions by IBM
Website	ibm.com [4]

International Business Machines (IBM) (NYSE: IBM [1]) is a multinational computer, technology and IT consulting corporation headquartered in Armonk, New York, United States. IBM is the world's fourth largest technology company and the second most valuable global brand[5] (after Coca-Cola). IBM is one of the few information technology companies with a continuous history dating back to the 19th century. IBM manufactures and sells computer hardware and software (with a focus on the latter), and offers infrastructure services, hosting services, and consulting services in areas ranging from mainframe computers to nanotechnology.[6] At the end of May 2010,

IBM bought the Sterling Commerce Unit from AT&T for about $1.4 billion. This is the second largest acquisition by IBM.

IBM has been well known through most of its recent history as the world's largest computer company and systems integrator.[7] With almost 400,000 employees worldwide, IBM is second largest (by market capitalisation)[8] and the second most profitable[9] information technology and services employer in the world according to the Forbes 2000 list with sales of greater than 100 billion US dollars. IBM holds more patents than any other U.S. based technology company and has eight research laboratories worldwide.[10] The company has scientists, engineers, consultants, and sales professionals in over 200 countries.[11] IBM employees have earned five Nobel Prizes, four Turing Awards, nine National Medals of Technology, and five National Medals of Science.[12] As a chip maker, IBM has been among the Worldwide Top 20 Semiconductor Sales Leaders in past years.

History

The company which became IBM was founded in 1896 as the Tabulating Machine Company[13] by Herman Hollerith, in Broome County, New York (Endicott, New York or Binghamton, New York), where IBM still maintains very limited operations. It was incorporated as Computing Tabulating Recording Corporation on June 16, 1911, and was listed on the New York Stock Exchange in 1916 by George Winthrop Fairchild. CTR's Canadian and later South American subsidiary was named International Business Machines in 1917, and the whole company took this name in 1924 when Thomas J. Watson took control of it.

Since November 1910, a Hollerith subsidiary existed in Germany, the DEHOMAG (Deutsche Hollerith-Maschinen GmbH), founded as a license holder from the Tabulating Machine Company. In 1922, the renamed CTR took over 90% of DEHOMAG, which was in license debt due to the German inflation 1914-1923. In 1949 DEHOMAG finally took the name IBM Germany.

IBM has an important history of acquisitions and spin-offs. Among the famous ones, German SAP was founded in 1972 by five former IBM engineers. Chinese Lenovo became world-famous after acquiring IBM's Thinkpad business in 2005.

Selected current projects

developerWorks

developerWorks is a website run by IBM for software developers and IT professionals. It contains how-to articles and tutorials, as well as software downloads and code samples, discussion forums, podcasts, blogs, wikis, and other resources for developers and technical professionals. Subjects range from open, industry-standard technologies like Java, Linux, SOA and web services, web development, Ajax, PHP, and XML to IBM's products (WebSphere, Rational, Lotus, Tivoli and DB2). In 2007, developerWorks was inducted into the Jolt Hall of Fame.[14]

alphaWorks

alphaWorks is IBM's source for emerging software technologies. These technologies include:

- **Flexible Internet Evaluation Report Architecture** – A highly flexible architecture for the design, display, and reporting of Internet surveys.
- **IBM History Flow Visualization Application** – A tool for visualizing dynamic, evolving documents and the interactions of multiple collaborating authors.
- **IBM Linux on POWER Performance Simulator** – A tool that provides users of Linux on Power a set of performance models for IBM's POWER processors.
- **Database File Archive And Restoration Management** – An application for archiving and restoring hard disk drive files using file references stored in a database.

- **Policy Management for Autonomic Computing** – A policy-based autonomic management infrastructure that simplifies the automation of IT and business processes.
- **FairUCE** – A spam filter that verifies sender identity instead of filtering content.
- **Unstructured Information Management Architecture (UIMA) SDK** – A Java SDK that supports the implementation, composition, and deployment of applications working with unstructured data.
- **Accessibility Browser** – A web-browser specifically designed to assist people with visual impairments, to be released as open source software. Also known as the "A-Browser," the technology will aim to eliminate the need for a mouse, relying instead completely on voice-controls, buttons and predefined shortcut keys.

Semiconductor design and manufacturing

Virtually all console gaming systems of the latest generation use microprocessors developed by IBM. The Xbox 360 contains a PowerPC tri-core processor, which was designed and produced by IBM in less than 24 months.[15] Sony's PlayStation 3 features the Cell BE microprocessor designed jointly by IBM, Toshiba, and Sony. Nintendo's seventh-generation console, Wii, features an IBM chip codenamed Broadway. The older Nintendo GameCube utilizes the Gekko processor, also designed by IBM.

IBM's Wii "Broadway" CPU

In May 2002, IBM and Butterfly.net, Inc. announced the Butterfly Grid, a commercial grid for the online video gaming market.[16] In March 2006, IBM announced separate agreements with Hoplon Infotainment, Online Game Services Incorporated (OGSI), and RenderRocket to provide on-demand content management and blade server computing resources.[17]

Open Client Offering

IBM announced it will launch its new software, called "Open Client Offering" which is to run on Linux, Microsoft Windows and Apple's Mac OS X. The company states that its new product allows businesses to offer employees a choice of using the same software on Windows and its alternatives. This means that "Open Client Offering" is to cut costs of managing whether Linux or Apple relative to Windows. There will be no necessity for companies to pay Microsoft for its licenses for operations since the operations will no longer rely on software which is Windows-based. One alternative to Microsoft's office document formats is the Open Document Format software, whose development IBM supports. It is going to be used for several tasks like: word processing, presentations, along with collaboration with Lotus Notes, instant messaging and blog tools as well as an Internet Explorer competitor – the Mozilla Firefox web browser. IBM plans to install Open Client on 5% of its desktop PCs. The Linux offering has been made available as the IBM Client for Smart Work product on the Ubuntu and Red Hat Enterprise Linux platforms.[18]

UC2: Unified Communications and Collaboration

UC2 (*Unified Communications and Collaboration*) is an IBM and Cisco Systems joint project based on Eclipse and OSGi. It will offer the numerous Eclipse application developers a unified platform for an easier work environment.

The software based on UC2 platform will provide major enterprises with easy-to-use communication solutions, such as the Lotus based Sametime. In the future the Sametime users will benefit from such additional functions as click-to-call and voice mailing.[19]

IBM Redbooks

Redbooks [20] are publicly available online books about best practices with IBM products. They describe the products features, field experience and do and don'ts, while leaving aside marketing buzz. Available formats are Redbooks, Redpapers and Redpieces.

Internal programs

Extreme Blue is a company initiative that uses experienced IBM engineers, talented interns, and business managers to develop high-value technology. The project is designed to analyze emerging business needs and the technologies that can solve them. These projects mostly involve rapid-prototyping of high-profile software and hardware projects.[21]

In May 2007, IBM unveiled Project Big Green [22], a re-direction of $1 billion per year across its businesses to increase energy efficiency.

On November 2008, IBM's CEO, Sam Palmisano, during a speech at the Council on Foreign Relations, outlined a new agenda for building a Smarter Planet.[23] In addition, an official company blog [24] exists. Smarter Planet @ IBM [25]

Environmental record

IBM has a long history in dealing with environmental problems. It established a corporate policy on environmental protection in 1971, with the support of a comprehensive global environmental management system. According to IBM, its total hazardous waste decreased by 44% over the past five years, and has decreased by 94.6% since 1987. IBM's total hazardous waste calculation consists of waste from both non-manufacturing and manufacturing operations. Waste from manufacturing operations includes waste recycled in closed-loop systems where process chemicals are recovered for subsequent reuse, rather than just disposing of them and using new chemical materials. Over the years, IBM has redesigned processes to eliminate almost all closed loop recycling and now uses more environmental-friendly materials in their place. IBM has also now built a modelling solution to help protect the environment and reduce its own Carbon Footprint using Lean and Six Sigma principles Green Sigma.[26]

IBM was recognized as one of the "Top 20 Best Workplaces for Commuters" by the United States Environmental Protection Agency (EPA) in 2005. The award was to recognize Fortune 500 companies which provided employees with excellent commuter benefits to help reduce traffic and air pollution.[27]

The birthplace of IBM, Endicott, suffered pollution for decades, however. IBM used liquid cleaning agents in circuit board assembly operation for more than two decades, and six spills and leaks were recorded, including one leak in 1979 of 4,100 gallons from an underground tank. These left behind volatile organic compounds in the town's soil and aquifer. Trace elements of volatile organic compounds have been identified in Endicott's drinking water, but the levels are within regulatory limits. Also, from 1980, IBM has pumped out 78,000 gallons of chemicals, including trichloroethane, freon, benzene and perchloroethene to the air and allegedly caused several cancer cases among the townspeople. IBM Endicott has been identified by the Department of Environmental Conservation as the major source of pollution, though traces of contaminants from a local dry cleaner and other polluters were also found. Despite the amount of pollutant, state health officials could not verify whether air or water pollution in Endicott has actually caused any health problems. According to city officials, tests show that the water is safe to drink.[28]

Solar power

Tokyo Ohkla industrial area Kogyo Co., Ltd. (TOK) and IBM are collaborating to establish new, low-cost methods for bringing the next generation of solar energy products, called CIGS (Copper-Indium-Gallium-Selenide) solar cell modules, to market. Use of thin film technology, such as CIGS, has great promise in reducing the overall cost of solar cells and further enabling their widespread adoption.[29] [30]

IBM is exploring four main areas of photovoltaic research: using current technologies to develop cheaper and more efficient silicon solar cells, developing new solution processed thin film photovoltaic devices, concentrator photovoltaics, and future generation photovoltaic architectures based upon nanostructures such as semiconductor quantum dots and nanowires.[31]

Green Sigma

Green Sigma is an Active Management Six Sigma system which is currently being developed and enhanced through the Innovation Centre in Dublin. Its goal is to Manage & Reduce Carbon Footprint while achieving associated economic and environmental benefits.

Green Sigma is focused around the elements of:

- Carbon
- Water
- Atmospheric emissions
- Liquid waste
- Solid waste
- Ground emissions
- Reporting

IBM Green SigmaTM consultants work with the client team to establish ongoing optimisation of core processes and KPMGs.

- Phase I: Define Key Performance Indicators (KPIs)
- *Phase II: Establish Metering*
- *Phase III: Deploy Carbon Console*
- *Phase IV: Optimise Processes*
- *Phase V: Control Performance*

IBM's goal with the Green SigmaTM offering is to partner with clients to drive innovation, achieving economic benefits for the business and reducing impact to the environment. [32]

Corporate culture

Big Blue is a nickname for IBM. There are several theories explaining the origin of the name. One theory, substantiated by people who worked for IBM at the time, is that IBM field representatives coined the term in the 1960s, referring to the color of the mainframes IBM installed in the 1960s and early 1970s. "True Blue" was a term used to describe a loyal IBM customer, and business writers later picked up the term.[33] [34] Another theory suggests that Big Blue simply refers to the Company's logo. A third theory suggests that Big Blue refers to a former company dress code that required many IBM employees to

1970s IBM System/3 with characteristic blue hardware

wear only white shirts and many wore blue suits.[33] [35] In any event, IBM keyboards, typewriters, and some other manufactured devices have played on the "Big Blue" concept, using the color for enter keys and carriage returns.

Sales

IBM has often been described as having a sales-centric or sales-oriented business culture. Traditionally, many IBM executives and general managers are chosen from the sales force. The current CEO, Samuel J. Palmisano, for example, joined the company as a salesman and, unusually for CEOs of major corporations, has no MBA or post-graduate qualification. Middle and top management are often enlisted to give direct support to salespeople when pitching sales to important customers.

The uniform

A dark (or gray) suit, white shirt, and a "sincere" tie[36] was the public uniform for IBM employees for most of the 20th century. During IBM's management transformation in the 1990s, CEO Louis V. Gerstner, Jr. relaxed these codes, normalizing the dress and behavior of IBM employees to resemble their counterparts in other large technology companies. Since then IBM's dress code is business casual although employees often wear formal clothes during client meetings.

IBM company values and "Jam"

In 2003, IBM embarked on an ambitious project to rewrite company values. Using its *Jam* technology, the company hosted Internet-based online discussions on key business issues with 50,000 employees over 3 days. The discussions were analyzed by sophisticated text analysis software (eClassifier) to mine online comments for themes. As a result of the 2003 Jam, the company values were updated to reflect three modern business, marketplace and employee views: "Dedication to every client's success", "Innovation that matters - for our company and for the world", "Trust and personal responsibility in all relationships".[37]

In 2004, another Jam was conducted during which 52,000 employees exchanged best practices for 72 hours. They focused on finding actionable ideas to support implementation of the values previously identified. A new post-Jam Ratings event was developed to allow IBMers to select key ideas that support the values. The board of directors cited this Jam when awarding Palmisano a pay rise in the spring of 2005.[38]

IBM launched another jam session called InnovationJam 2008.[39] This jam began on October 5 at 6:00 p.m. US EDT and continued for 72 hours through October 8. Unlike past jams, Innovation Jam 2008 involved wide participation from hundreds of IBM's clients, business partners and academics from around the world as well as thousands of IBM's own employees.

Open source

IBM has been a leading proponent of the Open Source Initiative, and began supporting Linux in 1998.[40] The company invests billions of dollars in services and software based on Linux through the IBM Linux Technology Center, which includes over 300 Linux kernel developers.[41] IBM has also released code under different open source licenses, such as the platform-independent software framework Eclipse (worth approximately US$40 million at the time of the donation),[42] the three-sentence International Components for Unicode [43] (ICU) license, and the Java-based relational database management system (RDBMS) Apache Derby. IBM's open source involvement has not been trouble-free, however (see *SCO v. IBM*).

Corporate affairs

Alleged business relations with Nazi Germany

In 2001, a book by Edwin Black was released contending that IBM played an integral administrative part in the systematic genocide of the European Jewish community from 1939 to 1944, by helping the Nazis organize and coordinate their efforts toward gathering and organizing all available information about their victims[44] by leasing their punched card equipment and support services to the Third Reich. Citing "recently discovered" Nazi government documents in the U.S. National Archives and Polish eyewitness testimony, Black claimed IBM's U.S. operations were linked directly to the operations of the Third Reich in occupied Poland.[45]

Historians have known for decades of Nazi use of Hollerith tabulators - the mainframe computer of its era sold and operated by the company's subsidiary, Deutsche Hollerith Maschinen GmbH (Dehomag) - to assist with the massive administrative task of the Final Solution.[46] However, IBM claims that it had no control over its subsidiaries after the Nazis took control of them.[47]

IBM asserts that any documents that existed on the subject from their archives had already been placed in the public domain to assist research and historical scholarship.[48] The records were transferred from the company's New York and German operations to New York University and Hohenheim University in Stuttgart, Germany. Independent academic experts at these universities now supervise access to the documents by researchers and historians.

Simultaneously with the release of Black's book, a lawsuit was filed against IBM based on his allegations. In April 2001, the lawsuit was dropped. Lawyers claimed that they feared proceeding with the suit would slow down payments from a special German Holocaust fund created to compensate forced laborers and others who had suffered due to the Nazi persecution. IBM's German division paid $3 million into the fund, although the corporation made clear that it was not admitting liability with its contribution.[49]

Kevin Maney, a leading biographer of Thomas Watson Sr., then CEO of the company, reports how, as a result of Watson's repudiation of Nazi Germany in 1940, the Nazi leadership heaped spite on him and renounced IBM to the point that Dehomag feared for its existence.[50] He further claims that "Watson declared war on Hitler".[51]

Diversity in the Workforce

IBM's efforts to promote workforce diversity and equal opportunity date back to 1899, when The Computing Scale Company, one of the three companies to later form what became IBM, hired Richard MacGregor, a Black employee, as well as three women: Lilly J. Philp, Nettie A. Moore and Emma K. Manske.[52] The company's first employee with a disability was hired in 1914.[53] IBM was the only technology company ranked in *Working Mother* magazine's Top 10 for 2004, and one of two technology companies in 2005 (the other company being Hewlett-Packard).[54] [55]

Research building in Haifa, Israel

On September 21, 1953, Thomas Watson, Jr., the company's president at the time, sent out a controversial letter to all IBM employees stating that IBM needed to hire the best people, regardless of their race, ethnic origin, or gender. He also publicized the policy so that in his negotiations to build new manufacturing plants with the governors of two states in the U.S. South, he could be clear that IBM would not build "separate-but-equal" workplaces.[56]

In 1984, IBM added sexual orientation to its nondiscrimination policy. The company stated that this would give IBM a competitive advantage because IBM would then be able to hire talented people its competitors would turn down.[57]

On October 10, 2005, IBM became the first major company in the world to commit formally to not using genetic information in employment decisions. The announcement was made shortly after IBM began working with the National Geographic Society on its Genographic Project.

The company has traditionally resisted labor union organizing, although unions represent some IBM workers outside the United States. In 2009 following the announcement in the UK of pension cuts that left many employees facing a shortfall in projected pensions, several hundred employees joined the Unite union.

In the 1990s, two major pension program changes, including a conversion to a cash balance plan, resulted in an employee class action lawsuit alleging age discrimination. IBM employees won the lawsuit and arrived at a partial settlement, although appeals are still underway. IBM also settled a major overtime class-action lawsuit in 2006.[58]

Historically, IBM has had a good reputation of long-term staff retention with few large scale layoffs. Recently, there have been cuts to the workforce in less profitable markets as IBM attempts to adapt to changing global market conditions. After posting weaker than expected revenues in the first quarter of 2005, IBM eliminated 14,500 positions, predominantly in Europe. In May 2005, IBM Ireland announced that the MD (Micro-electronics Division) facility was closing down by the end of the year and offered a settlement to staff. However, all staff that wished to stay with the Company were redeployed within IBM Ireland. The production moved to a company called Amkor in Singapore who purchased IBM's Microelectronics business in Singapore and is widely agreed that IBM promised this Company a full load capacity in return for the purchase of the facility. On June 8, 2005, IBM Canada Ltd. eliminated approximately 700 positions. IBM projects the moves as part of a strategy to "rebalance" its portfolio of professional skills and businesses. IBM India and other IBM offices in China, the Philippines and Costa Rica have been witnessing a recruitment boom and steady growth in the number of IBM employees due to lower wages, local revenue growth and increasing percentages of educated and skilled technical and business workers in other countries.

Gay rights

IBM provides same-sex partners of its employees with health benefits and provides an anti-discrimination clause. The Human Rights Campaign has consistently rated IBM 100% on its index of gay-friendliness since 2003 (in 2002, the year it began compiling its report on major companies, IBM scored 86%).[59]

In 2007 and again in 2010, IBM UK was ranked first in Stonewall's annual Workplace Equality Index for UK employers.[60]

IBM has won over forty gay, lesbian, bisexual and transgender awards globally.[60]

As part of IBM's diversity program, there is a GLBT Diversity Network Group, as well as a GLBT employee group (called EAGLE – Employee Alliance for Gay and Lesbian Empowerment) with over 1000 registered members worldwide.

Logos

The logo that was used from 1924 to 1946. The logo is in a form intended to suggest a globe, girdled by the word "International".[61]

The logo that was used from 1947 to 1956. The familiar "globe" was replaced with the simple letters "IBM" in a typeface called "Beton Bold."[62]

The logo that was used from 1956 to 1972. IBM said that the letters took on a more solid, grounded and balanced appearance.[63]

The striped logo was first used in 1967, and fully replaced the solid logo by 1972. The horizontal stripes suggest "speed and dynamism."This logo (in two versions, 8-bar and 13-bar), as well as the previous one, were designed by graphic designer Paul Rand.[64] [65]

IBM's current "8-bar" logo was designed in 1972 by graphic designer Paul Rand.[66]

Logos designed in the 1970s tended to be sensitive to the technical limitations of photocopiers, which were then being widely deployed. A logo with large solid areas tended to be poorly copied by copiers in the 1970s, so companies preferred logos that avoided large solid areas. The 1972 IBM logos are an example of this tendency. With the advent of digital copiers in the mid-1980s this technical restriction had largely disappeared; at roughly the same time, the 13-bar logo was abandoned for almost the opposite reason – it was difficult to render accurately on the low-resolution digital printers (240 dots per inch) of the time.

Board of directors

Current members of the board of directors of IBM are:

Entrance to IBM's secure headquarters complex in Armonk, New York

IBM PC 5150 with keyboard and green monochrome monitor (5151), running MS-DOS 5.0

- Alain J. P. Belda - Chairman of Alcoa Inc
- Cathleen Black - President of Hearst Magazines
- William R. Brody – Former President, Johns Hopkins University
- Kenneth Chenault – Chairman and CEO, American Express Company
- Michael L. Eskew – Former Chairman and CEO, United Parcel Service, Inc.
- Shirley Ann Jackson – President, Rensselaer Polytechnic Institute
- Andrew N. Liveris - CEO of The Dow Chemical Corp
- W. James McNerney, Jr. - Chairman, President, and CEO of The Boeing Company
- Taizo Nishimuro - Chairman of the board Tokyo Stock Exchange Group
- James W. Owens – Chairman and CEO, Caterpillar Inc.
- Samuel J. Palmisano – Chairman, President and CEO, IBM
- Joan Spero – Former President, Doris Duke Charitable Foundation
- Sidney Taurel – Chairman, Eli Lilly and Company
- Lorenzo Zambrano – Chairman and CEO, Cemex SAB de CV

Corporate headquarters

IBM's headquarters complex is located in Armonk, Town of North Castle, New York, United States.[67] [68] [69] The 283000-square-foot (26300 m^2) IBM building has three levels of custom curtainwall. The building is located on a 25 acre site.[70]

See also

- CP/CMS
- Extreme Blue
- Globally Integrated Enterprise
- History of IBM
- IBM AIX
- IBM Blue Gene
- IBM DB2
- IBM ESA/390
- IBM Fellow
- IBM Global Business Services
- IBM Lotus Notes
- IBM M44/44X
- IBM PC compatible (or IBM PC clone)
- IBM PC
- IBM PC DOS
- IBM Personal Computer
- IBM Personal System/2
- IBM Project Big Green
- IBM Rochester
- IBM Rome Software Lab
- IBM Selectric typewriter

- IBM Software Group
- IBM System/36
- IBM System/38
- IBM System/360
- IBM System/360 Model 67
- IBM System/370
- IBM System i
- IBM System p, POWER6
- IBM System z
- IBM System z9, IBM System z10
- IBM Systems Network Architecture
- IBM Toronto Software Lab
- IBM ViaVoice
- IBM VisualAge
- IBM WebSphere
- IBM's Deep Thought (chess computer)
- Institute of Electrical and Electronics Engineers
- Itty bitty machine company
- John Fellows Akers
- John Opel
- List of computer system manufacturers
- List of IBM products
- List of mergers and acquisitions by IBM
- Louis V. Gerstner, Jr.
- OS/2
- Samuel J. Palmisano
- *SCO v. IBM*
- Smarter Planet
- Thomas J. Watson
- TSS/360
- Watson (artificial intelligence software)

Further reading

Edwin Black	2008	*IBM and the Holocaust: The Strategic Alliance Between Nazi Germany and America's Most Powerful Corporation*	ISBN 0-914153-10-2
Ulrich Steinhilper	2006	*Don't Talk – Do It! From Flying To Word Processing*	ISBN 1-872386-75-5
Samme Chittum	2004	*In an I.B.M. Village, Pollution Fears Taint Relations With Neighbors* [71]	New York Times
Louis V. Gerstner, Jr.	2002	*Who Says Elephants can't Dance?* HarperCollins.	ISBN 0-00-715448-8
Doug Garr	1999	"IBM Redux: Lou Gerstner & The Business Turnaround of the Decade"	Harper Business
Robert Slater	1999	*Saving Big Blue: IBM's Lou Gerstner*	McGraw Hill
Emerson W. Pugh	1996	*Building IBM: Shaping an Industry*	Massachusetts Institute of Technology
Robert Heller	1994	*The Fate of IBM*	Little Brown
Paul Carroll	1993	*Big Blues: The Unmaking of IBM*	Crown Publishers
Roy A Bauer et al.	1992	*The Silverlake Project: Transformation at IBM (AS/400)*	Oxford University Press
Thomas Watson, Jr.	1990	*Father, Son & Co: My Life at IBM and Beyond*	ISBN 0-553-29023-1
David Mercer	1987	"IBM: How the World's Most Successful Corporation is Managed" [72]. Futureobservatory.dyndns.org.	Kogan Page
Richard Thomas DeLamarter	1986	*Big Blue: IBM's Use and Abuse of Power*	ISBN 0-396-08515-6
Buck Rodgers	1986	*The IBM Way*	Harper & Row
Robert Sobel	1986	*IBM vs. Japan: The Struggle for the Future*	ISBN 0-812-83071-7
Robert Sobel	1981	*IBM: Colossus in Transition*	ISBN 0-8129-1000-1
Robert Sobel	1981	*Thomas Watson, Sr.: IBM and the Computer Revolution* (biography of Thomas J. Watson)	ISBN 1-893122-82-4
William Rodgers	1969	*Think: A Biography of the Watsons and IBM*	ISBN 0812812263

External links

- IBM official website [73]
- IBM Archives Site [74]
- Article about IBM setting-up its new Global Healthcare Center of Excellence on the Côte d'Azur - 10/09/2009 [75]
- IBM Agrees to Acquire Sterling Commerce from AT&T for USD 1.4 Billion [76]
- IBM Workers [77]

Business data

- IBM Corp. [78] at Google Finance
- IBM Corp. [79] at Yahoo! Finance
- IBM Corp. [80] at Hoover's
- IBM Corp. [81] at Reuters
- IBM Corp. [82] SEC filings at EDGAR Online
- IBM Corp. [83] SEC filings at the Securities and Exchange Commission

References

[1] http://www.nyse.com/about/listed/quickquote.html?ticker=ibm

[2] Fortune global 500 list 2009, " (http://money.cnn.com/magazines/fortune/global500/2009/full_list/)".

[3] IBM 2009 Annual Report, " Complete 2009 Annual Report (http://www.ibm.com/annualreport/2009/2009_ibm_annual.pdf)".

[4] http://ibm.com

[5] "Business Week, Top Brands 2009" (http://bwnt.businessweek.com/interactive_reports/best_global_brands_2009/). .

[6] "Nanotechnology & Nanoscience" (http://domino.research.ibm.com/comm/research.nsf/pages/r.nanotech.html). .

[7] CNET Networks, " IBM challenges partner Cisco (http://news.cnet.com/8301-1001_3-10228455-92.html)".

[8] "The Global 2000: Sorted by Market Cap" (http://www.forbes.com/lists/2009/18/global-09_The-Global-2000_MktVal.html). *Forbes*. April 8, 2009. . Retrieved March 6, 2010.

[9] "The Global 2000: Sorted by Profit" (http://www.forbes.com/lists/2009/18/global-09_The-Global-2000_Prof.html). *Forbes*. April 8, 2009. . Retrieved March 6, 2010.

[10] "IBM maintains patent lead, moves to increase patent quality" (http://www.ibm.com/news/us/en/2006/01/2006_01_10.html). 2006-01-10. .

[11] "Worldwide IBM Research Locations" (http://www.research.ibm.com/worldwide/). IBM. . Retrieved 2006-06-21.

[12] "Awards & Achievements" (http://www.research.ibm.com/resources/awards.shtml). IBM. . Retrieved 2009-08-13.

[13] Martin Campbell-Kelly and William Aspray, "Computer a History of the Information Machine – Second Edition", Westview Press, p. 37, 2004.

[14] "developerWorks blogs : Michael O'Connell : dW wins Jolt Hall of Fame award; Booch, Ambler, dW authors also honored" (http://www.ibm.com/developerworks/blogs/page/moc?entry=dw_wins_jolt_hall_of). IBM. 2007-03-27. . Retrieved 2007-04-23.

[15] "IBM delivers Power-based chip for Microsoft Xbox 360 worldwide launch" (http://www.ibm.com/chips/news/2005/1025_xbox.html). IBM. 2005-10-25. .

[16] "Butterfly and IBM introduce first video game industry computing grid" (http://www.ibm.com/industries/media/doc/content/news/pressrelease/359248111.html). IBM. 2002-05-09. .

[17] "IBM joins forces with game companies around the world to accelerate innovation" (http://www.ibm.com/industries/media/doc/content/news/pressrelease/1551338111.html). IBM. 2006-03-21. .

[18] "IBM Client for Smart Work" (http://www-01.ibm.com/software/lotus/openclient/). 01.ibm.com. . Retrieved 2010-05-23.

[19] "IBM and Cisco: Attempt to Unite the Communication Software Developers" (http://www.infoniac.com/hi-tech/ibm-cisco-uc2.html). .

[20] http://www.redbooks.ibm.com/

[21] "Extreme Blue web page" (http://www-01.ibm.com/employment/us/extremeblue/). 01.ibm.com. 2007-09-07. . Retrieved 2010-05-23.

[22] http://www-03.ibm.com/linux/project_big_green_linux.html

[23] "Building a smarter planet" (http://asmarterplanet.com/blog/2008/11/building-a-smarter-planet.html). Asmarterplanet.com. . Retrieved 2010-05-23.

[24] http://asmarterplanet.com/

[25] http://www.ibm.com/ibm/ideasfromibm/us/smartplanet/index.shtml

[26] "ibm.com. "Environmental Protection" 3 May 2008" (http://www.ibm.com/ibm/responsibility/world/environmental/pollution.shtml). Ibm.com. . Retrieved 2010-05-23.

[27] "Environmental Protection", 3 May 2008 (http://www.ibm.com/ibm/responsibility/world/environmental/index.shtml).

[28] "In an I.B.M. Village, Pollution Fears Taint Relations With Neighbors." 15 March 2004. New York Times Online. 1 May 2008 (http://query.nytimes.com/gst/fullpage.html?res=9C00E4DF1631F936A25750C0A9629C8B63&fta=y).

[29] IBM and Tokyo Ohka Kogyo Turn Up Watts on Solar Energy Production (http://www.tok.co.jp/en/news/2008/pdf/080616.pdf).

[30] "Energy, the environment and IBM." (http://www.ibm.com/ibm/green/index.shtml). IBM. 2008-04-01. . Retrieved 2009-05-27.

[31] "IBM Press room - 2008-05-15 IBM Research Unveils Breakthrough In Solar Farm Technology - United States" (http://www-03.ibm.com/press/us/en/pressrelease/24203.wss). IBM. 2008-05-15. . Retrieved 2009-05-27.

[32] "IBM" (http://www-935.ibm.com/services/uk/bcs/pdf/ibm2216_02_green_sigma_final.pdf) (PDF). . Retrieved 2010-05-23.

[33] edited by Evan Selinger. (2006). *Postphenomenology: A Critical Companion to Ihde* (http://books.google.com/?id=Da1bPYRyltMC&pg=PA228&lpg=PA228&dq=big+blue+ibm). State University of New York Press. p. 228. ISBN 0-7914-6787-2. .

[34] Conway Lloyd Morgan and Chris Foges. (2004). *Logos, Letterheads & Business Cards: Design for Profit* (http://books.google.com/?id=5zAW7RntiD8C&pg=PA15&lpg=PA15&dq=big+blue+ibm). Rotovision. p. 15. ISBN 2-88046-750-0. .

[35] E. Garrison Walters. (2001). *The Essential Guide to Computing: The Story of Information Technology* (http://books.google.com/?id=AwrQsOW5SsQC&pg=PA55&lpg=PA55&dq=big+blue+ibm). Publisher: Prentice Hall PTR. p. 55. ISBN 0-13-019469-7. .

[36] Smith, Paul Russell (1999). *Strategic Marketing Communications: New Ways to Build and Integrate Communications* (http://books.google.com/?id=HYvbeQLf_gEC&pg=PA24&lpg=PA24&dq="sincere+tie"+ibm). Kogan Page. p. 24. ISBN 0749429186. .

[37] Samuel J. Palmisano (2004-04-27). "Speeches" (http://www.ibm.com/ibm/sjp/04-27-2004.html). IBM. .

[38] "Leading Change When Business Is Good: The HBR Interview--Samuel J. Palmisano". *Harvard Business Review* (Harvard University Press). December 2004.

[39] *InnovationJam 2008* (http://www.ibm.com/ijam2008). IBM. . Retrieved 2009-02-22

[40] "IBM launches biggest Linux lineup ever" (http://web.archive.org/web/19991110114228/http://www.ibm.com/news/1999/03/02.phtml). IBM. 1999-03-02. Archived from the original (http://www.ibm.com/news/1999/03/02.phtml) on 1999-11-10. .
[41] Farrah Hamid (2006-05-24). "IBM invests in Brazil Linux Tech Center" (http://lwn.net/Articles/185602/). LWN.net. .
[42] "Interview: The Eclipse code donation" (http://www.ibm.com/developerworks/linux/library/l-erick.html). IBM. 2001-11-01. .
[43] http://source.icu-project.org/repos/icu/icu/trunk/license.html
[44] Edwin Black (2001). *IBM and the Holocaust: The Strategic Alliance Between Nazi Germany and America's Most Powerful Corporation* (http://www.amazon.com/Holocaust-Strategic-Alliance-between-Americas/dp/0316857696/ref=sr_1_4?ie=UTF8&s=books&qid=1260899415&sr=1-4). ISBN 0316857696. .
[45] "IBM And Nazi Germany" (http://www.cbsnews.com/stories/2002/03/27/print/main504730.shtml). *CBS News*. 2002-03-27. .
[46] Robert Urekew (2002). *Justice Delayed: IBM's Collaboration with Nazi Germany. (Review Essays).(Brief Article) (book review): An article from: Harvard International Review(HTML - Digital)*. Harvard International Relations Council, Inc..
[47] "IBM Statement on Nazi-era Book and Lawsuit" (http://www-03.ibm.com/press/us/en/pressrelease/1388.wss). .
[48] http://www-03.ibm.com/press/us/en/pressrelease/1388.wss accessed 08/03/2010
[49] "Case profile: IBM lawsuit (Holocaust claim by Gypsies)" (http://www.business-humanrights.org/Categories/Lawlawsuits/Lawsuitsregulatoryaction/LawsuitsSelectedcases/IBMlawsuitHolocaustclaimbyGypsies). .
[50] Maney, K. (2003) The Maverick and his Machine: Thomas Watson Sr. and the making of IBM. Wiley, Hoboken, N.J., p. 222
[51] Op. cit. page 222
[52] "IBM Valuing Diversity: Heritage - 1900s" (http://www.ibm.com/employment/us/diverse/heritage_ibm_1900.shtml). IBM. .
[53] "IBM Valuing Diversity: Heritage - 1910s" (http://www.ibm.com/employment/us/diverse/heritage_ibm_1910.shtml). IBM. .
[54] "100 best companies for working mothers 2004" (http://web.archive.org/web/20041017073511/http://www.workingwoman.com/top10.html). Working Mother Media, Inc.. Archived from the original (http://www.workingwoman.com/top10.html) on 2004-10-17. .
[55] "100 best companies 2005" (http://www.workingwoman.com/top10.html). Working Mother Media, Inc.. . Retrieved 2006-06-26.
[56] "IBM's EO Policy letter is IBM's foundation for diversity" (http://www.ibm.com/employment/us/diverse/50/tc.shtml). IBM. .
[57] "IBM Valuing Diversity: Heritage - 1980s" (http://www.ibm.com/employment/us/diverse/heritage_ibm_1980.shtml). IBM. .
[58] "IBM settles overtime lawsuit for $65 million" (http://lisahome.blogspot.com/2006/11/ibm-settles-overtime-lawsuit-for-65.html). .
[59] HRC Corporate Equality Index Score (http://w3.hrc.org/Template.cfm?Section=Search_the_Database&Template=/CustomSource/WorkNet/srch_dtl.cfm&srchtype=QS&searchid=34&orgid=1238) *International Business Machines Corp. (IBM) profile*.
[60] "IBM Valuing Diversity - Awards and Recognition" (http://www-03.ibm.com/employment/us/diverse/awards.shtml#glbt). IBM. . Retrieved 2009-05-27.
[61] " IBM Archives: International Business Machines (1924-1946) (http://www-03.ibm.com/ibm/history/exhibits/logo/logo_5.html)." Retrieved January 16, 2007.
[62] " IBM Archives: IBM in transition (1947-1956) (http://www.ibm.com/ibm/history/exhibits/logo/logo_6.html)." Retrieved January 16, 2007.
[63] " IBM Archives: IBM continuity (1956-1972) (http://www.ibm.com/ibm/history/exhibits/logo/logo_7.html)." Retrieved January 16, 2007.
[64] " IBM Archives: IBM international recognition (1972-) (http://www.ibm.com/ibm/history/exhibits/logo/logo_8.html)." Retrieved January 16, 2007.
[65] IBM Logo History (http://worldsbestlogos.blogspot.com/2007/08/ibm-logo-history.html).
[66] IBM Archives (http://www-03.ibm.com/ibm/history/exhibits/logo/logo_8.html)
[67] " Contact Us (http://www.ibm.com/contact/us/en/)." IBM. Retrieved on October 20, 2009.
[68] " Armonk CDP, New York (http://factfinder.census.gov/servlet/MapItDrawServlet?geo_id=16000US3602649&_bucket_id=50&tree_id=420&context=saff&_lang=en&_sse=on)." U.S. Census Bureau. Retrieved on October 20, 2009.
[69] " North Castle town, Westchester county, New York (http://factfinder.census.gov/servlet/MapItDrawServlet?geo_id=06000US3611951693&_bucket_id=50&tree_id=420&context=saff&_lang=en&_sse=on)." U.S. Census Bureau. Retrieved on October 20, 2009.
[70] " IBM Corporate headquarters (http://204.94.126.60/projects/ibm-armonk.html)." The Whiting-Turner Contracting Company. Retrieved on October 21, 2009.
[71] http://query.nytimes.com/gst/fullpage.html?res=9C00E4DF1631F936A25750C0A9629C8B63&fta=y
[72] http://futureobservatory.dyndns.org/2013.htm
[73] http://www.ibm.com/
[74] http://www.ibm.com/ibm/history/
[75] http://www.cad.fr/en/newsletter/index.php?txt=act8820
[76] http://rfpconnect.com/news/2010/5/24/ibm-agrees-to-acquire-sterling-commerce-from-at-t-for-usd-1-4-billion
[77] http://www.endicottalliance.org/
[78] http://finance.google.com/finance?q=IBM
[79] http://finance.yahoo.com/q?s=IBM
[80] http://www.hoovers.com//--ID__10796--/free-co-factsheet.xhtml
[81] http://www.reuters.com/finance/stocks/overview?symbol=IBM
[82] http://google.brand.edgar-online.com/?sym=IBM

[83] http://www.sec.gov/cgi-bin/browse-edgar?action=getcompany&CIK=51143

Article Sources and Contributors

Software Testing Automation Framework *Source*: http://en.wikipedia.org/w/index.php?oldid=313676595 *Contributors*: 16@r, Andreas Kaufmann, Davidmcb64, Kbdank71, Rwwww, 1 anonymous edits

Open source *Source*: http://en.wikipedia.org/w/index.php?oldid=384958775 *Contributors*: 217.126.156.xxx, 24.218.142.xxx, 2CentsOfMine, 4twenty42o, AL SAM, AVM, Aaboelela, Aborg, Acelros, Adam Buteux, AdamWeeden, Addshore, Adriaan, Adrian7812, Ahoerstemeier, Ahy1, Alai, Alakon, Alex756, Alexandertsang, AlistairMcMillan, Aljullu, AllGloryToTheHypnotoad, Allan McInnes, Almafeta, Altermike, Alvatov, Alvin Seville, Anaines0210, Anastrophe, AndersL, AndersTR, Andonic, Andre Engels, Andrei.petcu, Andres, AndrewBellis, Andycjp, Angeline Lek, Angus Lepper, Animum, Anna Lincoln, Anonymous editor, Anonymous56789, Antaeus Feldspar, Antandrus, Apoc2400, Ara Qadir, Aranel, ArnoLagrange, ArnoldReinhold, Art LaPella, Ashawley, Askmar, Aspro, Audriusa, AutomaticWriting, Averagejoedude, Aviv007, Awickert, AxelBoldt, Axle2005, Azrael Nightwalker, Bact, Barf73, Bcrowell, Beachy, Becksguy, Behrod08, Beland, Benajnim, BenediktG, Betamod, Bevo, Bgoswami, Bill Cannon, BlacWorks, Blacken, BlueNovember, Blueteaw, Bobo192, Bolatan, Bonadea, Bongomatic, BonnySwan, Borisblue, Bpupadhyaya, Bruce Perens, Btw0, CJ, CSWarren, Calmypal, Camw, Capricorn42, Car031, Carpet9, Catamorphism, Catbar, Cedars, Ceros, Ceyockey, CharlesC, ChaseDave, Cherlin, Cheyinka, Chriced, Chris Pickett, Chrisch, Christian List, ChuckConnell, Ckatz, Clicketyclack, Clockwork Soul, Cmacd123, Collard, Cometstyles, Computerjoe, Conficio, Consumed Crustacean, Cpiral, CrazyLegsKC, Curps, Cwebster93, CyberSkull, D6, DCEvoCE, DGG, DMacks, Da monster under your bed, Daekharel, DagErlingSmørgrav, Damian Yerrick, Damicatz, Dan Guan, Danc, Daniel Quinlan, Danieljackson, Danimart, Dany4762, Darrien, Daverocks, David Gerard, DavidCary, DavidSpencer.ca, Davidds, Davidp, Davodavo, Dawnseeker2000, Dcljr, Debresser, Defrenrokorit, Delirium, Deltabeignet, Demian12358, Den fjättrade ankan, DerHexer, Dhinchcliffe, Dirk Riehle, DirkvdM, DixonD, Dlrohrer2003, Dmccreary, Dmsar, Donarreiskoffer, Dov Henis, Download, Dreadstar, DreamGuy, Dreamyshade, Dreftymac, Duffman, Durova, Dwheeler, Dwightjensen, Dwiki, Dynomites, Dzonatas, ESkog, Eagleal, Ecozeppelin, Ed Poor, Ed g2s, EdEColbert, Edcolins, Edjackiel, Edward Z. Yang, Edward321, Eeera, Elijahmeeks, Elkersh, Eloquence, Elsendero, Emperorbma, Enchanter, Enviro1, Enviroboy, Epastore, Eras-mus, Erianna, Eric S. Raymond, Esborg, Ethanco, EvanED, Evercat, Everyking, Evice, Excirial, Exit2DOS2000, Falcon Kirtaran, Falcon8765, Fbos, Feezo, Femto, Ffooxx 2006, Fheyligh, Finnegar, Fitzhugh, Foolswisdom, FoxxOTG, Francs2000, Frap, Frazzydee, Fred Bauder, Friday, Fsdfs, Fubar Obfusco, Fvw, Gadfium, Gadren, Gail, Gaius Cornelius, Gamaliel, Gaoos, Garo, Gdamasceno, Gdushanbabu, Geekdom04, GeneralAtrocity, GlassCobra, Gnomeraver, Gnp, Godawful82, GoodDamon, Goud, Goyo de la Brisa, Gpietsch, GraemeL, Graham Chapman, Graibeard, Grandscribe, Greenbreezegrl, GregAsche, GregPrice, GregorR, Gronky, Guanaco, Gudeldar, Guppie, Guppy, Gurubrahma, Haakon, Hadal, Hamitr, Hamster200, Hanacy, HarisX, Harry Wood, Harryboyles, Hashar, Hendrixski, Hgamboa, Hnobley, Hooperbloob, Hu12, Huffers, Hussy50, Hydrogen Iodide, I already forgot, I-20, IanOsgood, IanVaughan, Ijustam, Indicjade, Inebriation station, Infosoph, InnovatorM, Inter, Intgr, Ioannis Karamitros, Irtaza abbas, Isabela95, Isam, Isca team lisboa, J Di, J.delanoy, JCS2050, JForget, JLaTondre, JaGa, Jacius, Jack M., Jacoplane, Jahiegel, JakaryandJake, James Rycyk, JamesHenstridge, Jamesday, Jamesedixon, Jamesgeraldnacario, Janizary, Jay, Jclemens, Jefchip, Jeff3000, Jeffmcneill, Jeltz, JeremyA, Jesse Ruderman, JesseW, Jhballard, Jiddisch, Jikbag, Jim Henry, Jktoole99, Jmchuff, Jmk2008, JoCalejandro, Joanhuang, Joebeone, John Fader, John Quiggin, JohnArmagh, Johnny 0, Johntex, JonHarder, Jonik, Josh.anders, Joy, Jpbowen, Jtrainor, JunCTionS, Jusjih, Justbecause09, Jwissick, JzG, KHerbst, Karl-Henner, Keaswara, Keilana, KeithJonsn, Kesla, Kevin B12, Kevouze, Kh7, Khalid hassani, Khym Chanur, Kievite, Kimchi.sg, Kingpin13, Kitoba, Kl4m-AWB, Komunley, Korg, Kozuch, Kpjas, Kukini, Kuszi, Kutulu, L Kensington, Landon1980, Lcarscad, Lcmedia, LeadSongDog, Lee Carre, Leigh, Leithp, Lentower, Leuko, Liaojv, Liblamb, Liftarn, Linkspamremover, Lir, Lochan94, Lord Hawk, Lotje, Lsdr, Luna Santin, Lupin, Lysdexia, MER-C, MSGJ, MSTCrow, Mac, Madmardigan53, Magnus Manske, Majkl82, Makemi, Marek69, Mark Elliott, Markaci, Maroux, Martarius, Martijn Hoekstra, Martin Ankerl, Marudubshinki, Mathsinger, MattGiuca, Matthew Woodcraft, Mav, Maximaximax, Maximus Rex, Mbc362, Mboverload, McSly, Mcdonn, Mcgeester, Mczack26, Mdd, Meelar, Mfinney, Mgrennan, Michael Devore, Michael Hardy, Michael Tiemann, Michig, Midgley, MightyWarrior, MikeCapone, Mikeblas, Mikemill, Milan Keršláger, Mindmatrix, Minesweeper, Minghong, Mion, Misza13, Mmeiser, Mms, Mortenoesterlundjoergensen, Morwen, Mtribe, Mulligatawny, Mully308, Multixfer, MureninC, Nakon, Nanshu, Napalm Dragon, Naudefj, Nbherring, Neoaverroes, NicM, Nick Challoner, Nihiltres, Nikai, Nilsdavis, Njyoder, Nk, Noissime-wiki, Nurg, Nyenyec, OSS123, Octane, Officiallyover, Ohnoitsjamie, Olea, Olivier, Omar2abid, Omicronpersei8, Onursendag, Open source kg, OpenAdvantage, Openblargon, Opensourceteaching, Oscarthecat, Ospalh, Oxford Dictionary, Oxymoron83, P0lyglut, Pakaran, Paladin1979, Patbolger, Pengo, Pengu, Pete142, Peter Winnberg, Petermr, Pgan002, Phamernik, Pharaoh of the Wizards, Phil websurfer@yahoo.com, Pillefj, Piotrus, Pit, Pjamescowie, Pmcalduff, Politepunk, Poweroid, Prab, Prabasiva, Premeditated Chaos, PrezKennedy, Pseudomonas, Psychonaut, Putnik, QuadrivialMind, QualipsoEU, Qwertman, Qwerty8ytrewq, Qwmos, R27182818, RB972, Radagast83, RadioKirk, Ragib, Ragnarev, Raraoul, Raul654, RaviC, Razor X, Rbrwr, Rchamberlain, Rdikeman, Reboot, ReconTanto, Red Director, RedWolf, Reedy, Reliablesources, Reluctan, Res2216firestar, RexNL, Rgardler, Rhobite, Rich Farmbrough, Richard D. LeCour, Rick Block, Rjwilmsi, Rl, Rmstallman, Robbyyy, Robert Buzink, Robert K S, Robert Merkel, Roberta F., Robuis, Ronlevi2, Ronz, RossPatterson, Roux-HG, RoySmith, Rsm99833, RunOrDie, RussNelson, Ryguasu, S.venkataramesh, SEEcher, SF007, SJP, Safalra, Saibhaskar, Scarykitty, Sceptre, Schestowitz, Sdibb, SeanMack, Seanhan, Seansquared, Secfan, SecondV, Serlin, Sesamevoila, Sesu Prime, Shadowlynk, Sharkface217, ShaunMacPherson, Shne, SidP, Sift&Winnow, SilkTork, SimonP, Siniestra, SirGrant, Sjjupadhyay, SkeletorUK, Skyfaller, Slakr, Sleepyhead81, Sligocki, Smurfjones, Snigbrook, Soeren1611, Software-surprise, SpaceFlight89, Speaksleft, Spearhead, Specter01010, Splash, Squids and Chips, Starship Trooper, StaticGull, SteinbDJ, StephanDoerner, Stephen Gilbert, Stephenb, Stephenchou0722, SteveLoughran, SteveSims, Stevemidgley, Stevenj, Stevietheman, Stillmandrew, Stino v, Stirling Newberry, Stirwen, Stonehead, Strongbutbendy, StuffOfInterest, Sunja, Suruena, Sycthos, TPK, TRS-80, TakuyaMurata, TaranRampersad, Taranet, TastyPoutine, Technobadger, Techtonik, Tedickey, Teehee123, Terra Green, Texture, ThSoft, The Anome, The Belgain, The Thing That Should Not Be, The wub, Themfromspace, Thingg, Thomas H. Larsen, Thumperward, Tiddly Tom, Tide rolls, TigerShark, Tim Ivorson, Tisane, Titoxd, TittoAssini, Tobz1000, Tom harrison, Tombomp, Tomi, Tony Sidaway, Towsonu2003, Triona, Trollpedia, Trusilver, Tslocum, Ttudor, Turnstep, Tuxisuau, Twcook, Ubuntulistener, UkPaolo, Ultimus, Umapathy, Umutau, Uncle G, Underbelly02, Unforgettableid, Unixguy, Uogl, Useight, VARGUX, Vashtihorvat, Vecter, Veeven, Versageek, Victorgrigas, Vifir, Vik001ind, Vikramsinghchauhan, ViperSnake151, Visor, Voice of All, Vyuiv, Walter.bender, Wapcaplet, Wavelength, Wayiran, Webmink, Weel, Wemlands, West Brom 4ever, Wickethewok, Wik, Wiki Roxor, Wiki alf, Wikiborg, WikipedianMarlith, Willking1979, Winothmca, Wiretse, Wk muriithi, Wkonkel, Wolli, Xboy, Xeusman, Xibe, Xmachina, YUL89YYZ, Yamamoto Ichiro, Yerpo, Yitzhak, Yosri, Ysangkok, Yworo, ZeWrestler, Zginder, Zigger, Zincsalt8199, Zmauko, Zoganes, Zoicon5, ZooFari, Zslevi, Zvn, Zydeco, Zzuuzz, Ævar Arnfjörð Bjarmason, Хацкер, یرون س‌ارای, 1208 anonymous edits

Cross-platform *Source*: http://en.wikipedia.org/w/index.php?oldid=380709683 *Contributors*: -Majestic-, A plague of rainbows, Abdull, Adambro, AhmadSherif, AlistairMcMillan, Ancheta Wis, Andre Engels, Andrew Rodland, Arifsaha, Asmitford, Audiocow, Avenged Eightfold, Avillia, AxelBoldt, AyoubZubairi, Belovedfreak, BernardH, Bluemoose, Brz7, Butseriouslyfolks, Celestianpower, Ceroklis, Cometstyles, CommonsDelinker, Craigm71, Csabo, D.brodale, DARTH SIDIOUS 2, DStoykov, Davedx, Den fjättrade ankan, Dingfelder, Djcam, DopefishJustin, Dreftymac, Dyee, Dylan Lake, Edaelon, Edward, Efficacious, Evercat, EvilFlyingMonkey, EwokiWiki, FT2, Farm, FatalError, Feinoha, Felixcatuk, Ferkel, Flockmeal, Fractal3, Fuzzie, Ggeldenhuys, Ghettoblaster, Gronky, Gsp, Guy Harris, Harryboyles, Hectorthebat, Hede2000, Hm2k, Hooperbloob, Ian Moody, Ign0rance1sb11ss1166, Inuyasha5400, Isnow, JAF1970, Jamoche, Jdrhodes, Jeshan, Joeblakesley, JonHarder, Joowwww, Juhtolv, Jwcodling, Jwoodger, Kanzelsberger, Karl-Henner, Katecummings, Kbrose, Keilaron, KiaThr, Kurros, Labreuer, LazyEditor, Lexo, Liempt, Lightsup55, LilHelpa, LimoWreck, Lucidn, Lupin, Magnus Manske, MarkS, Marko75, Markpeak, Michael B. Trausch, Michael Hardy, Milly, Milowarmerdam, Minesweeper, Minghong, Mion, Morios, Music Sorter, NapoliRoma, Neelix, Nelson50, Norm, Numbo3, Oicumayberight, Oleg Alexandrov, Orderud, OsamaK, Pgr94, Piano non troppo, Pillefj, Piotrek54321, Poldi, Princess Lirin, R'n'B, Retodon8, Rhe br, Rjwilmsi, Romanc19s, RufusG, SF007, Sakari568, Sam Hocevar, Sand village, Sentencedtolife, Shlomif, SkyWalker, Slogan621, Stephan Leeds, Tdc6502, Tedickey, Teopetuk, Thumperward, Timwi, Tmcw, UncleDouggie, Updatehelper, Veinor, Velent, Vendettax, Waldir, Warren, Wengier, Wlievens, Wyatt Riot, Wysiwia, Yuuki Mayuki, Zoicon5, 210 anonymous edits

Software test *Source*: http://en.wikipedia.org/w/index.php?oldid=73419793 *Contributors*: 0612, 144.132.75.xxx, 152.98.195.xxx, 166.46.99.xxx, 192.193.196.xxx, 212.153.190.xxx, 2D, 2mcm, 62.163.16.xxx, A Man In Black, A R King, A.R., A5b, Abdull, AbsolutDan, Academic Challenger, Acather96, Ad88110, Adam Hauner, Ag2402, Agopinath, Ahoerstemeier, Ahy1, Aitias, Akamad, Akhiladi007, AlMac, Alappuzhakaran, Albanaco, Alhenry2006, AliaksandrAA, AliveFreeHappy, Allan McInnes, Allstarecho, Alvestrand, Amty4all, Andonic, Andre Engels, Andreas Kaufmann, Andres, Andrewcmcardle, Ankurj, Anna Frodesiak, Anna88banana, Annepetersen, Anonymous Dissident, Anonymous anonymous, Anonymous editor, Anorthup, Anthonares, Anwar saadat, Aphstein, Apparition11, Aravindan Shanmugasundaram, ArmadilloFromHell, Ash, Ashdurbat, Barunbiswas, Bavinothkumar, Baxtersmalls, Bazzargh, Betterusername, Bex84, Bigtwilkins, Bigwyrm, Bilbo1507, Bindu Laxminarayan, Bkil, Blair Bonnett, Blake8086, Bluerasberry, Bobdanny, Bobisthebest, Bobo192, Bonadea, Bornhj, Bovineone, Boxplot, Bpluss, Breno, Brequinda, Brion VIBBER, Brunodeschenes.qc, Bryan Derksen, Bsdlogical, Burakseren, Buxbaum666, Calton, CanisRufus, Canterbury Tail, Canterj, CardinalDan, CattleGirl, CemKaner, Certellus, Certes, Cgvak, Chairboy, Chaiths, Chaser, ChiLlBeserker, Chowbok, Chris Pickett, ChrisB, ChrisSteinbach, ChristianEdwardGruber, Chrzastek, Cjhawk22, Claygate, Cometstyles, Conan, Contributor124, Conversion script, CopperMurdoch, Corruptcopper, Cpl Syx, Cptchipjew, Craigwb, Cvcby, Cyberdiablo, CyborgTosser, DARTH SIDIOUS 2, DMacks, DRogers, Dacoutts, DaisyMLL, Dakart, Dalric, Danhash, Danimal, Davewild, David.alex.lamb, Dazzla, Dbelhumeur02, Dcarrion, Declan Kavanagh, Der Falke, DerHexer, Derek farn, Dicklyon, Diego.pamio, Digitalfunda, Discospinster, Dnddnd80, Downsize43, Drewster1829, Drxim, DryCleanOnly, Dvansant, Dvyost, ELinguist, ESkog, Ea8f93wala, Ebde, Ed Poor, Edward Z. Yang, Electiontechnology, Ellenaz, Enumera, Enviroboy, Epim, Epolk, Eptin, Ericholmstrom, Erkan Yilmaz, Esoltas, Excirial, Faught, Felix Wiemann, Flavioxavier, Forlornturtle, FrankCostanza, Fredrik, FreplySpang, Furrykef, GABaker, Gail, Gar3t, Gary King, Gary Kirk, Gdavidp, Gdo01, GeoTe, Georgie Canadian, Giggy, Gil mo, Gogo Dodo, Goldom, Gorson78, GraemeL, GregorB, Gsmgm, Guehene, Gurchzilla, GururajOaksys, Guybrush1979, Hadal, Halovivek, Halsteadk, HamburgerRadio, Harald Hansen, Havlatm, Haza-w, Hdt83, Headbomb, Helix84, Hemnath18, Honey88foru, Hooperbloob, Hsingh77, Hu12, Hubschrauber729, Huge Bananas, Hutch1989r15, IJA, IceManBrazil, ImALion, Imroy, Indon, Infrogmation, Intray, Inwind, J.delanoy, JASpencer, JPFitzmaurice, Ja 62, JacobBramley, Jake Wartenberg, Jeff G., Jehochman, Jenny MacKinnon, JesseHogan, JimD, Jjamison, Jluedem, Jm266, Jmax-, JoeSmack, John S Eden, Johndci, Johnny.cache, Johnuniq, JonJosephA, Joneskoo, JosephDonahue, Josheisenberg, Joshymit, Joyous!, Jsled, Jstastny, Jtowler, Juliancolton, JuneGloom07, Jwoodger, Kalkundri, KamikazeArchon, Kdakin, Kevin, Kgf0, Khalid hassani, Kingpin13, Kingpomba, Kitdaddio, KnowledgeOfSelf, Kompere, Konstable, Krashlandon, Kuru, LeaveSleaves, Lee Daniel Crocker, Leujohn, Little Mountain 5, Lomn, Losaltosboy, Lotje, Lowellian, Lradrama, Lumpish Scholar, M Johnson, MER-C, MPerel, Mabdul, Madhero88, Madvin, Mailtoramkumar, ManojPhilipMathen, Mark Renier, MattGiuca, Matthew Stannard, MaxHund, MaxSem, Mazi, Mblumber, Mdd, Mentifisto, Menzogna, Metagraph, Mfactor, Mhaitham.shammaa, Michael B. Trausch, Michael Bernstein, MichaelBolton, Michig, Mike Doughney, MikeDogma, Miker@sundialservices.com, Mikethegreen, Misza13, Mitch Ames, Miterdale, Moa3333, Mpilaeten, Mpradeep, Mr Minchin, MrJones, MrOllie, Msm, Munaz, Mxn, N8mills, NAHID, Nambika.marian, Nanobug, Neokamek, Newbie59, Nibblus, Nick Hickman, Nigholith, Nimowy, Nksp07, Noah Salzman, Notinasnaid, Nuno Tavares, Oashi, Ocee, Oddity-, Ohnoitsjamie, Oicumayberight, Oliver1234, Omicronpersei8, Ospalh, Otis80hobson, Oysterguitarist, PL290, Paranomia, Pascal.Tesson, Pashute, Paudelp, Paul August, Paul.h, Pcb21, Peashy, Pepsi12, PhilHibbs, PhilipO, PhilippeAntras, Phoe6, Piano non troppo, Pinecar, Plainplow, Pmberry, Pointillist, Pomoxis, Poulpy, Pplolpp, Prari, Praveen.karri,

Priya4212, Promoa1, Psychade, Puraniksameer, Pysuresh, QTCaptain, Qaiassist, Qatutor, Qazwsxedcrfvtgbyhn, RHaworth, Radagast83, Rahuljaitley82, Rajesh mathur, Randhirreddy, Ravialluru, Raynald, RedWolf, RekishiEJ, Remi0o, ReneS, Retired username, Rex black, Rgoodermote, Rhobite, Riagu, Rich Farmbrough, Richard Harvey, RitigalaJayasena, Rje, Rjwilmsi, Rmattson, Rmstein, Robbie098, Robert Merkel, Robinson weijman, Rockynook, Ronhjones, Ronz, Rowlye, Rp, Rror, Ruptan, Rwwww, S.K., SJP, SP-KP, SURIV, Sachipra, Sachxn, Sam Hocevar, Samansouri, Sankshah, Sapphic, Sardanaphalus, Sasquatch525, SatishKumarB, Scottri, Selket, Senatum, Serge Toper, Sergeyl1984, Shadowcheets, Shanes, Shepmaster, Shimeru, Shimgray, Shishirhegde, Shoejar, Shubo mu, Shze, Silverbullet234, Skalra7, Skyqa, Slowbro, Smack, Smurrayinchester, Snowolf, Softtest123, Softwaretest1, Softwaretesting1001, Softwaretesting101, Solde, Someguy1221, Sooner Dave, SpaceFlight89, Spadoink, SpigotMap, Spitfire, Staceyeschneider, Stansult, StaticGull, Stephen Gilbert, Steveozone, Stickee, Storm Rider, Strmore, SunSw0rd, Superbeecat, SwirlBoy39, Sxm20, Sylvainmarquis, T4tarzan, TCL India, Tagro82, Tdjones74021, Techsmith, Tedickey, Tejas81, Terrillja, Testingexpert, Testinggeek, Testmaster2010, ThaddeusB, The Anome, The Thing That Should Not Be, The prophet wizard of the crayon cake, Thehelpfulone, ThomasOwens, Thread-union, Thv, Tipeli, Tippers, Tmaufer, Tobias Bergemann, Toddst1, Tommy2010, Tonym88, Tprosser, Ttam, Tulkolahten, Tusharpandya, TutterMouse, Uktim63, Uncle G, Unforgettableid, Useight, Utcursch, VMS Mosaic, Vaniac, Venkatreddyc, Venu6132000, Verloren, Versageek, Vijaythormothe, Vishwas008, W2qasource, Walter Görlitz, Wifione, Wiki alf, Wikieditor06, Willsmith, Winchelsea, Wlievens, Wombat77, Yamamoto Ichiro, Yesyoubee, Yngupta, Yosri, Yuckfoo, ZenerV, Zephyrjs, ZhonghuaDragon2, ZooFari, Zurishaddai, 1770 anonymous edits

Distributed computing *Source*: http://en.wikipedia.org/w/index.php?oldid=384749644 *Contributors*: 64.104.217.xxx, APH, Adam Conover, Aervanath, Ahmed abbas helmy, Aitias, Ajtouchstone, Akiezun, AlbertCahalan, AlexChurchill, Alfio, Allan McInnes, Amwebb, Andrewpmk, Andyjsmith, Anonymous56789, AreThree, Ariedartin, Atlant, Autopilots, Barneyboo, Beetstra, Bejnar, Beland, Bender235, Bernfarr, Bihzad, Bobdoe, Bovineone, Brent Gulanowski, Brighterorange, BrokenSegue, Buyya, Cadence-, Capricorn42, CaptainMooseInc, CarlHewitt, CatherineMunro, Cdiggins, Chocmah, Chrischan, ChuckPheatt, Cincybluffa, Cmdrjameson, Codepro, Conversion script, CosineKitty, CrypticBacon, Curps, D104, D6, DLJessup, Damian Yerrick, Darkness Productions, David Eppstein, David Shay, David Woolley, David-Sarah Hopwood, Dawidl, Dbenbenn, Dbroadwell, Decrease789, DennisDaniels, Derek, Donarreiskoffer, Dori, Doulos Christos, Dreadstar, Drektor2oo3, Dust Filter, EdH, Edcolins, Edward, Eggstasy, El C, Ellisonch, Eng azza, Evice, Evil Monkey, Ewlyahoocom, EwokiWiki, Ezrakilty, FayssalF, Felix.rivas, Flata, Flubeca, Formulax, Frazzydee, Freakofnurture, Fred Bradstadt, Fredrik, Frehley, Gaius Cornelius, Gangesmaster, Garas, Georgewilliamherbert, Geozapf, Ghewgill, Giftlite, Glenn, Gorffy, Gortsack, Greg Lindahl, Guarani.py, Guy Harris, Gyll, Hadal, Haham hanuka, Hahutch298, Hala54, Hao2lian, Hazzeryoda, Herbee, Heron, Hervegirod, Howdoesthiswo, Ichatz, Ideogram, Iflipti, InShaneee, Indiedan, Iosef aetos, Irdepesca572, Ixfd64, JCLately, JFromm, Jacob grace, Jacobko, Janakan86, Jeff3000, Jeh, Jni, JoanneB, John Nixon, Jomifica, JordiGH, Joysofpi, Juliano, Karmachrome, Kasperd, Kbdank71, Kbrose, Khalid hassani, Kinshuk jpr19, Kizor, Kku, Koyaanis Qatsi, Kristof vt, Kurt Jansson, Kuru, Kuszi, LaggedOnUser, LedgendGamer, Lee Carre, Lee.Sailer, Lexor, LightningDragon, Lupine1647, M1ss1ontomars2k4, Machete97, Maria C Mosak, Mark Zinthefer, Markov12, Marvinfreeman, Matt Crypto, Maximaximax, Mboverload, Mdd, Mdsmedia, Metz2000, Michael2, Miguel in Portugal, Mika au, MikeHearn, Miym, Mkbnett, Monkeypooisgood, MrJones, MrOllie, Mrdude, Nanshu, Neilksomething, Nethgirb, Neum, Nickptar, Nigini, Nit634, Nixdorf, Nonlinear149, Nuno Tavares, Nurg, Only2sea, Optim, Page Up, Palaeovia, Papipaul, Pascal76, Paullaw, Philip Trueman, Powo, PrimeHunter, Proofreader77, Quaeler, R3m0t, Ramu50, Raul654, Reddi, Redxiv, Rjwilmsi, Rob Hooft, Rotem Dan, Ruud Koot, Rwwww, S.K., Sahkuhnder, Scwlong, SebastianHelm, Shafigoldwasser, SimonHova, SimonP, Slashem, Snorre, Softguyus, Sohil it, Sorry Go Fish, Spiffy sperry, Spl, Staffwaterboy, Statsone, Stephan Leeds, Stevag, SuperMidget, Suruena, Szopen, TallMagic, Tanvir Ahmmed, Tedickey, Thv, Tim Watson, Timwi, Trey56, TwoOneTwo, Unfactual POV, Vague Rant, Vary, Vespristiano, Viriditas, Vladrassvet, Walden, Wapcaplet, Warrior4321, Waxmop, Wayfarer, Whkoh, Wifione, WikHead, WikiLaurent, Wikiant, Wonderfulsnow, Worldwidegrid, Wsiegmund, Ww, Xe7al, Île flottante, 403 anonymous edits

STAX *Source*: http://en.wikipedia.org/w/index.php?oldid=258931779 *Contributors*: Andrew Levine, Auntof6, Catapult, Chart123, Ctong, Djinn112, FuriousFreddy, Grm wnr, Hooperbloob, Hugzz, Jay, KFP, Kam Solusar, Lgreen, Mirror Vax, Nichalp, Nikai, Spliced, Staxringold, Warpandas, 14 anonymous edits

HTML *Source*: http://en.wikipedia.org/w/index.php?oldid=384013506 *Contributors*: -bilal92-, 007spyguy7, 0612, 07w109, 10nitro, 194.82.103.xxx, 195.186.148.xxx, 213.3.148.xxx, 7DaysForgotten, A brisson, A10brown, A3RO, ACBest, Aapo Laitinen, Aaron Brenneman, Abb615, Abc518, Abdull, Acq3, Adambiswanger1, Addihockey10, Addshore, Adi necromancer, Ado, Adrian J. Hunter, Aervanath, Ageekgal, Ahoerstemeier, Aitias, Aka042, Akira-otomo, Aksi great, Alan Pascoe, Alansohn, AlecFTW, Alex earlier account, Alexfiles, Alexius08, Alexjohnc3, Alfio, Alfrin, AlistairMcMillan, Allmightyduck, Allstarecho, Alone363, Alsandro, Amatulic, Amerias, Amniarix, An7drew, Andonic, Andrejj, Andres, Andy, Angus Lepper, Animum, Anirvan, Anna Lincoln, Answerthis, Antique Rose, Anton Sergeev, Antonio Lopez, Aodonnel, Armstrong1113149, Arnon Chaffin, Arntuuri, Arronax50, Arthur3030, Ashenai, Asiansryummeh, AstareGod, Ataru, AtheWeatherman, Attlas, Av2917, Ayansen1988, BabuBhatt, Bachrach44, Bart v M, Bartledan, BaseballByrd, Bazza 7, Bazzargh, BeakerK44, Beano, Becritical, Beeshoney, Beland, Bencherlite, Bento00, Betax, Bettia, Binksternet, BioTube, Bitbit, Blackdenimgumby, Blade Hirato, Blanchardb, Blehfu, Bluemask, Bmsshubham, Bobo192, Bogtha, Bonadea, Bongwarrior, BonsaiViking, Booyabazooka, Boxing245, Braddunbar, Bradeos Graphon, Brat32, Breon, Brews ohare, Brianjd, Brianreavis, Briansince1988, Brion VIBBER, Brossow, Bubba73, Buidinhthiem, Bullzeye, Bunnyhop11, Burket, Burns28, Burschik, Bushytails, Buzgun, Cadderly, Caknuck, Caltas, Camw, Can't sleep, clown will eat me, CanadianLinuxUser, Canterbury Tail, Cap'n Refsmmat, Capricorn42, Captain panda, CarbonUnit, Carewolf, Carineduwez, Cenarium, Cenet47, CesarB, Cfust, Chaojoker, Charles Gaudette, CharlotteWebb, Chat de jutiapa guatemala horcones, Ched Davis, Chesshead123, Chesspapa, Chicgeek, Chickenandpasta, Chiman9321, China Crisis, Chinneeb, Chowbok, Chridd, Cic, Classicfilms, Cliffsblog, Closedmouth, Clovis Sangrail, Code E, Codetiger, Coffee, Cole1234567890, Cometstyles, Conrad.Irwin, Conversion script, Coolcaesar, Cornellrockey, Costadelsponz, Costello, Courcelles, Cpiral, Cplot, Cq142, Crazycomputers, Crazyhead4, Crissov, CrizCraig, Csdorman, CyberSkull, Cyde, D'oh!, D6, DKEdwards, DVD R W, Dabomb45, Damicatz, Dammit, Dan100, Danakil, Daniel5127, DanielVonEhren, Darth Mike, Dasani, Dave314159, Dave6, David Biddulph, David Gerard, David Levy, DavidL (usurped), Daviecat, Dawn Bard, DeadEyeArrow, Deagle AP, Decrease789, Dekisugi, Demmy, Den fjättrade ankan, DennisWithem, Dethme0w, Dfrg.msc, Dhavalhirdhav, Diegosolo, Diligent Terrier, Dionyseus, Dionyziz, Discospinster, Dispenser, DocSigma, Dodiad, Donovans, Doug Patriarche, Drake2007, Dramatic, Drappel, Drc79, Dreftymac, Drestros power, Dsolovay, Dumarest, Durrantm, ENeville, EVula, Eagleal, Egmontaz, ElDakio, Eliazar, Eliz81, Elizabeth Barnwell, Empty Buffer, EncMstr, Enigmaman, Enochlau, Enrique00a, Epbr123, EpiQ SkiLL, Ergative rlt, Eric-Wester, Eric119, EricCanada75, Esanchez7587, Escape Orbit, EstebanF, Euchiasmus, Eurleif, Everyking, Evlekis, Ewawer, Excirial, Eyreland, Fab, Faceboyjim, Falcon8765, Farosdaughter, Fastily, Favonian, Fayte, Feinoha, Fenring, Fert81, Fetofs, Fgnievinski, Fieldday-sunday, Filceolaire, Flashesarenight, Flewis, Florihupf, Folic Acid, Formerly the IP-Address 24.22.227.53, Frankenpuppy, Fred Bauder, Fredrik, FreplySpang, Frosted14, Frymaster, Fsminc, Funandtrvl, Furrykef, Fuzheado, GT5162, Gabrielhobro, Gaius Cornelius, Galanothowns, Galoubet, Galwhaa, Gamekid276, Gary King, Gdo01, Geekosaurus, GeoffPurchase, GeorgeMoney, Gerhard Loeb, Gfonetobe, Ghewgill, Gianfranco, Giftlite, Glane23, Glen, Gmd588, Goeagles4321, Gogo Dodo, Goobergunch, GorillazFanAdam, Goystein, GraemeL, Graf Bobby, GranterOfMercy, Gsmgm, Gtachiki, Guanaco, Guppy, Gurch, Gwandoya, Gwernol, Gwguffey, Gyre, Gökhan, HDrake, Haakon, Hadal, Haipa Doragon, Hamitr, HarlandQPitt, HarmonicSphere, HarryAlffa, Haukurth, Herbee, Hervegirod, Hetar, Hetzer, Heycam, Hightilidie, Hirzel, Hiuhuhihiuh, Hmsfrench, Hogman500, Homo sapiens, Horatio, Hornyman121, Hostime, Howcome, Hsivonen, Html, Hu, Huo Ma Ke, I already forgot, Ian Pitchford, Iancarter, Iball, IeditU4good, Ifinditfunny, Igoldste, Ikh, Illinoisavonlady, Impala2009, Incnis Mrsi, Inter, Interiot, Internoob, Intgr, Iridescent, Irishguy, IsaacGS, Islamicinfo, Isoft isoft, Ixfd64, Izno, J Di, J.delanoy, J2000ca, JAKEhp55, JForget, JLaTondre, JNW, JPG-GR, JRS124c41, Jacob.jose, Jacosi, Jake11899, James-Y2J-fan, Jamie C, Janadore, Jasrocks, Jatkins, Jaxad0127, Jay, JayJayKay, JeLuF, Jeff G., Jeffq, Jeffz1, Jeltz, Jennavecia, Jennica, Jens Meiert, Jerome Charles Potts, Jesse0986, Jetrink, Jgr 94, Jgrahn, Jh51681, Jhone29, Jj137, Jmh, Jmundo, JodyB, Joeyman111, John254, Johnnybravo2009, Jollybengali, JonathanCross, Jonathanischoice, Jor, Jordan Rothstein, Jorunn, Josh3736, Joshebosh, Joy, Joyous!, Jpatokal, Jswarchinghimer, Jtneill, Jumbuck, Jusjih, Just James, Kablammo, Kakomu, Karl Dickman, Kate, KathrynLybarger, Kbolino, Kcmartz, Kelson, Kennyluck, Kerttie, Kewp, Killr833, King Arthur6687, King Bob324, KingHippo777, Kingpin13, Kjoonlee, Klingoncowboy4, KnowledgeOfSelf, Koavf, Kocio, Kongr43gpen, Konstable, Koyaanis Qatsi, Kozuch, KramarDanIkabu, Ksn, Kubigula, Kukini, Kurt Shaped Box, Kuru, Kuyabribri, Kvdveer, Kwiki, L5138, LAX, LLarson, LOL, Lakeishikawa, LamCarLL71, Lantay77, Laurusnobilis, Lawrence Cohen, Lcarscad, Leafyplant, Lear's Fool, Leastminor, Ledgerbob, Lee Daniel Crocker, Leif, Lethe, Leujohn, Leuko, Lianmei, LibLord, Liberal Classic, Lightmouse, Lights, Lilgamer64, Lineplus, Lipyn, Liquid Flash, LittleBenW, LittleOldMe, Llbbl, Llull, Logiphile, Lomn, Lordofnerds, Lordtopcat, Loren.wilton, Lotje, LovinHTML, Lowellian, Lowercase, Lradrama, LtEarth, Lturbine, Luk, Luna Santin, Lurker, Lysdexia, MC10, MER-C, MOO, MZMcBride, Mabdul, Mac, MadMax45, Madda, Madhero88, Maebmij, Magic.Wiki, Majorly, Makeemlighter, Makemi, Mani1, Manishearth, Manjo mandruva, Markus Kuhn, Markymarkmagic, Martinvie, Master of Puppets, Mattbr, MattieTK, Mattworld, Maxim, Maxiom, Maypigeon of Liberty, Mbc362, Mboverload, McSly, Mecanismo, MelanieBeth, MeltBanana, Mentifisto, Message From Xenu, Methnor, Mgearfan, Mholland, Mianbao, MicahElliott, Michael Hardy, Michael Slone, Michaelbusch, Midnightcomm, Mig, Mike Rosoft, Mike Selinker, Mikeo, Mindmatrix, Minghong, Minkus, Minun, Mipadi, MithrandirAgain, Miyagawa, Mjb, Mmj, Moeron, Moneysaver67, Monkle, Moocowisi, Moondyne, Morefight, MorgothX, MorrisRob, MrDolomite, Mrfencey, Mrholybrain, Mrnobody228, Mrxwindows, Ms2ger, Msreeharsha, Mvjs, MySchizoBuddy, Myanw, Mydogategodshat, Mysidia, Mzajac, N-Man, NSK, Nacimota, Nako16, Nakon, Nasa-verve, Nasnema, Natalie Erin, Nations114, NawlinWiki, NeantHumain, Neelchauhan, Neilc, NeoChaosX, Nepenthes, NerdyNSK, NetOracle, Netkinetic, Neustradamus, NewEnglandYankee, Nezzadar, Niceguydave, Nifky?, NigelR, Nigelj, Nivix, Nixeagle, Nman252, Noctibus, Noldoaran, Nphase, Nsaa, NuclearWarfare, Nut er, Nutiketaiel, Odinjobs, Ohnoitsjamie, Okome, Oli Filth, Omegatron, Omicronpersei8, Onefreeinternet, Oneiros, Opgfss, Orphan Wiki, OsoLeon, OspreyPL, Oswald07, OverlordQ, OwenBlacker, OwenX, Oxymoron83, P Carn, P3Pp3r, PAK Man, PJTraill, Paine Ellsworth, Palfrey, PanagosTheOther, Pandamonia, Party, PatriceNeff, Patrick, Patstuart, Paul August, Pavel Vozenilek, Pbb, Pedro, Penguinboyroy, Penubag, Petree69, Pgk, Phantomsteve, Philip Trueman, Philwiki, Piano non troppo, Pigsonthewing, Pikminlover, Pinethicket, Plasticup, Plugwash, Poldi, Pomadgw, Popadooodle7, Possum, Postdlf, Potatoswatter, PranksterTurtle, Prapsnot, Prince-of-Life, Profoss, Prosenzweig, Protonk, Pseudomonas, Pudleek, Purple Sheep, Purplepickle10, Pursey, Pwt-wsu-ap, Pádraig Coogan, Qtoktok, Queux, QuiTeVexat, Qwertyus, R.e.b., RJaguar3, RP459, RainbowOfLight, Rajakhr, Ramesh Chandra, Rami R, Rand, Rangi42, Raven4x4x, Rcairnsjr, Reach Out to the Truth, Recurring dreams, RedHillian, RedWolf, Redfarmer, Rednblu, Redvers, Reisio, Remember the dot, RetiredWikipedian789, Rettetast, RexNL, Rharding13, Rholton, Rich Farmbrough, Rich13, Richard cocks, Rick Block, Rick Jelliffe, RickBeton, Rima p.r, Ringling9, Rizwanazizshaikh, RkOrton, Rl, Robert Skyhawk, Robert Wellock, RobertG, Rogper, Romestar, Ronz, Rory096, RossPatterson, Rougieux, RoyBoy, Rror, Rtc, Rufous, RunOrDie, RuneScapez, Rursus, Ruslik0, Ruud Koot, Rwellington, Rwwww, Ryoutou, Ryulong, SH84, Sade, Saga City, Saintrain, Sajidsa13, Sakurambo, Salix alba, Sander Säde, Sango123, Saoshyant, Saqib, Sarmenhb, Sarregouset, SarvenCapadisli, Satchy, Scarian, Sceptre, SchfiftyThree, Sciurinæ, Scjessey, Scott Paeth, ScriptingMaster, Sean Kelly, Sen Mon, Sepsis13, SergeiRichard, Sesu Prime, SetiHitchHiker, Shadow1, ShadowRangerRIT, Shadowjams, Shalom Yechiel, Shantavira, SharkD, Sharon08tam, ShaunL, Shawnhath, Sheehan, Shenme, Shervinafshar, Shirik, Shirulashem, Shonda13, Shyluv, Sidasta, Sidonuke, Simetrical, Simonkoldyk, Simplexplus, Sionus, Sitegod, Sjpr73, Sjö, Skaarlaw, Skew-t, SkyWalker, Skysmith, Smitty, Smjg, Snareklutz, Snarius, Snowolfd4, Soc5555, SpaceFlight89, Spainhour, Sparkmonkey7, SparrowsWing, Speck-Made, SpeedyGonsales, Spherems, SpikeJones, Spitfire, Spitfire19, SpuriousQ, Squash444, Squirrel Boy, Sreeriz, Static17, Stephenb, Studerby, StunitTeam, Suburbanslice, Subversive.sound, Sujgfjfgjhgjgj, Sumanthk, Sunroof, Supertouch, Svetovid, Swamilive, Swpb, Szhaider, TFunk, THEN WHO WAS PHONE?, TNLNYC, Taare, Tamfang, Tangotango, Tannin, Tannkremen, Tasc, Tbg connor, Tbisonman123, Tedickey, Teehee123, Tempmj, Terrx, TexMurphy, Texture, Thaqtipkilla, Thatguyflint, The Anome, The Rambling Man, The Random Editor, The Thing That Should Not Be, The Transhumanist, The gergster, The undertow, TheDJ, TheDrakoman, TheKMan, TheRealFennShysa, Theone00, Theymos, Thingg, Think outside the box, Think777, ThunderPeel2001, Tide rolls, Timbl, Tntc.tig, Tobias Bergemann, Todd Vierling, Tom-, TomasBat, Tombomp, Tommy2010, Tommyqiscow, TomyDuby, Tonyseeker, Torc2, Toussaint, Tpbradbury, Traal, Traroth, Traxs7, Tregoweth, Trevorpittz, Trevyn, Tribaal, Triona, Trusilver, Trustle, Tslocum, Tudorol, Tundra010, TwigsterX,

Typochimp, Tyrol5, Tysto, Tyw7, UU, UberScienceNerd, Ucanlookitup, Uirauna, Ultramince, Unbreakable comb, Uncle G, Unixguy, Unknown W. Brackets, Unyoyega, Urhixidur, Uriyan, Uxgeoff, V.v.vinaybabu, Vampic, Vbigdeli, Veinor, Versageek, Vianello, Vickey Xiong, Violetriga, Vipinhari, Virtual Loïc, Vivio Testarossa, Voidvector, Vonones, Vystrix Nexoth, Wackymacs, Waggers, Wapcaplet, Ward3001, Wasabie, Waterret, Wavelength, Wermlandsdata, West Coast Gordo, Weylinp, Whileupper, Whosyourjudas, WikHead, Wiki alf, Wikidemon, WikipedianMarlith, Wikipelli, Wikiuser00008, Wileyc427, Will052690, WillOakland, William Avery, Williamborg, Willking1979, Withoutmark, Wknight94, Wolf grey, Wolfhoundfeet, Worlddominater08, Wperdue, WriterHound, Wrs1864, Wtni, Wwmbes, Wwwqwerty, X!, XU-engineer, Xaagkx, Xander756, Xenophon777, Xerocs, Xhosan, Xieqi200, Xihix, Xiong Chiamiov, Xmonicleman, Xp54321, Xyzu, YUL89YYZ, Yaniv p, Yelling Bird, Yellow & Blue Music, YggY, Yt95, Yulelee, Zahid Abdassabur, Zcorpan, Zedla, Zenohockey, ZeroOne, Zondor, Zorgelo, Zotag, Zsinj, Zundark, Zy26, Zzymyn, Александър, 2198 anonymous edits

E-mail *Source*: http://en.wikipedia.org/w/index.php?oldid=374970254 *Contributors*: 100110100, 16@r, 194.236.5.xxx, 228086, 2D, 7, A More Perfect Onion, A purple wikiuser, Abkovalenko, AdSR, Adw2000, Aesopos, Aff123a, Agather, Agent2693, Ahoerstemeier, AlainV, Alan Liefting, Alanpratt05, Alansohn, Ale2006, AlexWaelde, Alexius08, Alexjohnc3, Aliza250, Allynnc, Alphathon, Amire80, Amniarix, Anastrophe, Andareed, Andrejj, Andrew Kelly, Andrzej P. Wozniak, Andyiou52, Andylkl, Angela, Ann Stouter, Anna Lincoln, Anomalocaris, Antoine854, AntonioMartin, Anwar saadat, Arakunem, ArchonMagnus, Arjuno3, Armando49, Art LaPella, Asdasd12324, Aspandphp, Bachrach44, Badcop666, Baiji, Barefootguru, Barry26, Battoe19, Bayle Shanks, Bearly541, Beesman, Beland, Belugaperson, Benq2010, Benwildeboer, Bettia, Bhadani, Bhobbit, Big Bird, Bigbluefish, Bigderom, Biggity, Birdman1, Bkil, Blitzinteractive, Blue520, Bluemask, Bnorrie, Bob98133, Bobzayton489, Bomac, Bonadea, Bongwarrior, Boothy443, Boyhampus, Bubba hotep, Buckinghampalace101, Butros, C Teng, C'est moi, C+C, C777, Caesura, Cafeduke, Calliopejen1, Callmejosh, Caltas, Calvin 1998, CambridgeBayWeather, Cameforu, Can't sleep, clown will eat me, Canaima, Canihaveacookie, Canterbury Tail, CapitalR, CapitalSasha, Capricorn42, CaptainCat, CardinalDan, CattleGirl, Causa sui, Cboy676, Ccacsmss, CellMan0677, CesarB, Cfp, Chadude, Charles Gaudette, Chato, Chithrapriya, Chivasboi345, Chmod007, Chowbok, Chris G, Chrislk02, Chrismaster1, Christopher Parham, Chuq, Ckatz, Classfun, Classicfilms, ClaudineChionh, Closedmouth, Cmartell, Cometstyles, Comm 212 8, Commander, Comodo, Compo, Computerjoe, Conan, Conversion script, CoolChris99, Corti, Crackerwashere, CrazyInSane, Crazyperson324, Credema, Crismas, Ctjf83, Cutechar, Cyanoa Crylate, Cybercobra, D. Recorder, DRosenbach, DXRAW, Da monster under your bed, Da.skitz, Dalesgay, Dan D. Ric, Dangerousdanman, Daniel C. Boyer, Daniel Quinlan, Daniel.Cardenas, Danorton, Darac, Darkride, Darth Panda, Dave souza, Davecrocker, David in DC, DavidCary, DavidWBrooks, Davidcannon, Davidx2, Dawn Bard, Dawnseeker2000, Dean, December21st2012Freak, Demitsu, DerHexer, Derek Ross, Dhaun, Dhoom4, Digitalme, Discospinster, Dmccreary, Doc marseille, Domitori, Dr.s.t.ruggling, DragonHawk, Dragory, Dreadstar, Dreammixtr, Drilnoth, Drj, DropDeadGorgias, Drumsac, Duncan Keith, Durcar86, Dwo, DylanW, Dysprosia, Dzordzm, Długosz, ESkog, Eaefremov, EagleEye96, Eastmain, Eclecticology, Ed Poor, Edgerck, El pobre Pedro, ElKevbo, Eliezer Aharon, Ellywa, Emailexperiencecouncil, Emily GABLE, Emmy.rose, Emperorbma, EncMstr, Encyeditor, Enric Naval, Enviroboy, Epbr123, Erdal Ronahi, Erianna, Eric-Wester, ErikWarmelink, EscapingLife, Etacar11, Etz Haim, Everyking, Ewlyahoocom, Extransit, FaisaLakeel, Falcon8765, Farawayfrom, FastLizard4, Fatbroker, FayssalF, Fearless Son, Feedmecereal, Fieldday-sunday, Fisc, Fl, Fleminra, Flockmeal, Fnlayson, Foodlol123, FrancoGG, Frecklefoot, Fredrik, Frehley, FreplySpang, Frodet, Fubar Obfusco, Funnyfarmofdoom, Furrykef, Fuzzie, Galaxy250, Galoubet, Garkbit, Gary King, Gdr, Gejigeji, Ghemachandar, Gianfranco, Giftlite, Gilliam, Giseburt, Gogo Dodo, Gollobt, Graham87, Green caterpillar, Gribeco, Grosscha, Grumpyyoungman01, Gsklee, Guppy, Gurch, Guy Harris, Guybrush, Gzkn, Hadal, Hairhorn, Hairy Dude, Hanoman, Hans Carlos Hofmann, Hardyplants, Harej, Harris7, Harryboyles, Headbomb, HeikoEvermann, Heinzi.at, Hello32020, Heron, Hew, HexaChord, Hilgers08, Hobomason, Hoplon, Hu12, Hullbr3ach, Hymek, IRP, Iainh, Ibizr, Icairns, Ida Shaw, Iflynet, Ignacioerrico, Ilmari Karonen, Ilya-108, Imran, Inkington, Insanephantom, Inspector 34, Intgr, Ioapetraka, Ionidasz, Iridescent, Irishguy, Itai, Ivan Pozdeev, J-Star, J.delanoy, JForget, JLaTondre, JRM, JTN, Jackzhp, Jafeluv, Jaizanuar, Jallar, Jan eissfeldt, JayJasper, Jddphd, Jdforrester, Jebba, Jeff G., Jer10 95, JeremyA, Jesse Viviano, Jfdwolff, Jfire, Jiddisch, Jimthing, Jj137, Jjl33, Jlandis, Jmundo, Jnc, Jnk, Jnothman, Jodi.a.schneider, JodyB, John Covert, John a s, JohnOwens, Johnny Bin, Jomunro, Jon Harald Søby, JonHarder, Joseph Solis in Australia, Josh the Nerd, Joshhirstwood, Joy, Jredmond, Ju66l3r, JuJube, Juliancolton, Jumbuck, Jusdafax, Jusjih, Jwoodger, KC., KF, KPH2293, KPWM Spotter, Ka-Ping Yee, Kafuffle, Kaliumfredrik, Karcamp, Kaszeta, Katalaveno, Kazikameuk, Kbrose, Kdammers, Keilana, Kiamde, Kingpin13, Kingturtle, Kjkolb, Klykken, KnowledgeBased, KnowledgeOfSelf, Koenige, Kooljay253, Kowey, Krushdiva, Kuru, Kwshaw1, LC, LX, La Parka Your Car, LaFoiblesse, Lacrimosus, LarryQ, Last Avenue, Lathama, Leandrod, Lee Daniel Crocker, LeighvsOptimvsMaximvs, Lerdsuwa, Levineps, Liamob1993, Liftarn, Lightdarkness, LilHelpa, Lilac Soul, Lineface, Lisabelleg, LittleBenW, Llykstw, Llywrch, Lomonline, Lonestarcowboy, Longhair, Lordmac, Louie Franco, Lucasik, Lucky 6.9, Luckylive, Lunboks, Lupo, MER-C, MFH, MIT Trekkie, MWelchUK, Mabdul, Mac, Magister Mathematicae, Magnus Manske, Maheshkale, Majorly, Makro, Mani1, Manticore, Maralia, Marcus Brute, Mark, MarkGallagher, MarkSweep, Martaw22, Masaruemoto, MattGiuca, Mattbr, Matteh, Maxis ftw, Mbekula, Mboverload, MccowattMAS229, Mcr314, Mdwyer, Meand, Meekywiki, Meelar, MelcomRSA, Mendors, Mentifisto, Mephistophelian, Merciadriluca, Merry Devil, Mets501, Mhackmer, Michaelbusch, Midnightcomm, Mifter, Mike Payne, Mike Rosoft, Mikker, MindlessXD, Minghong, Mm40, Mogglewump, Monkey Bounce, Moondyne, Motor, Mozillar, Mqduck, Mr. Prez, MrPrada, Mrlee321, Mschel, Msikma, Msrafiq, Mtlk, Mu, Muhandes, Mursyids, Mwalimu59, Mxn, Mystical504, NHRHS2010, Nabeth, Nanshu, Naohiro19, NatusRoma, NawlinWiki, Nealmcb, Nebula17, Nehtefa, Nelson50, Nemo, Neon white, Neurolysis, Neustradamus, NewEnglandYankee, Newportm, Nick, Nick C, Nick Garvey, NickdelaG, Nickptar, NigelR, Nightscream, Nikai, Nikola Smolenski, Nilfanion, Niqueco, Nivix, Njál, No barometer of intelligence, Nol888, NormDor, Not telling, Notsocoolkid, Novasource, Nsaum75, Nubiatech, Numbo3, Nuttycoconut, Nxu009, Nzseries1, Ohadgliksman, Ohnoitsjamie, Ojw, OlEnglish, Olgerd, Oliphaunt, Oliver Pereira, Oliver202, Olivier, OlivierM, Ombudsman, Omegatron, Omegium, Omicronpersei8, Omniplex, OneWeirdDude, Orayzio, Oxymoron83, P.L.A.R., PCHS-NJROTC, Param0r33, Parmesan, Pat80, Patrick, PatrickFlaherty, Paul August, Paul Stansifer, Paul-L, Pax85, Pd THOR, PengiFergie, Pernoctus, Peschomd, Pfahlstrom, PhJ, Phantomsteve, Pharaoh of the Wizards, Phatom87, Phgao, PiMaster3, Piano non troppo, PierreAbbat, PinchasC, Pinethicket, Pinotgris, Pipedreamergrey, Plasticup, Plugwash, Pomte, Poor Yorick, Porkchop28, Prof Wrong, Programarium, Prowikipedians, Prozac1980, Pseudomonas, Qaqaq, Qwertyus, Qwyrxian, Qxz, RCVenkat, RJaguar3, Rajeevtco, Ramrod 63, RandalSchwartz, Randallrobinstine, Raphel M. Markez, Raryel, Rasmus Faber, Rbpickup, Rcannon100, Rdsmith4, Red Sunset, Refsworldlee, Reliablesources, Retodon8, Rettetast, RexNL, Reyk, Rhsatrhs, Rich Farmbrough, Richard Arthur Norton (1958-), Richi, Rick Block, Rjwilmsi, Roedelius, Rohasnagpal, Roland45, Rory096, RoyBoy, Rrburke, Rubicon, Rulesdoc, Runningeek, Ryan Roos, Ryoung122, Ryulong, SCGC, SMC89, SPAMSLAVE, Safedoctor, Sam Blacketer, Sam Hocevar, Sam Staton, Samtheboy, Sander Säde, Sander123, Sandstein, Sarasvathi, SasiSasi, Sbluen, ScottyWZ, Sd324, Sean 1996, Sentausa, Serpent-A, Sexdemon89, Shadow1, Shadowjams, Shaior, Shanes, Sheehan, Sheliak, Shirik, Shotwell, Sidhekin, Sietse Snel, Silas S. Brown, Silvery, SimonD, Sina, Sionus, Sir Nicholas de Mimsy-Porpington, Sirping, Skarebo, SkerHawx, Skomorokh, Skpatel20, SkyWalker, Skyezx, Skylerfatfacewrwe, Skyscrap27, Slady, Slakr, Sleske, Slowking Man, Smalljim, Smit, Smokyjohnpipe, Smpwiki, Smtc123, Snori, Snowflake7, Snowmanradio, Snoyes, Sogle, Solipsist, Someoneinmyheadbutit'snotme, Sorsoup, Spaceman85, Spoirier, Spookfish, Spork the Great, Sroeben, Srpnor, Startvtk, SteinbDJ, Stephan Leeds, Stephen Gilbert, Stephenb, SteveSims, Steven Zhang, Stevietheman, Stirling Newberry, Stolen Account 1, Strait, Stratocracy, Stwalkerster, Styrofoam1994, Superm401, Supermennn, SusanLesch, Symane, SystemBuilder, Syvanen, TGNobby, THEN WHO WAS PHONE?, TNLNYC, Taargus taargus 1, Tabletop, Tad Lincoln, Tailchopper99, TakuyaMurata, Tasc, Taw, TeaDrinker, Tenebrae, Terence, TerriersFan, The Anome, The Epopt, The Thing That Should Not Be, The Wild Falcon, The wub, TheRealFennShysa, Thebigmc2, Thehornet, Thingg, Thomas H. Larsen, Thue, Thuja, Thumperward, Thunderboltz, Thunderwing, Tide rolls, TigerShark, Tikiwont, Tim Ivorson, Timir Saxa, Todd Gallagher, Tommy2010, Trevor mendham, Trnj2000, UkPaolo, Ukexpat, Uncle G, Unforgettableid, Unfree, UnicornTapestry, Unschool, Uogl, Uriah923, Useight, VQuakr, Vaikulepak, VasilievVV, Veinor, Versageek, Vinnivince, Viskonsas, WJake2009, WadeSimMiser, Wafulz, Warren, Wasell, Wavelength, Weregerbil, Wes!, Wfeidt, Who, WikHead, Wiki alf, Wikid77, Wikieditor1988, Wikilibrarian, WikipedianMarlith, WillV, WilliamRoper, Wimt, Wine Guy, Wizardist, Wj32, Wmahan, Wolfkeeper, Wolfmankurd, Woods229, Wrs1864, Xdenizen, Xp54321, Xwildfire316x, Yahel Guhan, Yama, Yekrats, Yonatan, Ysangkok, Yuva raju raj, Yzmo, Zanimum, Zer0faults, Zip123, Zivha, Zoe, Zointer, Zondor, Zouavman Le Zouave, Zundark, Zzuuzz, Саша Стефановић, علاء بوسيجم, सुभाष राऊत, ლევანი, 1519 anonymous edits

File system *Source*: http://en.wikipedia.org/w/index.php?oldid=384768968 *Contributors*: (, 100110100, 121a0012, 2mcm, Adamantios, Adrian, Ae-a, Ahoerstemeier, Ahy1, Aillema, Aj00200, Alba, Aldie, Aliekens, AlistairMcMillan, Alkrow, AmRadioHed, Ameen.crew, Anandbabu, Ancheta Wis, Andre Engels, Andy16666, Anthony Borla, Ark, Arnon007, Aron1, Arrenlex, Aschrage, AtheWeatherman, AxelBoldt, Badgernet, Baryonic Being, Becksguy, Beland, Bender235, BiT, Bitwise, Bletch, Bob007, Boborok, Bornhj, Brycen, Burschik, Byteemoz, COstop, Can't sleep, clown will eat me, Cander0000, Capricorn42, Carlosguitar, Catalina22, Cbayly, Ceyockey, Cgy flames, Chealer, Chipuni, Chris Chittleborough, Chris the speller, ChrisHodgesUK, Christian Storm, Claunia, Cmdrjameson, Cohesion, Colin Hill, Conversion script, Coolfrood, Corby, Cpiral, Crashmatrix, Creidieki, Csabo, Cspurrier, Ctachme, CyberSkull, DGerman, DMG413, DStoykov, DVD R W, Damian Yerrick, Damieng, Darklilac, Darrien, David Gerard, David H Braun (1964), DavidHalko, Davitf, Decoy, Dekisugi, Del Merritt, Delirium, DerHexer, Dexter Nextnumber, Dillee1, Dirkbb, Donhalcon, Druiloor, Dsant, Dsav, Dysprosia, EddEdmondson, ElBenevolente, Eltouristo, Emperorbma, Emre D., Eob, Everyking, Ewlyahoocom, Eyreland, Falsifian, Favonian, Ferrenrock, Firthy2002, Fogelmatrix, Foxxygirltamara, FrYGuY, Frap, Froggy454, Gaius Cornelius, Galoubet, Gazpacho, Ghakko, Ghettoblaster, Gpvos, GraemeL, Grafikm fr, Greg Lindahl, GregorB, Groogle, Guroadrunner, Guy Harris, Hadal, Hagedis, Hairy Dude, Hazel77, Helix84, Hif, Howdyboby, Ian Pitchford, Imroy, InShaneee, Ineuw, Info@segger-us.com, Intgr, J0m1eisler, JLaTondre, Jason Quinn, Jcorgan, Jec, Jeff G., Jeffpc, Jengelh, Jerryobject, Joeblakesley, Joeinwap, Jonathan de Boyne Pollard, Jotel, Jóna Þórunn, Kairos, Karada, Karmastan, Kate, Kbdank71, Kbolino, Kc2idf, Kendrick7, Kenyon, Kim Bruning, Kozaki, Kvedulv, Kwharris, Kwi, LHOON, Lament, Leon Hunt, Letdorf, Lightdarkness, LilHelpa, Lion.guo, Loadmaster, LocoBurger, Lofote, Logixoul, Lost.goblin, Lupo, MARQUIS111, MZMcBride, Mac, Mange01, ManuSporny, Marcika, MarekMahut, Marudubshinki, Marysunshine, Mat-C, MatthewWilcox, Mattisgoo, Maxal, Maximaximax, Mdd, Med, Miblo, MicahDCochran, MikeRS, Mindmatrix, Minghong, Mjk64, Mk*, Mlessard, Mmairs, Modster, Monz, Morte, Mrichmon, Mschlindwein, Mulad, Mushroom, Mwtoews, Nahum Reduta, Nanshu, Nbarth, NeaNita, NevilleDNZ, Nikitadanilov, Nixdorf, OccamzRazor, Oda Mari, Omicronpersei8, OrangeDog, Orzetto, Oscarthecat, Ovpjuggalo, PGSONIC, Palconit, Patrick, Paul.raymond.brenner, Peterlin, Phil Bordelon, PhilHibbs, PhotoBox, PichuUmbreon, Poccil, Poppafuze, Porterde, Psychonaut, Public Menace, Pythagoras1, Qaywsxedc, Quale, Questulent, Quiddity, R. S. Shaw, RJaguar3, Radagast83, Raffaele Megabyte, Reconsider the static, RedWolf, Reisio, Retron, Reyk, Rfc1394, Rhobite, Rich257, Rob Kennedy, Rockstone35, Rogitor, Rror, Runner5k, Ruud Koot, Rvalles, Ryulong, SEWilco, SMC, Sam Hocevar, SamCPP, Samfw, Saucepan, Scarlet Lioness, Sdfisher, SeanMack, Semifinalist, Sheehan, Slogan621, Smappy, Snaxe920, SolKarma, SolarisBigot, Sommerfeld, SpeedyGonsales, Splash, Squash, Ssd, Stephen Gilbert, Stephenb, Stuart Morrow, StuartBrady, Supertin, Suruena, Swift, Swpb, Tablizer, Taka, Tannin, Tarquin, Tawker, Tellarite, Tempel, The_ansible, Theone256, Thompsa, Thunderpenguin, Tim Ivorson, Tobias Bergemann, Traut, Tylerni7, Typhoon, Uli, Uncle G, Unixguy, Val42, Vasi, W163, W1tgf, Wai Wai, Walabio, Warpflyght, Wayiran, Wesley, Wknight94, Wli, Woohookitty, Ww, X7q, Yamla, Yapchinhoong, Yudiweb, Zemyla, Zetawoof, Zodon, Zoicon5, Ævar Arnfjörð Bjarmason, ם'אפר לורם, 682 anonymous edits

cron *Source*: http://en.wikipedia.org/w/index.php?oldid=383639774 *Contributors*: Adam Brody, Alan012, AllenJB, Altonbr, Amcbride, ArchiSchmedes, Arienh4, Artcava, Arto95, Arvindn, BioStu, Blanchardb, BraveryOnions, Breadtk, Brest, Bxj, Byraul, Callidior, Cameltrader, Centrx, CiaPan, Da monster under your bed, DancingMan, Danielx, DanilaKutkevich, DavidBlackwell, DavidDouthitt, DemonThing, Djkrajnik, DocRuby, Dogaru Florin, Durrantm, Ed g2s, Escaladix, Estevoaei, Felipe1982, FiskFisk33, Fribbler, Gal Buki, Galoubet, Ghettoblaster, Glenn, Globbet, Gwernol, Highpriority, Ilyaroz, Iviney, JackPotte, Jefe2000, Jlin, Jon077, KVDP, Kapow, Kriplozoik, Kromped, Kukini, Lavers, Ldfifty, Ling.Nut, Lotje, MDfoo, Madman91, Manop, Markluffel, Mdwyer, Meand, Meandtheshell, Mirkon, Morte, MrOllie, Neosys, Nicol, NormG, Nurg, Nádvorník, Oxymoron83, Peyre, Pimlottc, PuerExMachina, QuackGuru, Rich Farmbrough, Richard Taytor, Riksweeney, Rlb408, Rwxrwxrwx, SF007, Sceptre, Scottmacpherson, Sleske, Smeelsmudge, Snaxe920, Svick, Sydius, Tanketz, Tardis, Themfromspace, ThomasMueller,

Thumperward, Tide rolls, Tingrin87, TomMcCann, Triona, UKER, Ugen64, User A1, Versageek, Versus22, Vipinhari, Voyagerfan5761, William Graham, Wrs1864, Yanico, Zenecan, 196 anonymous edits

IBM *Source*: http://en.wikipedia.org/w/index.php?oldid=384635974 *Contributors*: -Majestic-, 0612, 142.177.92.xxx, 16@r, 28bytes, 3dom, 5735ashley, 73liam, 9-11 suicide bomber, 95jb14, A Man In Black, A. Carty, AEMoreira042281, AGToth, AK Auto, ALepik, AOLLLTTYYY, AThing, AV3000, AVM, Abductive, Aboutmovies, AbsolutDan, Acegikmo1, Achille, Adashiel, AdjustShift, Adraeus, Aeons, Aff123a, AgentCDE, Agiorgio, Ahoerstemeier, Ahy1, AlainV, Alan Rockefeller, Alansohn, Alchemy 142, Alerante, Alexa411, Alexandre linhares, AlexandreB, Alison9, AlistairMcMillan, Allen3, Alpertron, Alphachimp, Altenmann, Althepal, Aluvus, Amcl, Amehta02, Amniarix, Analyzit, Anaxial, Ancheta Wis, AncientToaster, Andonic, Andre Engels, Andries, Andromeda, Andy Marchbanks, Angela, Angelofdeath275, Animum, Anonymous Cow, Antandrus, Aomarks, Ap, Apoc2400, Aqwis, Arch dude, Archagon, Archeus, ArglebargleIV, ArinArin, Arjun01, Ashley Pomeroy, Astor14, Astuishin, Athepirate08, Autiger, Awatt6, Axeman89, AzaToth, Azbert, B, BBCWatcher, BMGRAHAM, Badgernet, BalderV, Barek, Baseball Bugs, Bboyskidz, Beano, Beirne, Belinrahs, Beltz, BenShade, Benandorsqueaks, Bender235, Benhocking, BerniceRogowitz, BitterTwitter, BjF, Bjh21, Bjmarfito, Bkell, Blackfinale, Blaxthos, Blondinm, Blow of Light, Bnitin, Bobblewik, Bobo192, Bobopower, BocoROTH, Bogdangiusca, Bogey97, Bongomatic, Bongwarrior, Bookandcoffee, Bootedcat, Boothy443, Boyhere, BradBeattie, Brandon, Brian Crawford, Brian0918, Brianhe, Bsadowski1, Bubba hotep, Bugur, Bull Market, Burgundavia, Buron444, CALR, CBMIBM, CMacMillan, Calmer Waters, Camembert, Camw, Can't sleep, clown will eat me, CanadianLinuxUser, Canaima, CanisRufus, Cannonball 248, Capek, CardinalDan, Cc68, Cccp71, Ccwaters, CecilWard, Cenarium, Centrx, Cew79, Cgs, Chaitanya.lala, Chaldor, Charliebone1, Ched Davis, Cheeesemonger, Chensiyuan, ChicosBailBonds, Cholga, Chovain, Chris-gore, ChrisRuvolo, Chrispy337, Christhi, Christsp, Chunkz29, Ck lostsword, Claricia, ClickRick, CliffC, Cliffb, Cmtam922, CoJaBo, Coachmark2, Coasterlover1994, Coasttocoast, Cohesion, Commander Keane, Commander-64, CommonsDelinker, Conrad.pramboeck, ConstantLearner, Conversion script, Cool Blue, Coolcaesar, Count of Cascadia, Crocodile Punter, Crown Counsel, Crowstar, Crusadeonilliteracy, Cryptic, Csrbabu, Ctkoobster, D, DAB-NYC, DB Durham NC, DGaw, DIEXEL, DMG413, DMacks, DS1953, DVD R W, DZiemke, Dan Guan, DanMS, Dania4, Dannyisawesome4, DantisS, Dave6, Davelee8675309, David Haslam, Deakinboi, Deathbyhornet, Deb.techno, DefinityCommunications, Delldot, Denelson83, Deor, DerHexer, DeweyQ, Dialectric, Diego pmc, Digital fuel, Dinosaur submarine, Discospinster, Dismas, District Nein, Djsasso, Dlfkja;lskj, Dlohcierekim, Do it, Docboat, Dod1, Doommaster1994, Dr. Blofeld, Dragonix, Dreadstar, Drunkenmonkey, Drux, Dtcdthingy, Duke of Geography, Dust Filter, Dustin gayler, Dv8tor, Dwo, Déjà Vu, ESkog, EagleOne, Eastlaw, Ecksemmess, Eclecticology, EdH, Edcolins, Edgar181, Editore99, Edroppontiii, Egil, ElationAviation, Elcobbola, Elegantprashant, Elonka, Eluchil, Emma Frost 481, Empoor, Epcostello, Eraserhead1, Erebus555, Esoteric Rogue, Ethan kee, Euler xlt, Eurobas, Evannewman830, Everyking, Excirial, Fabe3k, Falcon9x5, FarnhamJ, Fastfission, Fat pig73, Favonian, Fdrgx, Fgtr, Fibonacci, Fieldday-sunday, FinalRapture, Firsfron, Firstm8e, Flamurai, Floorwalker, Flowanda, Flowerpotman, Fluffykryptonite, Folajimi, Former user 2, Francs2000, Frap, Fredrik, Freshacconci, Fsiler, Fudoreaper, Funandtrvl, Funeral, Furby100, Futureobservatory, GOD ACRONYM, Gail, Gaius Cornelius, Gareth Jones, Garglebutt, Gary King, Gary Knackstedt, Gavin Wilson, Gazpacho, Geekosaurus, Ghettoblaster, Giftlite, Gilliam, Gjd001, Glen, Gnangarra, Gogo Dodo, GoingBatty, GotenXiao, Gotophilk, Gr1st, GraemeL, Graham87, GravityIsForSuckers, Grawity, Grayshi, Greenmind, Greenshed, Greg Grahame, Griggs08, Ground Zero, Grouse, GroveGuy, Guanaco, Gunter, Gurulegend, Gusash, Gwernol, Haakon, Hagindaz, Haham hanuka, Hahnchen, Hanacy, HarisPorobic, Harry the Dirty Dog, Harry7478, Harryboyles, Helmandsare, Hemanshu, Henriok, Heracles31, Hildanknight, Hillbilly Homo, Hillbrand, Hmains, Hobartimus, Hohenloh, Hooperbloob, Hoov182, Howcheng, Howrealisreal, Hschatz, Huwey, Hydrogen Iodide, Hylene, ICEBreaker, IChrisI, INkubusse, IScorpio, IW.HG, Ian Rose, Ike-bana, Imanpc101, Imroy, InShaneee, Intelligentsium, Ionut.shaggy, Iridescent, Irishguy, IronGargoyle, Ixfd64, J Di, J.delanoy, JCDenton2052, JDPhD, JJMG, JLaTondre, JNW, JPH-FM, JPInfo, Jaberwocky6669, Jackol, JackyR, Jakezing, Jamcib, James Seneca, Japanfan, Jareha, JarlinFo, Jasenlee, Jasonmcdonald, Javascap, Javier Donoso, Jayjg, Jayron32, Jc3, Jcbarr, Jdjonsson, JeffW, Jeffmsmith70, Jeffrey Mall, Jerem43, Jezstewart, Jhsounds, JiE, JiMidnite, JimBrammer, Jimmi Hugh, Jjjddd444222, Jkeene, Jkl, Jmalc, Jmundo, Joao.caprivi, Jodanw22, JoeSmack, Joedaddy09, Jogloran, John, John Broughton, John K, John Quiggin, JohnCongerton, Johnbrownsbody, Johninflamez, Johnleemk, Johnuniq, Jojhutton, Jonathunder, JonintheUK, Jopo, Joshkap18, Jpavlenyi, Julesd, Jusdafax, Justin Ormont, JustinCredible00, Jvcdude, K.lee, K39, KBi, KJS77, Kaiser matias, Kaisershatner, KansasCity, Kapoor.kanishka, Kareeser, Karonza21, Kbdank71, Kbh3rd, Keith D, Keithclandis, Kenhed93, Kesla, Kevin B12, Kgasso, Khfan93, KickahaOta, Kidburla, Kingk21, Kingkse, Kingkse1, Kingkse3, Kingpin13, Kippson, Kkm010, Klp363, Km2065, Kmiki87, Kmorozov, Knows stuff, Koavf, Kojarou, Kokito23, Kozuch, KrakatoaKatie, Krawi, Kristof vt, Kumioko, Kurieeto, Kurse 2799, Kuru, KymFarnik, Kyng, LG4761, LOL, Lady Rataxes, Lars Washington, Latka, Lc9zb495, Lee Daniel Crocker, Lehk, Leif, Leip, Leonardofp, Levin, Lightmouse, LilHelpa, Lilac Soul, Llort, Lockbox7, Longhair, Lpgeffen, Lsjzl, LuigiManiac, Lumaga, Luna Santin, Lupo, Lyricmac, M.nelson, M.thoriyan, M1ss1ontomars2k4, MBisanz, MER-C, MGriffit6619, MITalum, MJBurrage, MLRoach, MMuzammils, Mabdul, Mac, MacGyverMagic, MacMed, Macpl, Madchester, Madhero88, Mailer diablo, Malcolmxl5, Mangojuice, ManoaChild, Mapsax, Marc44, Mardus, Marek69, MarekTT, Marnanel, MarsRover, Martarius, Martin451, MartinPackerIBM, MartinSFSA, Mascdman, Masque 308, Mathinker, Matthew Yeager, Mauricio Godoy, Max Naylor, Meateater, MediaMangler, MementoVivere, Merovingian, Metamatic, Mfc, Mhkay, MiNombreDeGuerra, Michael Hardy, Michaeldavisgv, Mikemoral, Mikiher, Minkaishorea, Mirmo!, MisfitToys, Mitchrush, Mkamat, Mmccalpin, Mmkaram, Mms, Mmusiolik, Mo0, Modal Jig, Mohawks, Moin.max, Mojei, Mondaybox, Monkeyman, Mooncow, Mouchoir le Souris, Mr. 57, MrGraber, Mscudder, Mulad, Mwtoews, Mycroft.Holmes, Mygerardromance, Myscrnnm, Mysdaao, Mystelious, Mytwocents, N328KF, N5iln, Nakon, NapoliRoma, NatR, Natl1, Naveennarula, NawlinWiki, Necrothesp, Neep, Neilc, NellieBly, NeoPhyteRep, NerdyScienceDude, Netalarm, Neurillon, Neutrality, NewEnglandYankee, Newportm, Nezbie, Nick C, Nicool333, Night Gyr, Nikai, Nimur, Ninly, Nlyte.Software, Noctibus, Nokes15, Nrcprm2026, Nsaa, NuclearWarfare, Nufy8, Nwbeeson, Object.toString(), Ocrho, Officiallyover, OhanaUnited, Ohnoitsjamie, Old Guard, Oleg Alexandrov, Omicronpersei8, Omnedon, Oo64eva, Orilux, OtherPerson, Ou tis, OverlordQ, Ozdog, PL290, PM Poon, PSTC555, Pairadox, Pak21, Pamwooten90, Parisianphilosopher2008, Patrick-br, Patricknoddy, Paul C. Lasewicz, PaulHanson, Pchov, Pcpcpc, Persian Poet Gal, Peter Isotalo, Peter Winnberg, PeterSymonds, Phi beta, Phil Boswell, Philbutt, Philcluff, Philhower, PiMaster3, Pielover87, PigFlu Oink, Pigsonthewing, Pingveno, PinkDeoxys, PlayStation 69, Pmsyyz, Pointillist, Pol098, Polly, Postdlf, PrestonH, Prince of History, Prodego, Prolog, Psellis, Psyntium, Puchiko, Python eggs, Quadra630, Quebec99, Qutezuce, Qweedsa, RTC, Rabhyanker, Rcawsey, Rdsmith4, Reaper187, Red Thrush, RedWolf, Reece Hannam, Reedy, Reepnorp, Rees11, Reisio, RetiredWikipedian789, Rettetast, RexNL, Rholliday, Rhsatrhs, Riana, Ricardian92, Rich Farmbrough, Rich257, RichInSydney, RichMac, Rifleman 82, Ritson Pinheiro, Rj, Rjwilmsi, Rmosler2100, Rob G Weemhoff, Robert Buzink, Robert K S, Robin klein, Robo.mind, Rockslide 91, RodneyCornelius, Rossami, Rostz, Rouven Thimm, Roux, Roygbiv666, Rror, Rsshilli, Rst20xx, Rtcpenguin, Rwwww, Ryan Norton, RyanGerbil10, Ryantatar, SQL, SYx, Sabre23t, Saebjorn, SalvadorRodriguez, SamJohnston, Samanello, Sammy8912, Samotto, Samsara, Samuelsen, SamuraiClinton, Sandeep117, SarahSmiles, Saravanan rose, Sardanaphalus, Sathishvm, Scarian, Scepia, Schmiteye, SchuminWeb, Scott McNay, Sdxvi, Sean.hoyland, Seidenstud, Sensahuma, Seraphchoir, SexyBern, Sgeo, Sgfoote, Shadowjams, Shaeckel, Shail09, Shamesspwns, Shawnc, Shinmawa, Shivanshub, Shoaler, Siddthekidd, Siegfried1, Sigma 7, Siliconov, Silvie rob, SimonThird, Sink257, Skumarla, Skware, Skyworkeralan, Slambo, Slavon37, Sleepaholic, Smart Fox, Snigbrook, Snowmanradio, Snoyes, Soccer baker, Solarisworld, Somebody in the WWW, Sonyaleech, Spalef, Spangineer, Speer320, Srijnan, St33lbird, Starseeker shkm, Starwiz, Stefffm, Stephenb, Stere0123, Steven Hepting, Steven Walling, Stevertigo, Strangnet, Strode1, Stwalkerster, SueHay, Superm401, Suruena, Swaq, THEN WHO WAS PHONE?, THF, Tascha96, Tedder, Tellyaddict, Telsa, Templetongore, Texture, Thatdog, The Anome, The Thing That Should Not Be, The Tom, The wub, TheQuaker, TheQuandry, TheSlowLife, Thegn, Thegreatglobetrotter, Theodolite, Therealcolletepierre, Thewallowmaker, Thibaultvanthillo, Thivierr, Thomas de Bruin, Thunderbrand, Tibetologist, Tiddly Tom, Tide rolls, Timc, Timfletcher, Timneu22, TimothyHorrigan, Tinton5, Tjwolfe, Tkaizan, Tom harrison, Tony Sidaway, Tooki, Topbanana, TorontoStorm, Torswin, Tpbradbury, Tregoweth, Trevor MacInnis, TubularWorld, TutterMouse, Twiin, TwoOneTwo, TyrellC, Tysto, USA 5000, UTF-8, Ubiquity, Ucanlookitup, Ukexpat, Urban011, UriBudnik, Useight, UtherSRG, Valeria.depaiva, Vannguy, Vegaswikian, Veinor, Veritas 0273, Victor, Victorgrigas, Virtig01, Vkem, Vlad, Vmanjr, W2bh, Wackymacs, Waggers, Wagia, Walkiped, WallStreetJournal, Warpozio, Wavelength, Webteam fiorano, Wereon, Wernher, West81, Westcoastbiker, Wgungfu, WhaleyTim, WhatamIdoing, Whendoestheworlddie, WhisperToMe, WhizzBang, WiggettMonster, WikHead, Wikiklrsc, Wikimachine, Wikimothers, Wikiti, Wikiuser100, Winbuyer, Wine Guy, Wisdom002, Wisdom89, Wizardman, Wk muriithi, Wliuibm, Wmahan, Wpktsfs, Wuhwuzdat, Wyatt Riot, Xaminmo, XelaRellum, Xgmx, Xnatedawgx, Xpclient, XvirusX, Yamamoto Ichiro, Yamla, Yensin, Ylee, Yuyudevil, Zanter, Zaphraud, Zazpot, Zeerus, Zeus 032, Zigger, Zr2d2, Žiedas, Јованвб, סורנר, سارای روس، 大西洋鮭, 1677 anonymous edits

Image Sources, Licenses and Contributors

Image:MediaWiki-smaller-logo.png *Source*: http://en.wikipedia.org/w/index.php?title=File:MediaWiki-smaller-logo.png *License*: Public Domain *Contributors*: Klapaucjusz

File:Distributed-parallel.svg *Source*: http://en.wikipedia.org/w/index.php?title=File:Distributed-parallel.svg *License*: Creative Commons Attribution-Sharealike 3.0 *Contributors*: User:Miym

Image:HTML-old.gif *Source*: http://en.wikipedia.org/w/index.php?title=File:HTML-old.gif *License*: unknown *Contributors*: Mabdul

Image:Tim Berners-Lee April 2009.jpg *Source*: http://en.wikipedia.org/w/index.php?title=File:Tim_Berners-Lee_April_2009.jpg *License*: Creative Commons Attribution 2.0 *Contributors*: Enrique Dans from Madrid, Spain

Image:HTML.svg *Source*: http://en.wikipedia.org/w/index.php?title=File:HTML.svg *License*: Attribution *Contributors*: Anihl, Bender235, DieBuche, Nagy, Str4nd, Tael, €, 6 anonymous edits

File:@@@.svg *Source*: http://en.wikipedia.org/w/index.php?title=File:@@@.svg *License*: Public Domain *Contributors*: User:Yug

File:email.svg *Source*: http://en.wikipedia.org/w/index.php?title=File:Email.svg *License*: GNU Free Documentation License *Contributors*: Original uploader was Yzmo at en.wikipedia

File:Mozilla-thunderbird-3.0.1.png *Source*: http://en.wikipedia.org/w/index.php?title=File:Mozilla-thunderbird-3.0.1.png *License*: unknown *Contributors*: Old Marcus

File:DirectoryListing1.png *Source*: http://en.wikipedia.org/w/index.php?title=File:DirectoryListing1.png *License*: Public Domain *Contributors*: User:Loadmaster

Image:IBM logo.svg *Source*: http://en.wikipedia.org/w/index.php?title=File:IBM_logo.svg *License*: Trademarked *Contributors*: Althepal, Artem Karimov, Bryan, Chaldor, Hautala, Imalipusram, O, OsamaK, Yarl, 1 anonymous edits

Image:Broadwaycpu.JPG *Source*: http://en.wikipedia.org/w/index.php?title=File:Broadwaycpu.JPG *License*: Trademarked *Contributors*: Alx 91, Tulikettu

Image:IBM System3.JPG *Source*: http://en.wikipedia.org/w/index.php?title=File:IBM_System3.JPG *License*: Creative Commons Attribution-Sharealike 3.0 *Contributors*: User:Jonathunder

Image:IBM-Denia.JPG *Source*: http://en.wikipedia.org/w/index.php?title=File:IBM-Denia.JPG *License*: Creative Commons Attribution-Sharealike 3.0 *Contributors*: User:Ooh

Image:Original IBM Logo.png *Source*: http://en.wikipedia.org/w/index.php?title=File:Original_IBM_Logo.png *License*: Public Domain *Contributors*: User:OgilvyOne

Image:Older IBM Logo 2.png *Source*: http://en.wikipedia.org/w/index.php?title=File:Older_IBM_Logo_2.png *License*: unknown *Contributors*: Original uploader was Christsp at en.wikipedia

Image:Old IBM Logo.png *Source*: http://en.wikipedia.org/w/index.php?title=File:Old_IBM_Logo.png *License*: Public Domain *Contributors*: User:OgilvyOne

Image:Ibmcorporateheadquartersentrance.jpg *Source*: http://en.wikipedia.org/w/index.php?title=File:Ibmcorporateheadquartersentrance.jpg *License*: GNU Free Documentation License *Contributors*: Hnc197, WhisperToMe

File:IBM PC 5150.jpg *Source*: http://en.wikipedia.org/w/index.php?title=File:IBM_PC_5150.jpg *License*: GNU Free Documentation License *Contributors*: User:Boffy b, User:Dpbsmith

License

GNU Free Documentation License Version 1.2, November 2002 Copyright (C) 2000,2001,2002 Free Software Foundation, Inc. 59 Temple Place, Suite 330, Boston, MA 02111 -1307 USA Everyone is permitted to copy and distribute verbatim copies of this license documen t, but changing it is not allowed.

0. PREAMBLE

The purpose of this License is to make a manual, textbook, or other functional and useful document "free" in the sense of freedom: to assure everyone the effective freedom to copy and redistribute it, with or without modifying it, either commercially or noncommercially. Secondarily, this License preserves for the author and publisher a way to get credit for their work, while not being considered responsible for modifications made by others. This License is a kind of "copyleft", which means that derivative works of the document must themselves be free in the same sense. It complements the GNU General Public License, which is a copyleft license designed for free software. We have designed this License in order to use it for manuals for free software, because free software needs free documentation: a free program should come with manuals providing the same freedoms that the software does. But this License is not limited to software manuals; it can be used for any textual work, regardless of subject matter or whether it is published as a printed book. We recommend this License principally for works whose purpose is instruction or reference.

1. APPLICABILITY AND DEFINITIONS

This License applies to any manual or ot her work, in any medium, that contains a notice placed by the copyright holder saying it can be distributed under the terms of this License. Such a notice grants a world -wide, royalty -free license, unlimited in duration, to use that work under the conditio ns stated herein. The "Document", below, refers to any such manual or work. Any member of the public is a licensee, and is addressed as "you". You accept the license if you copy, modify or distribute the work in a way requiring permission under copyright l aw. A "Modified Version" of the Document means any work containing the Document or a portion of it, either copied verbatim, or with modifications and/or translated into another language. A "Secondary Section" is a named appendix or a front -matter section o f the Document that deals exclusively with the relationship of the publishers or authors of the Document to the Document's overall subject (or to related matters) and contains nothing that could fall directly within that overall subject. (Thus, if the Docu ment is in part a textbook of mathematics, a Secondary Section may not explain any mathematics.) The relationship could be a matter of historical connection with the subject or with related matters, or of legal, commercial, philosophical, ethical or political position regarding them. The "Invariant Sections" are certain Secondary Sections whose titles are designated, as being those of Invariant Sections, in the notice that says that the Document is released under this License. If a section does not fit the above definition of Secondary then it is not allowed to be designated as Invariant. The Document may contain zero Invariant Sections. If the Document does not identify any Invariant Sections then there are none. The "Cover Texts" are certain short passages of text that are listed, as Front -Cover Texts or Back -Cover Texts, in the notice that says that the Document is released under this License. A Front -Cover Text may be at most 5 words, and a Back -Cover Text may be at most 25 words. A "Transparent" copy of the Document means a machine -readable copy, represented in a format whose specification is available to the general public, that is suitable for revising the document straightforwardly with generic text editors or (for images composed of pixels) generic p aint programs or (for drawings) some widely available drawing editor, and that is suitable for input to text formatters or for automatic translation to a variety of formats suitable for input to text formatters. A copy made in an otherwise Transparent file format whose markup, or absence of markup, has been arranged to thwart or discourage subsequent modification by readers is not Transparent. An image format is not Transparent if used for any substantial amount of text. A copy that is not "Transparent" is called "Opaque". Examples of suitable formats for Transparent copies include plain ASCII without markup, Texinfo input format, LaTeX input format, SGML or XML using a publicly available DTD, and standard -conforming simple HTML, PostScript or PDF designed f or human modification. Examples of transparent image formats include PNG, XCF and JPG. Opaque formats include proprietary formats that can be read and edited only by proprietary word processors, SGML or XML for which the DTD and/or processing tools are not generally available, and the machine -generated HTML, PostScript or PDF produced by some word processors for output purposes only. The "Title Page" means, for a printed book, the title page itself, plus such following pages as are needed to hold, legibly, the material this License requires to appear in the title page. For works in formats which do not have any title page as such, "Title Page" means the text near the most prominent appearance of the work's title, preceding the beginning of the body of the te xt. A section "Entitled XYZ" means a named subunit of the Document whose title either is precisely XYZ or contains XYZ in parentheses following text that translates XYZ in another language. (Here XYZ stands for a specific section name mentioned below, such as "Acknowledgements", "Dedications", "Endorsements", or "History".) To "Preserve the Title" of such a section when you modify the Document means that it remains a section "Entitled XYZ" according to this definition. The Document may include Warranty Disc laimers next to the notice which states that this License applies to the Document. These Warranty Disclaimers are considered to be included by reference in this License, but only as regards disclaiming warranties: any other implication that these Warranty Disclaimers may have is void and has no effect on the meaning of this License.

2. VERBATIM COPYING

You may copy and distribute the Document in any medium, either commercially or noncommercially, provided that this License, the copyright notices, and the license notice saying this License applies to the Document are reproduced in all copies, and that you add no other conditions whatsoever to those of this License. You may not use technical measures to obstruct or control the reading or further copying of t he copies you make or distribute. However, you may accept compensation in exchange for copies. If you distribute a large enough number of copies you must also follow the conditions in section 3. You may also lend copies, under the same conditions stated ab ove, and you may publicly display copies.

3. COPYING IN QUANTITY

If you publish printed copies (or copies in media that commonly have printed covers) of the Document, numbering more than 100, and the Document's license notice requires Cover Texts, you must enclose the copies in covers that carry, clearly and legibly, all these Cover Texts: Front -Cover Texts on the front cover, and Back-Cover Texts on the back cover. Both covers must also clearly and legibly identify you as the publisher of these copies. The front cover must present the full title with all words of the title equally prominent and visible. You may add other material on the covers in addition. Copying with changes limited to the covers, as long as they preserve the title of the Document and s atisfy these conditions, can be treated as verbatim copying in other respects. If the required texts for either cover are too voluminous to fit legibly, you should put the first ones listed (as many as fit reasonably) on the actual cover, and continue the rest onto adjacent pages. If you publish or distribute Opaque copies of the Document numbering more than 100, you must either include a machine-readable Transparent copy along with each Opaque copy, or state in or with each Opaque copy a computer -network location from which the general network -using public has access to download using public -standard network protocols a complete Transparent copy of the Document, free of added material. If you use the latter option, you must take reasonably prudent steps, when you begin distribution of Opaque copies in quantity, to ensure that this Transparent copy will remain thus accessible at the stated location until at least one year after the last time you distribute an Opaque copy (directly or through your agents or retailers) of that edition to the public. It is requested, but not required, that you contact the authors of the Document well before redistributing any large number of copies, to give them a chance to provide you with an updated version of the Document.

4. MODIFICATIONS

You may copy and distribute a Modified Version of the Document under the conditions of sections 2 and 3 above, provided that you release the Modified Version under precisely this License, with the Modified Version filling the role of the Do cument, thus licensing distribution and modification of the Modified Version to whoever possesses a copy of it. In addition, you must do these things in the Modified Version: A. Use in the Title Page (and on the covers, if any) a title distinct from that o f the Document, and from those of previous versions (which should, if there were any, be listed in the History section of the Document). You may use the same title as a previous version if the original publisher of that version gives permission. B. List on the Title Page, as authors, one or more persons or entities responsible for authorship of the modifications in the Modified Version, together with at least five of the principal authors of the Document (all of its principal authors, if it has fewer than f ive), unless they release you from this requirement. C. State on the Title page the name of the publisher of the Modified Version, as the publisher. D. Preserve all the copyright notices of the Document. E. Add an appropriate copyright notice for your modi fications adjacent to the other copyright notices. F. Include, immediately after the copyright notices, a license notice giving the public permission to use the Modified Version under the terms of this License, in the form shown in the Addendum below. G. Preserve in that license notice the full lists of Invariant Sections and required Cover Texts given in the Document's license notice. H. Include an unaltered copy of this License. I. Preserve the section Entitled "History", Preserve its Title, and add to it an item stating at least the title, year, new authors, and publisher of the Modified Version as given on the Title Page. If there is no section Entitled "History" in the Document, create one stating the title, year, authors, and publisher of the Document as given on its Title Page, then add an item describing the Modified Version as stated in the previous sentence. J. Preserve the network location, if any, given in the Document for public access to a Transparent copy of the Document, and likewise the netwo rk locations given in the Document for previous versions it was based on. These may be placed in the "History" section. You may omit a network location for a work that was published at least four years before the Document itself, or if the original publish er of the version it refers to gives permission. K. For any section Entitled "Acknowledgements" or "Dedications", Preserve the Title of the section, and preserve in the section all the substance and tone of each of the contributor acknowledgements and/or d edications given therein. L. Preserve all the Invariant Sections of the Document, unaltered in their text and in their titles. Section numbers or the equivalent are not considered part of the section titles. M. Delete any section Entitled "Endorsements". S uch a section may not be included in the Modified Version. N. Do not retitle any existing section to be Entitled "Endorsements" or to conflict in title with any Invariant Section. O. Preserve any Warranty Disclaimers. If the Modified Version includes new f ront-matter sections or appendices that qualify as Secondary Sections and contain no material copied from the Document, you may at your option designate some or all of these sections as invariant. To do this, add their titles to the list of Invariant Secti ons in the Modified Version's license notice. These titles must be distinct from any other section titles. You may add a section Entitled "Endorsements", provided it contains nothing but endorsements of your Modified Version by various parties --for example , statements of peer review or that the text has been approved by an organization as the authoritative definition of a standard. You may add a passage of up to five words as a Front -Cover Text, and a passage of up to 25 words as a Back -Cover Text, to the end of the list of Cover Texts in the Modified Version. Only one passage of Front-Cover Text and one of Back -Cover Text may be added by (or through arrangements made by) any one entity. If the Document already includes a cover text for the same cover, previously added by you or by arrangement made by the same entity you are acting on behalf of, you may not add another; but you may replace the old one, on explicit permission from the previous publisher that added the old one. The author(s) and publisher(s) of the Document do not by this License give permission to use their names for publicity for or to assert or imply endorsement of any Modified Version.

5. COMBINING DOCUMENTS

You may combine the Document with other documents released under this License, under the terms defined in section 4 above for modified versions, provided that you include in the combination all of the Invariant Sections of all of the original documents, unmodified, and list them all as Invariant Sections of your combined work in its lic ense notice, and that you preserve all their Warranty Disclaimers. The combined work need only contain one copy of this License, and multiple identical Invariant Sections may be replaced with a single copy. If there are multiple Invariant Sections with the same name but different contents, make the title of each such section unique by adding at the end of it, in parentheses, the name of the original author or publisher of that section if known, or else a unique number. Make the same adjustment to the sectio n titles in the list of Invariant Sections in the license notice of the combined work. In the combination, you must combine any sections Entitled "History" in the various original documents, forming one section Entitled "History"; likewise combine any sect ions Entitled "Acknowledgements", and any sections Entitled "Dedications". You must delete all sections Entitled "Endorsements".

6. COLLECTIONS OF DOCUMENTS

You may make a collection consisting of the Document and other documents released under this Lice nse, and replace the individual copies of this License in the various documents with a single copy that is included in the collection, provided that you follow the rules of this License for verbatim copying of each of the documents in all other respects. Y ou may extract a single document from such a collection, and distribute it individually under this License, provided you insert a copy of this License into the extracted document, and follow this License in all other respects regarding verbatim copying of that document.

7. AGGREGATION WITH INDEPENDENT WORKS

A compilation of the Document or its derivatives with other separate and independent documents or works, in or on a volume of a storage or distribution medium, is called an "aggregate" if the copyright resulting from the compilation is not used to limit the legal rights of the compilation's users beyond what the individual works permit. When the Document is included in an aggregate, this License does not apply to the other works in the aggregate which are not themselves derivative works of the Document. If the Cover Text requirement of section 3 is applicable to these copies of the Document, then if the Document is less than one half of the entire aggregate, the Document's Cover Texts may be placed on covers that bracket the Document within the aggregate, or the electronic equivalent of covers if the Document is in electronic form. Otherwise they must appear on printed covers that bracket the whole aggregate.

8. TRANSLATION

Translation is considered a k ind of modification, so you may distribute translations of the Document under the terms of section 4. Replacing Invariant Sections with translations requires special permission from their copyright holders, but you may include translations of some or all I nvariant Sections in addition to the original versions of these Invariant Sections. You may include a translation of this License, and all the license notices in the Document, and any Warranty Disclaimers, provided that you also include the original Englis h version of this License and the original versions of those notices and disclaimers. In case of a disagreement between the translation and the original version of this License or a notice or disclaimer, the original version will prevail. If a section in t he Document is Entitled "Acknowledgements", "Dedications", or "History", the requirement (section 4) to Preserve its Title (section 1) will typically require changing the actual title.

9. TERMINATION

You may not copy, modify, sublicense, or distribute th e Document except as expressly provided for under this License. Any other attempt to copy, modify, sublicense or distribute the Document is void, and will automatically terminate your rights under this License. However, parties who have received copies, or rights, from you under this License will not have their licenses terminated so long as such parties remain in full compliance.

10. FUTURE REVISIONS OF THIS LICENSE

The Free Software Foundation may publish new, revised versions of the GNU Free Documentat ion License from time to time. Such new versions will be similar in spirit to the present version, but may differ in detail to address new problems or concerns. See http://www.gnu.org/copyleft/. Each version of the License is given a distinguishing version number. If the Document specifies that a particular numbered version of this License "or any later version" applies to it, you have the option of following the terms and conditions either of that specified version or of any later version that has been pub lished (not as a draft) by the Free Software Foundation. If the Document does not specify a version number of this License, you may choose any version ever published (not as a draft) by the Free Software Foundation. ADDENDUM: How to use this License for yo ur documents To use this License in a document you have written, include a copy of the License in the document and put the following copyright and license notices just after the title page: Copyright (c) YEAR YOUR NAME. Permission is granted to copy, distr ibute and/or modify this document under the terms of the GNU Free Documentation License, Version 1.2 or any later version published by the Free Software Foundation; with no Invariant Sections, no Front -Cover Texts, and no Back-Cover Texts. A copy of the li cense is included in the section entitled "GNU Free Documentation License". If you have Invariant Sections, Front -Cover Texts and Back -Cover Texts, replace the "with...Texts." line with this: with the Invariant Sections being LIST THEIR TITLES, with the Fr ont-Cover Texts being LIST, and with the Back -Cover Texts being LIST. If you have Invariant Sections without Cover Texts, or some other combination of the three, merge those two alternatives to suit the situation. If your document contains nontrivial examp les of program code, we recommend releasing these examples in parallel under your choice of free software license, such as the GNU General Public License, to permit their use in free software.

CPSIA information can be obtained at www.ICGtesting.com
Printed in the USA
LVOW041153150712

290136LV00007B/129/P